The World's Business Cultures and How to Unlock Them

Barry Tomalin and Mike Nicks

Viva Books

New Delhi | Mumbai | Chennai | Kolkata | Bangalore | Hyderabad | Kochi

First Indian Edition 2009

VIVA BOOKS PRIVATE LIMITED

- 4737/23 Ansari Road, Daryaganj, New Delhi 110 002
  E-mail: vivadelhi@vivagroupindia.net, Tel. 42242200
- 76, Service Industries, Shirvane, Sector 1, Nerul, Navi Mumbai 400 706
  E-mail: vivamumbai@vivagroupindia.net, Tel. 27721273, 27721274
- Jamals Fazal Chambers, 26 Greams Road, Chennai 600 006
  E-mail: vivachennai@vivagroupindia.net, Tel. 28290304, 28294241
- B-103, Jindal Towers, 21/1A/3 Darga Road, Kolkata 700 017
  E-mail: vivakolkata@vivagroupindia.net, Tel. 22836381, 22816713
- 7, Sovereign Park Apartments, 56-58, K. R. Road, Basavanagudi, Bangalore 560 004
  E-mail: vivabangalore@vivagroupindia.net, Tel. 26607409, 26607410
- 101-102 Mughal Marc Apartments, 3-4-637 to 641, Narayanguda, Hyderabad 500 029
  E-mail: vivahyderabad@vivagroupindia.net, Tel. 27564481, 27564482
- First Floor, Beevi Towers, SRM Road, Kaloor, Kochi 682 018, Kerala
  E-mail: vivakochi@vivagroupindia.net, Tel: 0484-2403055, 2403056
- H. No. 12, P. B. Road, Near Arya Hospital, Rehabari, Guwahati 781 008
  E-mail: vivaguwahati@vivagroupindia.net, Tel: 0361-2735624

www.vivagroupindia.com

Published by arrangement with

Thorogood Publishers Limited
10-12 Rivington Street
London EC2A 3DU,
UK

ISBN-10: 81-309-0852-2
ISBN-13: 978-81-309-0852-6

Published by Vinod Vasishtha for Viva Books Private Limited, 4737/23, Ansari Road, Daryaganj, New Delhi-110 002. Printed and bound by Anand Sons, Delhi - 110 092.

Acknowledgements

We would like to thank Richard D Lewis, of Richard Lewis Communications, whose research, enthusiasm and sheer practicality have been a major influence, and David Solomons of CultureSmart Consulting, whose charisma and presentation skills have been so valuable in building cultural awareness. Also John Farrer of POD, whose interactive training skills are second to none. Finally, Barry's colleagues at International House, Steve Brent and Michael Carrier, have provided invaluable guidance. Special thanks to colleagues, Ulla Ladau-Harjulin, Jack Lonergan, Susan Stempleski and Rob Williams for their energy, ideas and support. Thanks too to Rupert Jones-Parry, who introduced us to Thorogood.

To Mary and Paul Tomalin and to Carole Nicks and Emilsa Estrada Espinosa.

Foreword

You're feeling harassed, overworked and nervous as you wait in the airport lounge. You're flying to meet a client in a foreign country, and you don't know why but there's something not right about the relationship. You can't seem to get your point across clearly, and you can't figure out just what they're thinking. The situation's muddy and the deadlines are drawing nearer.

If you've ever found yourself in that situation, this book is for you. We have written it to help international business travellers build relationships and achieve deals instead of running into dead-ends or committing embarrassing blunders. We want to help you to see the world from the other person's point of view: the process is called cultural awareness and, in the era of globalization, there has never been a greater need for it.

Barry Tomalin and Mike Nicks

The authors

Barry Tomalin is a cross-cultural consultant and the Director of Cultural Training at International House in London. He works with companies and organisations to improve their cultural skills and awareness, and runs the Business Cultural Trainers Certificate for teachers and coaches. Barry has worked as a language teacher, as an Overseas Development Administration adviser in West Africa, and as editor and marketing director of the English language teaching division of the BBC World Service. He speaks French and some Spanish and German. Barry lives in Surrey with his wife Mary. Their son Paul is a television drama scriptwriter.

Mike Nicks a journalist, media coach and language enthusiast. He has launched or redesigned more than 30 magazines and newspapers in the UK, France, the USA and Australia, and writes for national newspapers in London including the *Guardian*, the *Independent* and the *Observer* on motorcycle racing, business cultures and language learning. He is a tutor with PMA Training, Britain's largest media training organisation, and he coaches businesses on communication skills. Mike speaks Spanish and French. He lives in Cambridgeshire, and has three children.

Contents

ONE

Risky business

ONE

Risky business

To do business worldwide it isn't enough just to understand and apply a universal business model. You also have to understand the culture of the people you are dealing with.

We are in a light engineering company in central England. As you walk through its comfortable, purpose-built offices on an industrial estate on the outskirts of the city, designers work on-screen, creating products that will improve travellers' safety and comfort. The business, as its sales director cheerfully admits, is into rubber. The firm's trademark rubber fittings ensure that the moving parts of trains, boats and planes, and many other forms of transport, run smoothly, giving passengers an easier ride. Trains on the Indian Railways network, ferries in the Baltic Sea and Boeing and Airbus aircraft, all benefit from their work. The company's headquarters are in Sweden, but it has around 100 plants in 40 countries, and it sources rubber from agents in India, China and other countries in South East Asia.

Gary, an Englishman in his thirties, is the firm's purchasing manager, responsible for ensuring a supply of rubber to the factory. This is done through local agents, who liaise with rubber plantations. He's negotiating with Indians, Chinese, Malaysians and Thais, and he knows that it's not just about computerized product specifications and emailed draft contracts, backed up with a few phone calls. He needs to meet his overseas suppliers face to face. "Until I meet them, I don't know if we speak the same business language," Gary says. "Do they understand what I understand about product specification? Do they understand the need for exactness in what we do? Do they appreciate the importance of on-time delivery so that we can complete our side of the bargain with our clients?"

This is why we are in the Midlands: to advise the company on how its suppliers see the business world, what the suppliers' concerns are and what the company needs to do to get the best out of them. It's called cross-cultural training, and it's become a key management tool in the globalized business community.

Richard, the head of manufacturing, is interviewing us. Are we suitable for his needs? We're here to talk about India, which is predicted by the bankers Goldman Sachs to be the world's third largest economy by 2050. Can we tell him how to get the best results from his Indian suppliers? Can we advise him how not to offend people and how to ensure that the company builds good relations with its Indian customers? Indian Railways is one of the world's biggest employers – it has a workforce of 1.5 million – and is a vital client. "It's sometimes like a war out there," Richard says. "You're just trying to do your job, but it seems like everybody is doing their own thing in their own way. What I need to know is, what are the rules of engagement?"

You may worry about his military analogy, but in global selling and purchasing, a battlefield is very often what it feels like for the people involved. In military language, the rules of engagement describe the conditions under which it is acceptable to open fire against the enemy in war. Culture isn't war, but it engenders the same kind of tension about the right way to proceed to get results. Doing business internationally often seems like you're moving in a fog: people can be late or miss appointments altogether, don't do what they say they will when they say they will, and have to be constantly chased up. For busy managers it feels like an irritating and inefficient waste of time. But for Ian, the sales director, it's literally part of the day's work. An experienced hand on every continent, he's sat in more waiting rooms for more hours than he cares to count. The secret for him is knowing 'when to pounce' and to do that, he says, you have to know the culture. In Sweden, where the parent firm is based, business is clear, planned and organized. You sign the contract, you complete the task to the required specification and you get paid within due dates. But in most of the countries where he works, Ian says that you have to 'feel the people, as it were'. You must build good relationships, sometimes before you do any business. For him, understanding his clients' culture is perhaps his key triumph in a thirty-year career. He knows in depth how the system works.

To do business worldwide it isn't enough to apply a one-style-fits-all universal business model. You also have to empathize with a country's culture. This means understanding how your clients and suppliers see and do business, and recognizing that their processes may be very different to yours. Luckily, there is now enough research and information on the subject that, if you do your homework, you won't need thirty years to master the cultural rules of engagement.

> Understanding a culture too often becomes something you do after the event, when your relationship with a client has broken down. But that's shutting the stable door after the horse has bolted.

Failure to relate to another culture can lead to business disaster. At a conference of the Chartered Institute of Personnel and Development in Harrogate in the north of England, we asked the director of an international relocation firm at what point in a negotiation companies consider their partners' business culture. His reply was chilling: "When the project's crashed and they can't find any other reason for it." Cultural awareness too often becomes something you do after the event: shutting the stable door after the horse has bolted.

In the international automotive business there have been spectacular examples of business merger failures, epitomized by the Daimler-Benz sale of the American company Chrysler in 2007 after an unhappy nine-year union between the two organizations. London's *Financial Times* said of the break-up: "The 'merger of equals' was never really that, and early decisions were driven by politics rather than commercial reality. Many of Daimler's German managers seemed reluctant to see the makers of Mercedes associate with the makers of Dodge."

That failure to achieve cultural understanding proved expensive: the price paid by the new owners Cerberus, a venture capital group, was a fifth of the $35bn paid by Daimler back in 1998. But there have also been successful international mergers in the automotive world, notably Renault's turnaround of Nissan in Japan. This is mainly attributed to Carlos Ghosn, the head of Renault, who guided the revival of Nissan and has now achieved celebrity status in Japan. Ghosn was born in Brazil to Lebanese parents, and graduated with engineering degrees from the École Polytechnique in France. He worked in the USA, South America and France before masterminding the Renault-Nissan fusion, and his vast experience of different cultures undoubtedly contributes to the business judgements he makes. Successful international business depends increasingly on getting the cultural chemistry right as well as the financial plan and the due diligence process.

You might think that it's appropriate to talk about cultural differences when you're dealing with distant parts of the world, but surely not with our neighbours in say, France, Germany or the Netherlands. We were once talking to the sales director of an engineering firm in Kent in the south of England. "Of course we don't have cultural problems," he insisted. At that moment his PA told him that his Dutch representative was on the line. "Oh, I don't want to talk to him now," he exploded. "He's always so bloody rude!" The director clearly hadn't recognized the Dutch cultural preference for outspokenness and calling a spade a spade. But maybe Dutch frankness is a quality that should be appreciated in the business world, and not something to get annoyed about.

John Mole is one of the most knowledgeable commentators on business in the European Union. After a career at the prestigious INSEAD management college in France, he wrote a number of successful books, of which the most famous is *Mind Your Manners*, a guide to European business cultures and etiquette. He warns: "Remember, the people whose faces are most like yours may conceal the greatest cultural differences." The problem lies in our expectations. We expect the Chinese and, to a lesser extent, the Indians to be different. We assume, often to our cost, that the Dutch, Germans and Americans will be the same.

The people whose faces are most like yours may conceal the greatest cultural differences.

Panasonic, JVC and Technics are among the brand names of the Matsushita Electric Industrial Company, based in Osaka, Japan, and named after its founder, Konosuke Matsushita. Matsushita has manufacturing plants and sales operations worldwide: it makes electronic components for avionics in France, Saudi Arabia, the UK and the USA, plasma TV screens in Central and Eastern Europe, and batteries, video recorders and computers in various countries. Although a firmly European Company, Matsushita sends Japanese managers overseas for up to five years or so before rotating them back home or transferring them to another country. Matsushita trains its managers how to live in Europe, and how to operate in global business cultures. Its native European managers also learn how best to work with one another across borders and, above all, how to cooperate with their Japanese colleagues and bosses. One of the things the Europeans learn is how to earn the trust of their Japanese managers. Trust is of inestimable importance in Japanese business: with it comes responsibility and freedom of action. Trust is built by hard work (putting in the hours, both in working time and afterwards), loyalty and availability (being around when needed). Above all, it means learning to be a good team player, which in individualistic Europe can be difficult.

Examples like these illustrate the importance of cultural awareness in today's business world, but they don't explain what that awareness is. Read books on the subject and you'll find a range of definitions from the academic to the gnomic. One of our favourite definitions is: "Culture is the software of the mind." In terms of the rules of engagement, culture is very simple, as it has only two components:

- Different ways of doing business;
- Different client expectations.

Different business communities do things in different ways. In my culture it may be more important to be polite than to tell it like it is, so I will always say yes and never say no. I will come across to you as at best wishy-washy and at worst as a liar. But your straight-talking policy will seem impolite and arrogant to me. This is not a good basis for a business relationship.

We may also have different expectations about one another. In my community it's important to build a good personal relationship. If I don't know you and like you, how can I work with you? So I need you to come and see me, to keep in regular contact, give me presents and be my friend. But you have a horrific schedule to keep, and you just want to finish the meeting and get on the plane home or to your next destination. You consider that relationships are time consuming, and time is money. I feel that you are not a good business partner for me as you don't understand the meaning of friendship. You believe that I am not a good business partner because I insist, as you see it, in putting pleasure before business and using up too much of your precious management time. My business expectation is for friendship. Yours is to get the job done as fast and as efficiently as possible.

The two definitions of the role of culture in business were neatly summed up by Chrysler, the US automotive firm, in this sentence: "Our culture is the way we view things and the way we do things round here." This is sometimes paraphrased as the 'view and do' theory of culture.

David Solomons is English, born and brought up in north London, where he now lives. His father ran a chain of grocery stores. David speaks English, Spanish, French and Hebrew and has lived in Barcelona, San Francisco, Avignon and Tel Aviv. He presented the cultural slot on BBC World Service Television's *Fast Track* travel programme. For David, doing business internationally is all about a change in perspective – a change of mindset, he calls it. All business people are trained to do a task well. They are promoted and sent abroad to perform that task as efficiently as they can. But all too often, they are frustrated by a series of unknowns – different attitudes to timekeeping, negotiating and decision-making – which have nothing to do with the business process they are used to. The answer is simple. Business managers need educating in a new way of thinking. They must add to their task-based skills a range of culture-based considerations. In our terms, they need to learn new rules of engagement.

Managers must add to their task-based skills a range of culture-based considerations.

Learning new ways of thinking becomes even more important when we realize that many companies are having to relinquish control of parts of their manufacturing and service delivery processes. This is part of the accelerating movement known as globalization.

Thomas Friedman is the writer and *New York Times* journalist who has charted the progress of globalization and become one of its chief advocates. In two influential books, *The Lexus and the Olive Tree* and *The World is Flat,* he demonstrates in a series of eye-opening case studies how globalization has become not just an economic necessity for the developed world, but a road to regeneration for the developed and developing worlds alike. Globalization is a complicated and controversial concept, and has political and economic, as well as social and cultural ramifications. Let's explore what it means for the rules of engagement, and why it makes the understanding of other communities' business methods and expectations absolutely crucial. And let's take, as Friedman does, the case of India.

What globalization means is that any part of a manufacturing or service process that can be done more cheaply in an overseas country, will be.

India is in the forefront of the globalization movement, as it does considerable trade with the USA, the world's richest economy; the UK, the world's fourth or fifth largest economy (Britain vies with France in these positions); Australia; New Zealand; Canada, and anywhere else that English is spoken as a native language. What globalization means is that any part of a manufacturing or service process that can be done more cheaply in an overseas country, will be. Minute tasks, such as the transcribing of doctors' prescriptions, can be emailed to India, fed into a computer and sent for processing. Globalization as we understand it today is increasingly the product of international computer and telecommunications networks. We are most aware of it when we use a call centre based in India, but far more important is the huge back-office programming and data processing work handled largely by computing experts who do not need good spoken English.

A major insurance company is setting up a joint venture in India. We are training the board, the project team and operational staff to work with Indians. Personnel seconded from India are already working in the UK headquarters, but the contract hasn't been signed yet. At this stage everything is being done on trust and the board has had to accept the value of patience in negotiation. Equally, the British managers have had to learn that what they understand by design specification, quality, performance and delivery may not be perceived in the same way by their Indian partners. They have also realized that these matters cannot always be resolved by emails and teleconferences. India is ultimately a face-to-face culture, so managers frequently board planes to attend meetings to reiterate the rules of engagement and set in place ways of monitoring performance and establishing agreed service levels. All this is taking time, but the rewards will be great: a committed and highly qualified workforce is available for a third of the UK price. The insurance company is coming to terms with the cost of understanding and dealing with the workforce's culture because it sees the benefits of achieving synergy with Indian business practices.

The key issue for companies is that in outsourcing, you are giving away part of the responsibility for management performance and customer service to people who may not recognize and share your values and management behaviour.

Many companies don't achieve this breakthrough, which is why overseas joint ventures and mergers and acquisitions so often fail. The key issue for companies is that in outsourcing, you are giving away part of the responsibility for management performance and customer service to people who may not recognize and share your values and management behaviour. It would be a huge and unacceptable risk not to find out about your new supplier's or client's management culture and values, and to assume that a one-size-fits-all international management style will work. Which is why international business without understanding local business culture is risky business.

International business without understanding local business culture is risky business.

As a recent advertisment in *The Economist* pointed out: "Understanding culture is the power behind globalization."

The problem managers face, however, is – what culture? What is the best way to find out how to approach another culture? Is there a model we can use? The answer is yes, and how to unlock it is the subject of Chapter 2.

Conclusion

- Successful international business depends on getting the cultural chemistry right.
- Culture is about different ways of doing things and different client expectations in different business communities.

- Managers must understand a client's culture as well as the logistical requirements of the project in order to succeed in international business today.
- Globalization means putting part of your business in foreign hands.
- Not to understand your partner's business culture is risky and irresponsible.

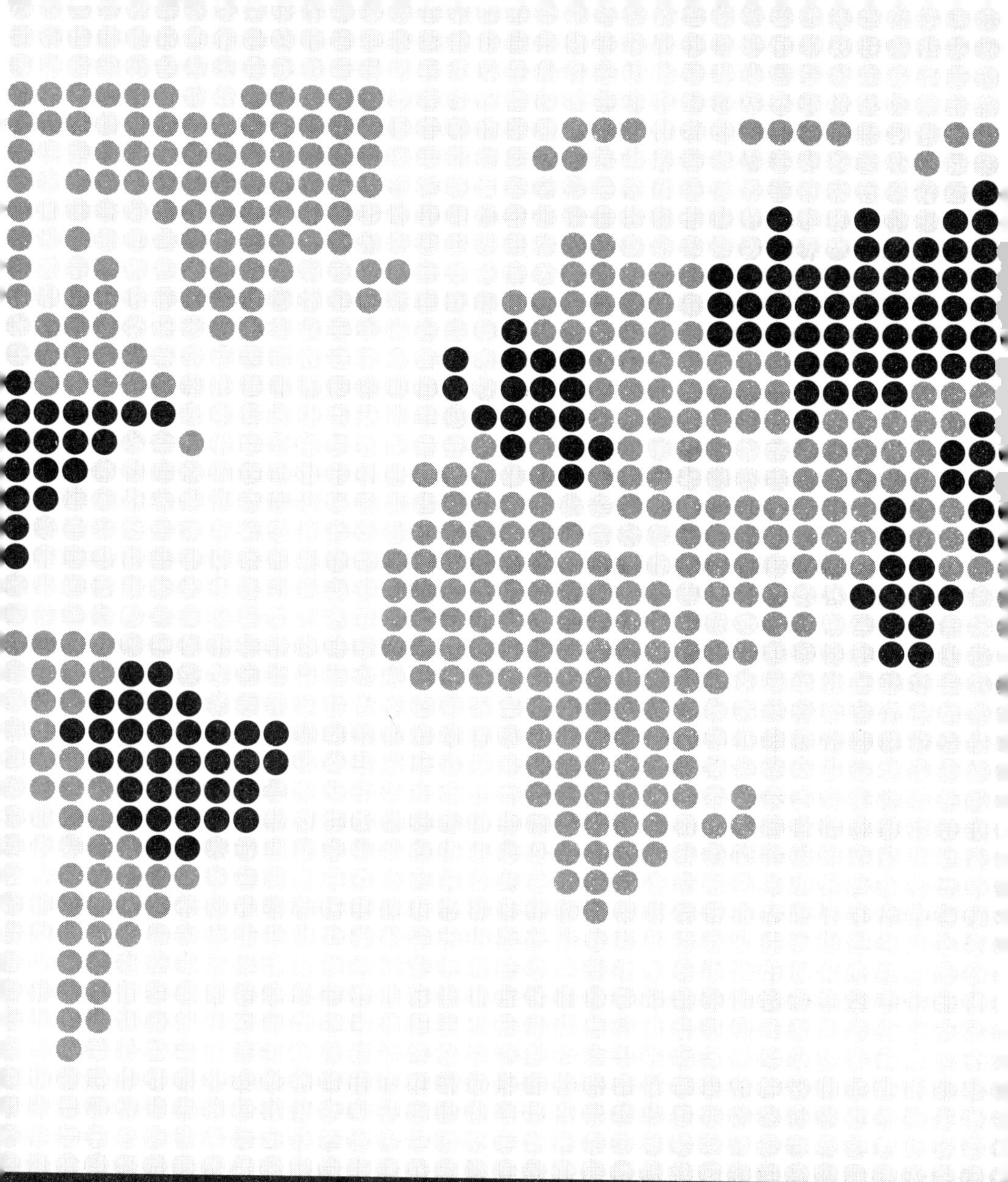

TWO

How to unlock any culture in the world

TWO

How to unlock any culture in the world

> **To do business worldwide it isn't enough just to understand and apply a universal business model. You also have to understand a country's culture.**

- The curse of anecdotes
- The TRUST model
- The three ingredients of culture
- The Five C's of culture
- Stereotypes and generalizations
- Race, religion, sexual orientation and disability

The curse of anecdotes

Learning about management is about understanding management models and applying them to business. Is there a similar model we can apply to understanding other business cultures? John Farrer follows a successful formula when he trains banking executives in The Square Mile, the City of London's financial centre, in personal development and leadership qualities. A typical session in a two- or three-day programme run by his company, POD, might contain the task, team and individual (TTI) model, the Belbin model of the ideal team, and ideas from other sources. Farrer introduces an activity, shows the lessons to be learned from it, and then demonstrates how they apply to the banking business. Clients enjoy the light-hearted but systematic approach that he and his consultants bring to business training.

A key to any successful training course, says Farrer, is the narrative, a story that runs through the programme and binds it together in a consistent whole, with a series of core messages that delegates can apply in their business lives. For Farrer and many like him, cultural training has in the past lacked that unifying thread: clients have been presented with too many details and bits of unrelated information, which has made it difficult for them to feel that they can quickly grasp how to deal with a new business culture. Cultural training has been, in short, too anecdotal.

Is it possible, Farrer asks, to find a consistent narrative that would allow a business person to unlock a culture? And not just one culture, but any culture. Is there a framework that can be applied?

Two approaches offer the kind of consistency that he is looking for. One is the TRUST model, and the other is the Five C's of culture. Used together, they offer a key to understanding and comparing any culture.

The TRUST model

In the early days of the London Stock Exchange, the brokers' motto was, 'My word is my bond'. In a slightly less complicated world, it was possible for people of honour to exchange money on a verbal commitment only. Today a vital part of any of the world's stock exchanges is the back office, which processes the paperwork filed by the front office traders on the floors. But to an extraordinary degree, international business dealings still rely on trust. Trust is an attribute created by two elements: rapport and credibility. The relationship between them is often presented in the following diagram.

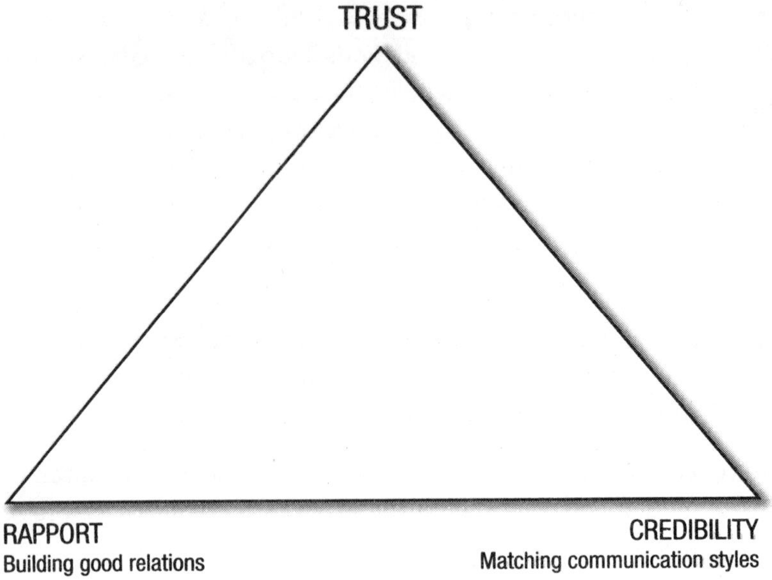

THE TRUST DIAGRAM

Rapport means having the ability to build good relations. In some business communities, these are established by doing a good job. We meet, we work together, we may go out to eat, we may play golf and may even become family friends over time. The point is that the relationship is developed and articulated through work. If the working arrangement didn't exist, the social relationship could never be built. But the work comes first, and in most cases a poor working relationship will signal the end of the social bond. This is the model broadly followed by Northern European countries and by the USA, Canada, Australia and New Zealand. What you need to understand in these countries are the rituals and signals by which the move from a business to a social relationship takes place; they can be quite subtle.

At the other extreme are business cultures that believe that you only deal with people you like and trust, and that the building of a personal and social relationship precedes the business arrangement. In these societies an extended courtship is undertaken, with eating and drinking together and socializing as part of an extended negotiation process, which can strain the nerves and the pocket of people from northern cultures. China, Japan and Russia are examples of this kind of approach. The business pattern in the USA and the UK is fairly easy to recognize and fit in with, but the 'social first' position demands a major effort of adaptation, and it's essential to do this if you want to achieve success. For Johnny Kim, a Korean businessman, based in Geneva, the process is automatic. "Build a successful relationship and business follows naturally," he says.

The other point of the TRUST triangle is credibility. Credibility is about how you demonstrate your ability. How do you show that you mean what you say? One way is to match your counterparts' communication style: watch how they communicate and replicate it (we'll explain more about this in Chapters 4 and 5). Another tactic is to adopt and respond to your client's core attitudes and values, a subject we approach later in this chapter.

The TRUST diagram demonstrates what is needed, but it doesn't tell you how to do it. You need to understand three things about another culture in order to deal with it:

- Basic information about the country
- Its people's attitudes and values
- Their behaviour

These are the three ingredients of understanding another business culture.

The three ingredients of culture

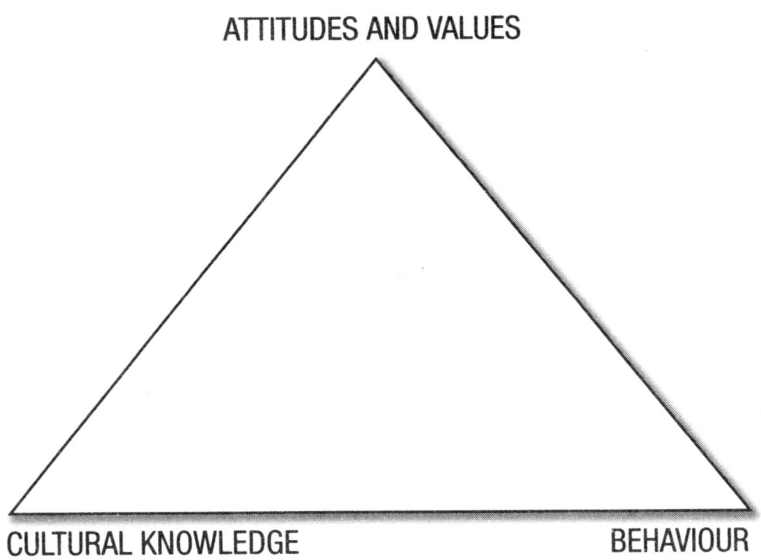

THREE INGREDIENTS DIAGRAM

The importance of cultural knowledge

Networking is important in building business relationships and knowing common cultural references is a key part of successful networking. You'd feel a fool if you went into a pub and didn't know how to pay for a drink, so why would you go to another country and not even know its currency, or what its capital city is? You need to look as if you've done your homework when you're doing business abroad. Make sure you find out the name of the president or head of government, the currency, the main sport (it's not always soccer) and its leading teams and, if you can, details of a couple of entertainment or sports personalities. These are basic elements of networking. Nothing stops a conversation faster than if a name or team is dropped into a conversation and you suddenly ask: "Excuse me – what's Real Madrid?" (Answer: one of Madrid's two leading soccer teams – the other is Atlético Madrid).

Useful and taboo subjects of conversation

When you know someone well, there are few taboo subjects of conversation. But, in the early days of a relationship, there might be areas that make you feel too outspoken, too insensitive or too indiscreet. It's worth researching what to talk about and what to avoid: certain topics get everyone going, but some just lead to an embarrassed silence. And they are not the same everywhere. In some countries, such as China or Italy, you can talk endlessly about food and regional delicacies. In Italy you can ask about families. In China this is a much more delicate area because of the one-child policy, but you can discuss children's education, as that is a basic concern for all families. Normal topics of conversation in Britain or the US may be unwelcome or even taboo in other communities. It's also worth finding out about a country's main information sources – how do people get their news and basic data about everyday living? Since the media has such an influence on how we think and our topics of conversation, it's worth knowing the names of some of the key outlets.

Use the airport for information

Georgina Howard is a language and cultural consultant, based in Spain. Her company 'The Pyrenean Experience' offers management and language walking tours in the Pyrenees mountain range in Spain's Basque country.

When she arrives at a new airport or train station, Georgina scans the local newspapers on display. An international sales manager and a skilled networker, she notes which are the most prominently displayed; if they are in a language she doesn't understand, she looks for names and pictures she recognizes. She can then mention or ask about these subjects, and use them as a talking point. Networking is all about making yourself seem familiar, part of the furniture, so that people feel at ease with you. By showing familiarity with the main media, even superficially, and taking an interest, people immediately feel: "Oh, you know our country!" This may not be entirely true, but at least Georgina's research gives her a chance to gain more insights.

Georgina has other techniques that she uses to absorb almost subliminal information about a country. In the airport she surveys the people, particularly those in the arrivals hall waiting to meet passengers. Rich, poor, how many women, people in families or on their own, styles of dress – all these details give her impressions that she can test in conversation.

The same strategy applies when she visits a new company. In the office foyer she watches how people deal with and greet receptionists (one of the best ways to judge a company's atmosphere and degree of formality or informality), and she scans the trade literature lying around for references to the business she is visiting. She notes the decorations on the walls – what certificates, awards, company photos or sponsorship photos there are. All this gives her a starter impression of what the organization might be like, and offers potential topics of conversation. Above all she is showing interest, and that's what clients need to see.

"Have you heard the one about ....?"

Everyone has a sense of humour and everyone likes jokes. The trouble is, they don't like the same jokes and they don't necessarily like to tell them in the same environment as you do. The British sense of humour is very varied but it depends ultimately on irony and sarcasm, which can make it hard for foreigners to enjoy, even if they have the language levels to understand it.

Worse still, the British use jokes in business meetings to lighten the atmosphere, get through difficult moments and to prick pomposity and self-importance. In communities where meetings are taken fairly seriously, the British sense of humour may be seen as inappropriate and suggest a lack of commitment or interest. Old hands in international business will say, leave the jokes for the bar and replace them with charm until you really know those you are dealing with. Even the traditional British speech opener, "I am reminded of the story about...", followed by a joke, may not be appropriate in societies expecting something more serious.

Preparing to travel

How do you find out all this stuff? Instead of analyzing your spreadsheets, are you expected to spend your scarce time studying business etiquette? How do professionals prepare to deal with another culture?

Kimo Sassi, Finland's former Minister of Overseas Trade, meets overseas business people and government officials both in the EU and worldwide. As well as understanding business issues, he also plans for the social side of an official visit.

It's always useful to learn something about the customs of the country you are going to visit," he says. "What is also very important is the CV of the person you are going to meet so that you know his or her background and can discuss things that they are most likely to be interested in. When I meet ministers, it's very important to get a good atmosphere from the very beginning; for that you need some social talk and some areas where you can agree with your counterpart."

Peter Westerlund, a Finnish IT entrepreneur, confirms Sassi's views.

"Generally, I buy a book when it's a new place," he says. "Nowadays I often go to a country's home pages on the Internet. And I try to talk to people who have been there earlier and know something about the place and the people."

A checklist of things you can do is:

- Buy a book: The Heathrow School of Management, aka the business section of WH Smith, stocks dozens of titles, as do other airport bookshops;
- Ask colleagues who have been there for their three most important Do's and Don'ts;
- Search the web. Enter the name of the country into a search engine and download information on business culture, customs and etiquette. A useful approach is to type Indian (or the name of the country you will be visiting) business culture into the Google search engine;
- Learn a few phrases. *Hello, goodbye, please, thank you. How are you? Fine, thank you. Excuse me, do you speak English?* These basic expressions will demonstrate courtesy to your hosts and suggest that you don't automatically expect them to speak English, although you probably do. (More on this in Chapter 4);

- Use the briefings at the back of this book. There we give you the information you need on the world's ten major economies: more countries will become available on our website and in future books in this series.

Ultimately, however, says Kimo Sassi, "You learn by doing. So when you travel, you notice what's appropriate in any country and what is useful." Above all, adds Peter Westerlund, "Be natural, but get to know about the country and the people."

Understanding values and attitudes

Values and attitudes make up the second pole of our three ingredients of cross-cultural communication. They constitute what the Indian trainer, Liz Kapoor, describes as 'the psyche of a country', and they determine clients' and partners' expectations of one another and their business behaviour. Values and attitudes also form the third C of our five-point business framework for cultural awareness. Recognizing and responding to them is vital to building cultural chemistry in sales, teamwork and joint ventures, and especially in mergers and acquisitions.

Understanding behaviour

Values and attitudes are reflected in business behaviour. If you believe in the importance of community and relationships, developing a friendship with your business partner will be a core behaviour. If your community values systems, clarity and organisation, it will be more important for you to focus on job efficiency. If your core value is directness, your business behaviour will reflect it, but if you favour politeness and courtesy, your approach will be more indirect. Understanding a community's business profile, and anticipating the points at which communication may break down – how to deal with any problems – is a vital skill for international managers.

The need for a cultural business model

So far we have offered two blueprints that indicate how the understanding of culture can help or hinder international business performance. First we introduced the TRUST model of business culture, which says that trust is built on rapport and credibility. Next we identified the three ingredients of building rapport and credibility – showing interest by gathering information about the culture, understanding values and attitudes, and understanding business behaviour. We can now move towards a framework which offers a clear process for building and using cultural knowledge in international business. It is the framework we call the Five C's.

The Five C's of culture

The Five C's offers a simple and clear approach to cultivating your own cultural competence and to selecting the information and understanding you need to unlock any business culture in the world. It enables experienced managers to codify and understand their knowledge, and allows managers relatively new to the international scene to make sense of what could otherwise be a confusing array of signals and impressions.

The Five C's are:

- **Cultural knowledge**

  What is the basic information you need to understand about another culture in order to show interest in it and familiarity with everyday patterns of life?

- **Cultural behaviour**

  How do you identify the basic profile of a country you are dealing with and compare it to your own?

- **Cultural values and attitudes**

  How do you identify what makes a business community tick, and what turns people off?

- **Cultural preferences**

  How can you verify your own cultural preferences and compare them with those of the communities you deal with? And how can you anticipate or get over the problems you encounter?

- **Cultural adaptation**

  What are the six key areas of cultural difference where communication can break down? How can you adapt, or train others to adapt to you?

Going through these five steps with any countries you deal with will allow you to build knowledge of and confidence in dealing with the people you encounter. Succeeding chapters show you how to carry out each step, but first there is one factor that you must consider before we move on.

Stereotypes and generalizations

It's very easy to stereotype people from other business communities, especially when things go wrong. One rule in culture is: Never forget that people are individuals. They don't conform to the cultural profile in all respects. The opposite is also true. People who appear fully integrated into your business culture may suddenly do things which are totally in tune with their culture and totally out of tune with yours.

Vikram is Indian, and a successful fashion and show business photographer. He's a good example of international culture not being recognized locally. He was born and brought up in Mumbai, where he attended school and college. Later he studied photography in London and worked in fashion photography in New York before he returned to the Bollywood movie scene in Mumbai. Vikram is wealthy and cosmopolitan, but when he visits his parents they still ask him when he's going to get a proper job. For an Indian family it is especially important for the sons to do well in business or the respected professions. Photography and the cinema count as neither.

Neeta was born and brought up in London, and works as an underwriter for a leading British insurance company. She recently surprised her HR manager by asking for extended leave of absence to return to India at a time when she was desperately needed in the office. "Why now?" asked the manager. "If I don't go now," Neeta replied, "I won't be able to get married." She was referring to the marriage market, the time in India when marriages are brokered between families and an auspicious moment to be on the spot. Many Indian marriages are arranged, and superstition plays an important part in the timing of the engagement and marriage ceremonies. In observing traditional engagement and marriage customs she was, as an international manager, reverting to her own traditional culture.

Both examples illustrate how sophisticated and worldly people can be constrained or influenced by traditional factors, and why we need to consider this when we look at cultural characteristics.

One of the effects of globalization is that we are all culturally mixed. We carry multiple cultural influences by virtue of the TV we watch, the movies we see, the fashions we wear and the food we eat at restaurants or at home from supermarkets or take-aways. Therefore it is all the more important to recognize the difference between cultural influence and personal experience. We do this by distinguishing between stereotypes and generalizations.

Stereotypes fix people. *All English people are cold and reserved.* No we're not! Some are on first acquaintance, but many foreigners are happily surprised when they discover later that the stereotypical image of English people is false. *Most British people respect and value privacy.* As a general principle that statement is much truer, and is one that more gregarious foreigners fail to take into account, which can cause misunderstandings. "No thank you, I don't want to go out every second of my weekend and attend all your family outings and gatherings. Nothing personal, *but I just want to be alone!"*

What we try to do in understanding another culture is to make generalizations about it, but also to recognize that they may be modified by a number of factors. The principal ones are:

- Region
- Company
- Personal experience
- Generation
- Gender

Region

People behave differently according to the region they come from. The differences may be based purely on geography (northern and southern Britain, for example) or they may include a racial element. Russian Lithuanians in the east of the country display significant behavioural differences from Western Lithuanians, as do French-speaking Walloons from Flemish-speaking Belgians.

It's important to know culturally whom you are dealing with by asking the simple question: "Where are you from (in Lithuania)?" or "What language do you speak at home?" National cultural characteristics exist in every country, but there are usually regional variations.

Company

Company culture may also influence national or regional characteristics, especially in multinational organizations. It's important to find out if the person you are dealing with has experience of working in a multinational. An executive brought up in a community traditionally relaxed about time and punctuality will have had to learn a different system if she is operating in a multinational. Unilever or Shell, for example, simply cannot function in a 'loose' time environment.

Personal experience

Personal experience may also influence a person's cultural characteristics. As we saw from Vikram's and Neeta's situation, an Indian born and brought up entirely in India will be very different from one who has had extensive overseas experience, although even they may be constrained by certain national attitudes and customs. An individual brought up in a 'loose' time environment, such as Brazil or India, may feel that they are never actually late, even though they consistently arrive long after the scheduled moment for an appointment or meeting. But a person from a 'tight' time environment – the USA and the UK are examples – can feel irritated if someone is as little as five minutes late. More importantly, a manager who has studied and worked in two or three countries will be a different person to one who has never experienced any other than his native business culture.

Working with international managers who have experience abroad can be both a blessing and a curse. Although Japan is changing rapidly, it still has quite a closed business community with definite codes of behaviour, particularly in the manufacturing sector. And it doesn't always have total confidence in some of its widely travelled, more expansive 'westernized' managers. Koji was Japanese, had had two overseas postings, one of them to the US, spoke good US-accented English and adopted US mannerisms and style. "Good," we thought, "someone we can do business with." But he wasn't. His manner and style meant that he wasn't considered Japanese enough to be fully trusted by his colleagues, and our image was affected by our association with him. The lesson is to make sure that the foreign manager who is 'just like you' is also 'just like them' as well.

We can represent the different levels of influence like this:

National culture	National characteristics
Regional culture	Regional variations on the national cultural profile
Company culture	Multinational Local SME Family owned
Individual culture	Ethnic background Religion Generation Gender

Generation

Western societies may have age-discrimination laws, but we don't actually respect age. We prefer to respect achievement regardless of age. But in many societies, reaching 55 and having white hair is in itself regarded as an achievement and earns respect. Japan is like this, as is China. In countries like these, age is second only to seniority. In a meeting, spend time with the oldest member present. Others will be watching and they will appreciate your respect. In Russia it is still the custom to give way to older people on public transport. And being a direct people, Russians will tell you if you fail to observe this courtesy.

A more sensitive age factor often arises in companies and countries that have experienced major social, economic or political upheavals. Central and Eastern

Europe moved from communism to capitalism very rapidly in the 1990s: there, 'old school' managers may be efficient and experienced, but they may also be reluctant to take initiatives and may defer unnecessarily to rules and authority (not doing this could have lost you your job or got you thrown in jail even 20 years ago). In Japan there is a generation gap in the way industrial and commercial society functions, such as with the gradual change from womb-to-tomb employment to contract work, and the revolt of the young against the 'My company comes first' work culture. In Japan, too, a modernizing manager (often in his thirties or early forties) may be replaced by a more conservative manager in his forties or early fifties. You may think that this is just the natural effect of ageing, but social and cultural factors have a big influence on the way managers see their jobs, especially when they are dealing with managers overseas. For example, an older foreign manager may expect respect by right of age that they simply don't get in the UK or the US, where you are as good as your performance. Similarly, an older UK or US manager may be embarrassed by receiving what he sees as exaggerated respect or deference in more age-respectful societies, such as China, Japan or Russia.

Gender

Catherine is an associate in a British law firm, and hopes to become a junior partner in a few years. She is young for her level of responsibility, very competent, very presentable and Afro-Caribbean. On a consultancy visit to Brazil, it took a while for her and her colleagues to realize that she was not being treated in the same way as the others in her team. Over a private drink in the bar one night with one of the male members of the team, a Brazilian lawyer assumed that she was obviously simply the mistress of one of the partners, on a 'jolly' with her boss. Crudely put, he simply didn't believe that a beautiful, black, young female could be anything other than a plaything. This is not typical of Brazilians, but nevertheless such attitudes are more common than you might expect.

Even in the USA and the UK, sexism hasn't been fully resolved. But in economies where women still hold relatively junior positions or are normally expected to leave work on marriage, male executives may find it difficult to deal with female counterparts at their level. There are two rules for female managers to help you to maintain parity and ensure respect:

1. Lead with your business card. Make sure it states clearly your level of seniority within the company;

2. Make sure that your male colleagues support your position and defer to you if, for example, a foreign manager automatically addresses them rather than you.

Don't be embarrassed to establish the ground rules with your team before you go into meetings: there should be no joking about women, they should respect your position, and if someone on the other team puts a question to a man that you should deal with, make sure they refer it across. You can establish the rules lightly and quickly, but they do need establishing.

Other factors: Race, religion, sexual orientation and disability

In multicultural, equal-opportunity societies such as the UK or the USA, where managers can be white, black, brown, or yellow, Christian, Hindu, Buddhist or Jewish and gay or straight, it is a crime to discriminate on the grounds of race, religion and sexual orientation. It can therefore be a shock when we encounter different attitudes held quite openly in other cultures. But we have to recognize that in some business cultures there is an aversion to people of different races and religion, or who are gay. You may feel extreme distaste for the attitudes expressed, for example, by one Eastern European businessman who said: "I'll tell you right out – we don't like Jews."

How do you deal with that in a business meeting? Do you confront it or remain silent? In a negotiating team it is vital at all times to reinforce the status and position of your key members, so here is a strategy that will help you to cope with discrimination should it arise:

1. **Remain true to your principles**. Don't back down because of fears of non-acceptance of race, religion or sexual orientation, nor indeed of disability.
2. **Assess the risk**. Is the person representing you confident enough to deal with these kinds of issues if they arise? Do they need support?
3. **Lead with the business card**. Make sure it is clear about your title and seniority.

4 **Ensure that team support is absolute**. Team members must defer to the appropriate colleague when appropriate and not take responsibility for things that are not in their remit.

5 **Be sensitive**. When a team member is ignored or not consulted by the other side, it may be that they are making negative assumptions based on their traditional attitudes to gender, race, religion or sexual orientation differences. It can be quite difficult to judge what is going on, so if you think that this is the case, it's important to establish the credentials (experience and qualifications) of the colleague concerned so that they can feel confident in making their full contribution to the meeting or negotiation.

On the whole, we have not found that disability is an area that provokes discrimination in business cultures. However, it is often a practical issue, as facilities for the disabled in many parts of the world are not as well developed as they are in the UK, Western Europe and North America. It's always worth advising your hosts of any disability issues that might arise, as they could influence room and transport bookings, the availability of help with wheelchairs and other aids, and other matters.

Conclusion

In this chapter we have presented the TRUST diagram as the basis of successful international business dealing, and the Five C's of culture as a framework to unlock any culture in the world. We have also identified the danger of stereotyping and suggested how to avoid it, and looked at how diversity issues (race, religion, age, gender, sexual orientation and disability) might be viewed in other countries.

In the next chapters we offer the keys to the framework. We begin with how to discover the behaviour profile of the country you are dealing with, and how you might need to adapt.

Key learning points

- In international business, trust assumes enormous importance.
- Trust is established by building rapport and credibility (matching your communication style to theirs).
- To unlock any culture in the world you need to apply the Five C's: knowledge, behaviour, values and attitudes, an awareness of your cultural preferences and techniques to adapt it.
- Use generalizations about national, regional and company culture as a platform to understand the individuals you deal with.
- Different cultures have different attitudes to issues such as gender, race, religion, sexual orientation, age and disability. You need to establish strategies beforehand to deal with issues.

THREE

How people think

where do our values and attitudes come from, and how can we know those of other people? The way we think and what we expect from other people are affected by six main influences, which are strongly swayed by national and regional traditions. This chapter explains where these influences come from, and how to use them to achieve greater international business success. The influences are: parents, social environment, education, religion, history and media.

Parents

Parents embody not just their personal experience, but also the history of the nation they grow up in. They are a repository of values, and as the first people we 'meet' they influence massively the way we subconsciously think. But there are also national and regional patterns in the way people regard the family, and differences in social environments. In Italy, family relationships are the prime motivation for doing business: it still has one of the largest percentages of family-run enterprises in Europe. In dealing with an Italian business, it's essential to appreciate the family's role. In the same way, an Italian will look for evidence of your family. Family means you have roots, you have something to lose and therefore you are less likely to behave irresponsibly. Where extended families are common, as in India or Africa, it's crucial to accept that people are motivated by a range of domestic responsibilities that may affect how business is done. In British companies, Indian executives resident in the UK may still be sending a portion of their salary to India to support relatives back home. An African businessman once confided to us how he hated going abroad because of the huge number of presents he was expected to buy for his extended family when he got back home. A teddy bear bought for a kid at the last moment on the flight home just didn't hack it!

Social environment

If you live in Britain you will take for granted that we have four nationalities – English, Irish, Scottish and Welsh – plus significant immigration from the Commonwealth countries and, more recently, the expanded European Union. You will also be aware of the cultural differences in the UK, principally between the north and the south. Where you are brought up – region, country or town, deprived area or affluent neighbourhood – will affect your outlook, as will the political system you grow up in.

The six metros or metropolitan cities, as they are known in India, of Delhi, Mumbai, Kolkata, Hyderabad, Bangalore and Chennai, have very different cultures. Spain has three major business cultures – those of Madrid, Barcelona and Andalusia – but there are also significant differences between northern and central Spain and the Basque Country. And Spaniards would add at least two more, Valencia and the cold north-west of Galicia. In Italy there is a fundamental difference between the business cultures of the north, focused on Milan, and the south – the *mezzogiorno* – based around Naples. Some northerners even suggest that the *mezzogiorno* begins above Rome! Belgium has a major linguistic and cultural divide between the Flemish and French speaking parts of the country.

These are what we call cultural fault lines, the equivalent of the geological fault lines caused by the overlapping of the earth's tectonic plates. They indicate sometimes subtle but often fundamental contrasts in cultural approach which can cause tension within the domestic population and externally with foreigners. As we have seen in Iraq, there is an explosive fault line between the Shia majority and Sunni minority, and between them and the Kurds. In spite of their common Muslim faith, these divisions can pull a country apart.

Education

"There is no problem about leadership in Italy," an Italian businessman said. "The Holy Father tells us what to believe, our teachers tell us what to think and our fathers tell us how to behave." Education systems largely define how people think, how they feel about authority and how they go about solving problems. Understanding the principles and psychology of a country's school and university system is vital to interpreting its people's social and psychological ideas. Of course, tradition can distort reality. Foreigners dealing with British companies retain images of public schools and the old school tie, which both amuses and irritates the Brits. Educational priorities explain the preponderance of engineers with PhD's who lead German companies, the lawyers who manage American corporations and the accountants who run many British organizations.

Religion

Britons and Americans are brought up and work in a Judeo-Christian environment. Religion doesn't impinge on their daily working life and is not a part of business processes, although it often influences individual practice and decisions. However, in the Middle East and in the Muslim Far East, the Five Pillars of Islam dominate life and business, including the concept of mortgages and money-lending. In India business is not guided by Hinduism or any of the country's six other main religions but it is affected, as in China, by superstition. Decisions to sign contracts, to travel and to get married are taken on auspicious days. In China, decisions as to where to site buildings may be made according to the principles of Feng Shui and there is superstition, as in Japan, about the number four, which will affect the naming of offices and floors in buildings. On Golden College Day in Shanghai, when Chinese upper middle schools enrol pupils, taxis with the number four in their registration plate were pulled off the streets, according to a BBC Radio 4 report. In China, philosophical tradition governs the culture of respect that is so crucial in Chinese life. Respect for authority and age, frugality, the giving of alms and a passion for education are the five principles of Confucianism.

History

History also affects how a country views foreigners and the rest of the world. A huge example of this is the work that Central and Eastern European countries are doing to rebuild their economies and financial and governmental structures, after as much as 70 years of Communist rule. Banks and political institutions are having to reach back before the Second World War and even to the 19th century to discover their organizational roots. In countries where such upheaval is taking place, business visitors who show an interest in this vivid history and the way it affects people's lives today are really appreciated. In ancient civilizations such as those of China and India, events and achievements from their long history crop up frequently in conversation, and the foreigner who can contribute at least something to the debate will be valued over one who remains sadly ignorant.

Media

The media has shrunk the world. From the internet, CNN, BBC World TV, the financial channel Bloomberg, the Arabic TV channel and website Aljazeera, as well as global news agencies such as Reuters, we learn of natural disasters, conflicts and economic crises as they happen. What the media says about a country can have an immediate effect on levels of business confidence and stock market prices, and on the travel decisions of the business community and holidaymakers. An isolated incident in one place can cause wholesale business flight. In Pakistan, for example, stories of honour killings of Muslim women can affect the image of the country and overall business confidence.

In both positive and negative ways, the media contributes to our images of countries and regions as desirable business partners. A new branch of cultural studies, known as cultural branding or nation branding, now identifies the ways in which national profiles can be enhanced. Its aim is to raise a country's political and economic standing, increase exports and inward investment, and attract tourism. Countries compete to host major world events such as football's World Cup, the Olympic Games and the G8 Summit of major economic powers, and strive to achieve membership of international organizations such as the World Trade Organization.

In his book *On Brand*, brand management expert Wally Olins shows how the perception of Spain changed after the death of the dictator General Franco in 1975 from that of a land of cheap plonk, peasants and fascism to one of a modern democracy, a key member of the European Union, and a desirable holiday and second-home destination. Spain now trains managers in a network of business schools, produces international personalities such as Javier Solana, secretary-general of the Council of the EU and former NATO secretary-general, the film director Pedro Almodóvar, the Iglesias family (father Julio and son Enrique), who have done so much to popularize Latin music, and the country's first Formula 1 world champion, Fernando Alonso. How the media treats countries and regions influences how both their citizens and outsiders see them.

Cultural brand management is an increasingly important industry, with one of its pioneers, Simon Anholt, advising governments worldwide on how to improve their international image to encourage inward investment and increase external influence.

How to understand values and attitudes

How do you apply your new knowledge of values and attitudes to make good business decisions? The answer is break it down into five key component parts. Understand these, and you're on your way to successfully conducting international deals.

1 Core values

Core values are the principles that guide people's behaviour: honour them, and you'll forge strong business relationships. They're often expressed in national slogans. The French celebrate *liberté, égalité, fraternité* (freedom, equality and brotherhood), so it's hardly surprising that individual freedom and independence is especially important to them. It goes some way to explaining why the French always strive for individual solutions and refuse to follow the general consensus, to the despair of other countries. It also accounts for their ingenuity in finding solutions to problems, especially for getting round their government's sometimes arcane bureaucracy. The USA shares similar values, which is not surprising as both countries went through revolutions in the late eighteenth century that inspired many similar movements. However, the USA differs in its 'can do' culture and its belief that anything is possible providing you work at it hard enough. It's important to Americans that foreigners empathize with this attitude rather than oppose it. The value that the Chinese most cherish in others is sincerity, while the British prefer transparency about the business process and privacy about personal life. Germans will look for efficiency, clarity and order in their dealings with others, whereas the Japanese appreciate above all the time taken to build trust. Romanians often say that showing hospitality is one of their virtues. In many countries, including Russia, the USA and France, patriotism and national interest are high on the values agenda, and you must be careful about criticizing their country, even if they themselves feel free to do so. Core values are what you appeal to in every stage of the business process.

2 Cultural fears

These are the hidden and deep-rooted anxieties held by any society. Avoid triggering them and you will prosper; set them off and you'll find yourself in a minefield that will destroy your business relationship. Probably even more so than cultural values, cultural fears can cause real problems. In cultures that value respect, such as China, Korea and Japan, a failure to show courtesy and to defer to the right people will lead to a downgrading of your status and, in Korea, your unofficial designation as a 'non-person'. You'll be treated with punctilious politeness, but you'll find that somehow all decisions and information-sharing pass you by. Losing face is a prospect particularly feared in the Far East, India and the Middle East. This is the dread of your personal dignity being insulted by someone's remarks or actions. Your sensitivity to these issues will really increase your standing in such societies.

Country names are another area of sensitivity. Don't call Austrians Germans, even when joking; Canadians are Canadians or North Americans, but never Americans. The PRC (People's Republic of China – mainland China) must never be confused with the ROC (Republic of China – the island of Taiwan). Mainland Chinese call it Taiwan or sometimes Greater China, but never by its former name, Formosa. The English are less sensitive to national issues and often call themselves British in order not to embarrass the Scots, Northern Irish or Welsh. But it's important to treat seriously other cultures' concerns about nationality.

The fear of being patronized is especially common in former colonial countries or economic dependencies. Indians, Africans and Afro-Caribbeans are very sensitive to what they may see as condescending comments about their country and its system of government and business, and will freeze up if they hear them. Latin Americans will react in the same way if they hear derisory comments from their US neighbours. On a less serious note, we asked a group of Indian managers what their cultural fears were. The answer came as one: "God and our mothers!" Cultural fears: avoid them, or if you can't, treat them with healthy respect.

3 Motivation

Many people believe that business is solely about making money and generating wealth. But even in free-market societies that's not necessarily true. Other factors may influence decisions and may be more important in the long run. You therefore need to understand the key motivators for different communities and to respond to them appropriately. Throwing money at people isn't necessarily the best way of solving a business problem or cementing a relationship.

The five key areas of motivation are:

- Money
- Status

- Power
- Security
- Working conditions and professional development – fun, in short

MONEY

Money is the driving force in business communities like the United States or India. So the key argument in building a business relationship is: how much money will this proposal generate, and when? This is not so much greed, as a response to a feeling that you're very much on your own. Safety nets and social security are limited in such countries, and people have to provide for their dependants. Indian families share the aspiration that their sons will do well in business, which is why the Indian education system turns out so many MBA graduates.

The US is a nation of immigrants, many of whom were – and are – driven there by poverty and a lack of economic opportunity in their own countries. In Central and Eastern Europe, money was and remains a scarce commodity, so in those countries short-term economic gain is usually the prime motivation in a business relationship.

STATUS

Where cash is not the prime worry, other motivations begin to take over. In many business communities, particularly in countries with an established safety net based on state provision, the emphasis might be less on short-term income and more on building social status. Having the right car or an office suite equal to your opposite number's becomes important as a symbol of your economic success, as in Germany. In countries like Britain, successful business people often make sizeable charitable donations or devote time to voluntary work. This can lead to knighthood, attendance at royal garden parties at Buckingham Palace and other status symbols that announce that you've truly arrived. In Britain, Sir Richard Branson has launched The Virgin Foundation to aid African causes. In the USA, Bill Gates provides one of the best-known examples of a business person channelling his efforts into philanthropical work, with the multi-billion dollar Bill and Melinda Gates Foundation, launched by the Microsoft co-founder and his wife.

POWER

In other countries, including Russia, Spain, Italy and Latin America, the route to money may be by acquiring power. If you control things, you will enrich yourself. This is less to do with your social position and the esteem in which you are held. It is more to do with the resources you control, your power to make things happen and to get others to do things. Status and power in some ways go together, but there is a subtle difference. It is possible to have low social status but a lot of power. The mafia is an obvious example.

SECURITY

A fourth motivation may be security. During recessions or periods of insecurity, people might desperately need to make money, yet their economy may have become risk-averse. So a business deal might be seen as a means of providing security for the family. This is especially the case in Eastern and Central Europe where people have emerged from the relative security of Communism into the insecurity and opportunity of the free market. In some cases this has led to massive opportunism, in others a retreat into a wish for security. Understanding the need for security is a very important way of motivating people in an insecure environment. A solid foundation rather than a get-rich-quick strategy may be the approach to go for.

FUN

The fifth motivator is what we call fun. People often stay in poorly paid jobs because they provide a regular income, stimulating working conditions and opportunities for professional development. In this instance, people weigh the profit motive against the desire to enjoy a congenial working environment. This is often the case in British companies, for example, and in countries like Switzerland. Professional development and good working conditions tend to be important in countries with a reasonably high and secure standard of living and may be particularly important to clerical workers, supervisors and junior and middle managers. However, in a country like India, creating a family or campus atmosphere for workers, especially in the call centre industry, is considered important for retaining employees and reducing attrition.

4 Space

We all have a personal comfort zone: how close do you like to stand to people? Roger Axtell, in his amusing books on international business etiquette, suggests that the acceptable difference between people of the same nationality who don't know each other well varies from 30 centimetres to 1.5 metres. So if an Italian – comfort zone between three and 60 centimetres, according to Axtell – stands at what he feels is an appropriate distance from me, a Brit –

comfort zone around 1.2 metres – I will feel that he's being too familiar. But if I move away, he could think that I'm being stand-offish. It's important to be sensitive to local practice and not get upset if people seem to stand too close to you.

Similar rules apply to the question of touch. In India handshakes are common, but you should wait for a woman to extend her hand first. She may be more accustomed to the traditional *namaste* greeting (hands joined together in prayer at chest height) and might find a handshake too personal and embarrassing. The Japanese are the world's least tactile people, whereas Latins are highly touchy-feely. In India, Pakistan and Arab countries, male friends may hold hands in the street but this doesn't mean that they're gay.

Even smiling carries social meaning. The French, Russians and Japanese all profess to be amazed at the American and British habit of smiling for the sake of it. *They* smile when there's something to smile about or, in the case of people from the Far East, to hide embarrassment or to be courteous. A Japanese manager told us: "We smile because we know you Westerners like it." In a famous case, when McDonalds opened in Moscow in the eighties, they trained their front of house staff to greet the customer cheerfully with a nice smile. "What?" was the unanimous protest, "They'll think we're idiots!"

Distance, touching and body language are customs that you can learn by watching how people go about their business. If in doubt, ask someone you know and trust. And if a Greek businessman hugs your arm as you cross the street or go for a walk, it's a sign of trust and confidence, nothing more.

5 Time

In some countries, government officials make you hang around to demonstrate how important they are. Two British company directors were in Libya, waiting for an appointment with the chief secretary at one of the ministries in Tripoli. How long did they have to sit outside his office? *Six hours!* In the end, they were ushered into his presence. He looked them both in the eye and pointed. "I like you," he said to one director, and then, "I like you," to the other. Then he turned to his personal secretary and told him: "See to it." Painful and frustrating as the delay had been, the visitors agreed that the investment had been worth it for the huge contract they had just clinched.

Nothing in international business makes people angrier than the conflict between 'loose' and 'tight' timekeeping. 'Loose' timekeeping means that schedules are not maintained and appointments are elastic. 'Tight' timekeeping means that appointment and meeting times are adhered to rigidly. There is almost a desperation to the American feeling that time is important and urgent, whereas the British believe that it's simply courteous and efficient to arrive at the agreed hour. In France, meetings normally begin on schedule but never end on time, due to the French propensity for discussing all aspects of the subject at length and in philosophical depth. In Germany and in Scandinavia, meetings start and end exactly when they say they will. Toni, the chairman of a group of Swiss companies based in Zurich, says that he always allows an extra hour for important meetings, just in case longer is needed: it's testimony to his country's attitude to time that even overruns have to be tightly scheduled. In Britain, ten minutes spent in small talk at the start of a meeting is not uncommon to allow attendees to relax but, in Finland and Sweden, the same will be accomplished in three minutes.

How do I find out what's what?

There are six rules for finding out what's really going on in a culture.

RULE 1	Don't assume	RULE 4	Listen
RULE 2	Be quiet	RULE 5	Feel
RULE 3	Look	RULE 6	Ask questions

It will also help if you read about the country or culture that you're dealing with. In the chapters at the back of this book you'll find detailed information about the values and attitudes in the ten countries that are forecast to be the world's leading economies in 2050. The guidelines they contain will help you to plan drama-free business relationships.

Conclusion

The first key to appreciating another culture is to learn about it, and the second is to understand its values and attitudes. Then you can apply these values and see how they affect the business process.

Key learning points

- Understanding a country's values and attitudes is crucial to doing successful business.
- Values and attitudes come from families, geographical, social and political environments, education, religion and history, and are deeply influenced by media treatment.
- Pay special attention to the following areas: core values, cultural fears, motivation (money, status, power, security or 'fun'), and attitudes to personal space and to time.

FOUR

Cultural behaviour

FOUR
Cultural behaviour

Richard Gesteland is the founder of Global Management LLC and trains managers in cross-cultural negotiating techniques. In his book *Cross-Cultural Business Behaviour* he identifies four factors that provide a quick insight into how a foreign business culture works. They are:

Relationship-focused	**Deal-focused**
Does business depend on building good relationships?	Is getting the job done the prime criterion?
Formal	**Informal**
Are business relationships formal and respectful? Is the business style top-down? Are reporting lines strict and respected?	Are business relationships informal and casual? Is the business style egalitarian? Is a matrix system of reporting in operation?
Monochronic	**Polychronic**
Strict timekeeping Tight scheduling Long-term planning	Unpunctuality Flexibility Crisis management
Reserved	**Expressive (emotional)**
Don't show emotion	Show emotion

The best way to begin to compare behaviour is to analyze your own culture. Broadly speaking, British and North American cultures have similar behaviour profiles. They are both deal-focused, informal, monochronic and reserved. Incidentally, we prefer the term 'emotional' to Gesteland's choice of 'expressive' as will be apparent in Chapter 6. Gesteland considers the UK to be 'variably formal', whereas we rate it as very informal, but these distinctions often depend on your country of origin. If you use his guide to evaluate two contrasting cultures, China and Brazil, you find that China is relationship-focused, formal, polychronic and emotionally neutral, whereas Brazil is relationship-focused, formal, polychronic and emotional.

Given these two profiles, how should you adjust your behaviour to match the expectations of your client or partner? In China you should spend time building the relationship (usually through regular visits, exchanges of formal dinners and so on). You should respect Chinese authority by not criticizing it, praise Chinese culture and understand that the way to change Chinese behaviour is by persuasion from a position of loyalty, not opposition. You should allow for the fact that meetings may start and certainly finish late, and that people may leave during the proceedings. Finally, you will realize that the Chinese, although very hard in business negotiations, will always expect you to preserve the niceties of the social relationship.

The Brazilians will want a good relationship with you. Even if the business relationship starts formally it will be important to extend it to first name terms as soon as you both feel at ease. Expect socializing after work to be an important part of the business, including family occasions. Once again, make allowances for delays in all events and, above all, be prepared to show your human side.

If you can create a business behaviour profile for the country you're dealing with, it's one of the easiest ways of assessing how you might need to adapt. Gesteland made a list of the key behavioural characteristics of many countries, which we include below.

Why me?

This is such a common complaint by business people dealing with issues of intercultural awareness. Why do *I* have to change? Why not *them*? And what happens if we both change? Do we collide in the middle? Well, yes, as it happens. The head of Japan Airlines in London met me (Barry Tomalin) at his offices off Regent Street in the centre of the West End. He had previously been head of the US bureau, and had just returned from a trip to New York; I had just returned from Tokyo. I turned up ahead of schedule and was invited to wait next to his office. As I heard steps coming down the corridor, exactly on time, I stood up, tightened my stomach ready to bow and checked that my name card was in my breast pocket ready to present. As he turned into the office anteroom I bowed to show how aware I was of Japanese culture. "Hi, I'm Kimura!", he said. He bounded forward, hand outstretched and our heads met in the middle! We got on fine after that.

Traditionally, it is the provider who adapts to the client. But although training in intercultural awareness is relatively well established in the Netherlands, Germany and the US, and increasingly so in Britain, it is not yet seen as an essential skill elsewhere. Therefore it's often necessary for the client to adapt to the provider, at least until the relationship is well established. What is important is not to get resentful, and above all not to get aggressive and make unpleasant jokes about your partners. They usually understand what is happening, even if you talk in asides to your colleagues in your own language, and they don't respond well. Assume that it's down to you to take the first step.

To help you, take a look at Gesteland's behaviour profiles of key business cultures below. He places world cultures in eight groups. To compare the UK with another country, match its profile against the culture you are interested in.

UK	**US, CANADA, AUSTRALIA**
Deal-focused	Deal-focused
Informal	Informal
Monochronic	Monochronic
Reserved	Variably emotional

In 2050, according to Morgan Grenfell investment bank, the world's leading economies will look like this.

1 China

2 USA

3 India

4 Japan

5 Brazil

6 Russia

7 UK

8 Germany

9 France

10 Italy

All these countries have very different cultural profiles but by using Gesteland's cultural behaviour profile we can begin to understand the differences and understand how to adapt our behaviour to suit the culture we are dealing with.

The UK and Germany have quite similar behaviour profiles and differences are a matter of degree rather than opposition. Both countries, for example, are deal-focused in that it is possible to do business without building a personal relationship and personal relationships are often built through successful business.

One significant difference is that German business is still quite formal, whereas British business is usually very informal. For us, as Brits working with Germans, we know we need to watch our P's and Q's and be just a little bit more formal, more deliberate and a little less casual and jokey than we might be at home.

Germans need to learn to relax a bit more with British and Americans and sometimes their efforts to do so feel quite heavy-handed.

On the other hand, the British and the Germans both believe in punctuality, although the Germans possibly stress being on time a little more than the British do.

Both the British and the Germans share the 'stiff upper lip'. Showing emotions is not what you do in the business environment. So a British business person adapting to a German environment will pay more attention to time, and to respect and taking a serious approach in the workplace.

If you apply the same principles to the USA, you discover that the UK and the US have similar profiles but the Americans are more inclined to share how they feel. Therefore, when we are advising a Brit or a German on how to adapt their behaviour to the US environment we will always stress the importance of showing your human side, being positive and sharing your personal dreams and aspirations in order to get the support of American colleagues.

Let us now apply Gesteland's behaviour profile to a Mediterranean country, such as Italy. Here the differences are much greater. Italian business is built on good personal relationships. So entertainment, invitations home and the creation of a good family spirit are an important part of making the business work. Similarly, a Brit will need to realize that alongside this family atmosphere there is a lot of respect for the boss and for senior figures in the organization, and that a certain amount of respectful distance should be observed.

All British business people have to adopt a more relaxed attitude to time. Meetings will go on longer. Meals will be an important part of the business process, and availability in the evenings and at weekends will be expected. Monochronic Brits will have to adapt to the more polychronic Italians, not an unpleasant process.

Finally, Italians display and expect enthusiasm and emotion. Showing how you feel is important for many Italians and some British love it. Others however, find it wearing and even embarrassing! If you're in this group, just remember that Italians may find your deadpan expression and slightly pursed lips equally off-putting.

Relationships are not just important for the Italians. They also matter to the Chinese, the Japanese, the Russians and the Brazilians. These are people who feel a need to know what kind of person you are and, to do so, socializing is important. This may be done through eating (Chinese), through drinking (traditionally, Russians), through going out (Brazilians), and singing karaoke (Japanese). All these have the same function, creating a social environment where people can get to know each other. In the ritualistic environment of the Chinese or Japanese office, the banquet or the karaoke bar is the place where people feel they can unwind and reveal their real selves. If all you want to do after the working day is be alone, you will miss out on an important part of business relationship building.

All these cultures are marked by a degree of formality in business relationships, especially in the attitude towards the boss. It can be surprising for a Brit or an American to find the person they refer to by their first name, addressed as Sir or Mrs Wu, by everyone else.

The attitude to time, however, is different. Like the British and the Americans, the Chinese and the Japanese believe in punctuality. For the Brazilians and the Russians time is more a question of what is needed in relation to the task at hand. If it's not absolutely important to be somewhere on time, relax and get there when you can. What can be galling for British and Americans is that others often expect them to arrive on time 'because that's their culture' while reserving their own right to turn up when they are ready!

The other difference is the attitude to emotion in a meeting or negotiation. For the Brazilians and the Russians emotion is important and, particularly on the Russian side, anger may be used as a bargaining tool. However, for the Chinese and the Japanese emotion has no place at the negotiation table and to show anger or loss of temper may be seen as a sign of weakness and loss of control.

That leaves two cultures unaccounted for in our top ten, France and India.

According to Gesteland, France is less deal-focused compared with Britain but much more so than India, where business is built entirely on relationships. Personal warmth and goodwill are vital to Indian business relationships. Indian business people work hard to build relationships as they are the basis on which a contractual relationship can be established.

Both France and India have a formal business structure and relationship with a high degree of respect shown to the boss. Where the British often come unstuck is in confusing relationship building with lack of respect. If I have a good relationship with you I can make jokes at your expense, right? That *may* be the case but it is important not to take informality for granted. We have seen many business relationships fail after a lot of effort put into establishing them because of a misplaced familiarity with the boss.

In India, as we have said elsewhere, people refer to Indian Standard Time as Indian *Stretchable* Time, which gives a fair impression of most Indians attitude to timekeeping. The French are much more time sensitive but although things may start on time, they rarely finish on time as it would be considered rude to end before the business is completed.

Another difference between the French and the Indians is that Indians, although emotional under the surface, prefer to keep their emotions under control in business and in negotiations, whereas the French are much more likely to show anger or appreciation openly.

How should British business people react to these differences in behaviour?

First, recognize your own national profile and decide to what extent you personally respond to it or differ from it. Secondly, understand the other nationality's profile and decide to what degree your colleague or client responds or differs from it. Thirdly, decide how much you need to adapt and in what area or how much you want them to adapt to you, remembering that the supplier normally adapts to the client.

As a quick guide to how to adapt, if you come from a country that is deal-focused, informal, monochronic and reserved:

- If you're dealing with emotional cultures, take time to build the relationship.
- With formal cultures, respect hierarchy and age.
- In polychronic cultures, relax your schedule, expect things to take longer and do more business at social occasions.
- With cultures that are more emotional, share personal experiences and show your human side.

Scheduled, flexible and listening cultures

Richard Lewis is an internationalist, a linguist and one of the most accessible authors on cross-cultural communication. He has taught among others the Crown Prince of Japan and the President of Finland, and founded and ran for many years the language school chain, Linguarama. Today he trains individuals and small groups in the UK. His Lewis model is a framework that organizes business cultures according to how they think about and use time.

He divides business cultures into three categories: linear-active, multi-active and reactive. For simplicity, we have retitled them, Scheduled, Flexible and Listening. Understanding each type of society adds detail to the Gesteland model, and offers insight into how different cultures perform in business.

Our reformulation of the Lewis model looks like this:

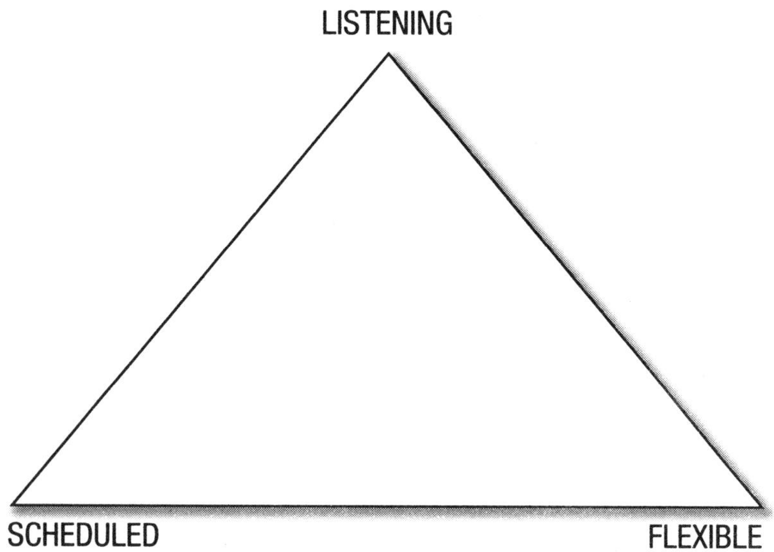

THREE TYPES OF CULTURE

Characteristics

SCHEDULED	LISTENING	FLEXIBLE
Schedules	Listens	Blocks of time
Times	Questions	Flexible
Punctual	Clarifies	Unpunctual
High pre-planning	Little feedback	Responds to circumstances
Medium- to long-term	Slow decisions	Short-term
Formal agreement	Silence	Informal agreement
Facts important	Mainly relationship important	Relationship important

Scheduled cultures

A scheduled culture does things by the clock: examples are Germany, the USA and Japan. It's important to have a detailed plan for everything, to keep to it and to adhere to strict timetables. This involves the development of medium- and long-term strategies, and a complicated system of business cases, revenue projection, agendas, memos, milestones, benchmarking and minutes to record plans and progress. This is the armoury of a scheduled business community. There is a preference for written communication, usually by email, and decisions are based on facts and figures rather than instinct and intuition.

Other cultures that conform to this model include the Netherlands, the Nordic countries (Norway, Sweden, Denmark and Finland), Canada, Australia, New Zealand, Korea, Taiwan, Hong Kong and Singapore. Cities which are industrializing or have strong links with scheduled societies will also have a more planned business culture, even when they operate in a largely non-scheduled society. Barcelona in Spain, Prague in the Czech Republic and Sao Paulo in Brazil fall into this category.

Flexible cultures

Countries from this category are almost diametrically opposed to scheduled cultures. They substitute vision for planning. They know where they want to go, but are flexible about how they get there. The watchword of a flexible culture is improvisation. Meetings may or may not start on time, and will never finish on time. This means that flexibility is needed in adjusting to timings and locations, since punctuality is not seen as a virtue. The great advantage of a flexible society is that it is quick to find unexpected solutions and can deal with crises faster than a scheduled culture. The reason is that effort is put into building social relationships over time, so that the relevant players know each other well and can do things easily and quickly on a personal basis. There is less need to write things down in a flexible business culture, so agendas and memos tend to go by the board. Above all, it's important to spend time building relationships: a face-to-face meeting or a phone call is more important than emails and letters. The majority of the world conforms to this pattern, including the Mediterranean countries, France, Central and Eastern Europe, the Middle East, Africa, South America and most of Asia-Pacific, including India.

This is not to say that people from scheduled business communities are all highly organized – many are not. Nor does it mean that everyone in a flexible society is adaptable: many are highly scheduled. But the distinction explains why the two groups often don't get on. Scheduled managers often describe those from flexible business cultures as inefficient, and even lazy and incompetent, while managers from flexible cultures often regard scheduled business culture managers as rigid, arrogant and inflexible. Both think they're right, but a mixture of both styles is probably the most effective.

Listening cultures

This category of management style is found mainly in the Asia-Pacific region. These business communities may be either scheduled (Japan) or mainly flexible (China), but they share an additional characteristic – they listen. A listening culture is one that is comfortable with silence. Managers listen more and often respond with pauses and longish silences, which Westerners can find unsettling. The trick is to just relax and sit it out, but it's difficult to restrain yourself if you're used to a fast and fluent interchange.

As Lewis points out, one Western business culture is also noted for its comfort with silence – Finland. Many Finnish managers, especially men, can be taciturn, direct to the point and – very quiet. The silent Finn has long been a cliché in European business cultures.

A more serious issue for Western managers dealing with listening cultures can be the difference in negotiation styles. Westerners often have an individualistic management style in which they take decisions within their budgets and responsibilities, and justify them to a more senior executive. In the Asia-Pacific region, and in Japan particularly, decisions are made collectively. The principle is that everyone should agree on a policy before moving forward. Depending on the organization, this can extend to quite low level matters and cause major delays in communicating decisions. A Japanese company might use an intermediary to keep its foreign partners unofficially abreast of developments, but otherwise it can be frustrating for Westerners to be kept waiting and not to know what is going on.

A third feature of the Asia-Pacific listening culture is the focus on respect and face. Face involves your personal dignity and the esteem that we are held in by others. This is a feature of all business communities, but is particularly important in Asia-Pacific, especially in the Far East, where its functioning can be extremely subtle. Managers try to find ways of giving face and to avoid losing it, which explains why there is so much ritual and politeness in Asian business. It also explains the preference for indirectness over directness in discussions and the need to read between the lines.

The last characteristic of listening societies is very strict seniority. Junior managers don't talk in the presence of seniors, do not volunteer information unless asked and certainly don't interrupt. This is very different from the practice of many independent-minded European managers. It's important to identify the senior person in a group and address queries and questions to him or her. If they wish to redirect the question to another member of the group, they will do so.

In many respects, British and US business has democratized in order to allow processes to move faster. Accountability has replaced respect for seniority as a principle of management. There is no doubt that this will influence Asia-Pacific companies as international trade develops – it is already doing so in China and India – but you need to be ready to do business in ways that may be very different from what you are used to in the UK or US.

The Lewis model identifies broad cultural differences in doing business and illustrates some of the frustrations UK and US business people experience in dealing with other communities. So if you are from a scheduled culture, what can you do if you're working with a flexible or listening society? Here are some guidelines.

In working with a flexible society:

- Relax your schedule, and expect fewer but longer meetings.
- Expect more 'getting to know you' sessions – a longer period of socialization is preferred.
- Plan more trips to flexible countries to build trust and contact even before any business is done.
- Expect business to extend into lunch, evening and even weekend social activities.
- Take the trouble to get to know your counterpart, where they come from and other personal details.
- If a partner from a flexible business community visits you, look after them socially as well in the office: they will do the same for you when you visit their country.

In a listening society:

- Observe conventions of respect and seniority.
- Learn to be comfortable with silence, and don't make jokes about it.
- Be careful not to cause loss of face (although the Chinese are quite tolerant of foreigners in this respect).
- Be aware that decisions may be slow in coming due to the principle of internal collective negotiation. You probably can't rush this but a personal contact or intermediary may be able to give you an informal 'heads up' on developments.

Conclusion

Understanding a business community's behaviour profile will tell you how they expect to be treated. But don't assume that everyone will conform to the pattern: many of those you deal with will have lived or studied in the US or the UK, and will have learned different ways of working. They may be as confused or as frustrated as you are by their compatriots' approach to the business process. Use these guidelines as tools to test the water and to help you understand why business may not proceed in the way you expect.

In Chapter 5 we will help you use these tools to identify your own cultural preference, compare it with another business community and show you how to recognize and deal with problems.

Key learning points

- To understand another culture's expectations you must first establish its business profile.
- Although the supplier traditionally adapts to the culture of the client, as a culturally aware manager you may need to take the first step.
- Gesteland's four factors in business negotiation identify cultural differences between business communities. They are relationship/deal, formal/informal, monochronic/polychronic and reserved and expressive (emotional).

- The UK tends to be deal-focused, informal, monochronic and reserved.
- The Lewis model highlights differences in business processes between cultures. We have used the model to identify scheduled, flexible and listening societies. Britain and the US are broadly scheduled business cultures.
- In dealing with a different business culture, adapt your style to theirs to achieve business success.
- These are guidelines, not rules. The person you are dealing with may have experienced a scheduled business community and have adopted its values, especially in a multinational corporation.

FIVE

How to increase your cultural sensitivity

FIVE

How to increase your cultural sensitivity

To understand another culture, you first have to understand your own personal cultural style. That's the only way that you can usefully compare the way you approach life and how other people do, and then see where you need to adapt. You can also evaluate your company and your country in the same way. It's not complicated: a number of cultural indicators will help you to understand the process.

It's all about perception

In cultural awareness, how you feel about things is important. Perception is how we see things from our own point of view. Our perceptions may change when we start to understand the people we are dealing with or the circumstances surrounding a project, but initially our perceptions affect our reactions and our willingness to cooperate with other nationalities. Even if you don't like the way other people do things – if they're always late for appointments, for example – understanding their cultural background allows you to adapt yourself, or to help adapt their behaviour to yours. There is less risk of confrontation. So how can you discover your cultural style, and then compare it with others?

The Personal Cultural Profile

This is a way of understanding your business style: the way you communicate, your approach to hierarchy and formality, your attitude to change, how you negotiate and make decisions, and your entire attitude to work. Ten major areas of business life are listed in bold on the left hand side of the chart. For each category, there is a word or phrase on each side of a row of ten squares. The middle square represents a minimal approach and the far left or right an extreme one. You can chart your personal cultural profile by putting a cross in the square in each row that represents your attitude.

For example, if you always arrive at the office ten minutes before your scheduled start time, if you maintain a list of tasks that you intend to complete during each hour of your working day, and if you begin to feel irritated if three minutes have gone by since the agreed start of a meeting and the other person still hasn't arrived, then you'd put a cross on the far left of the Scheduled side of the Attitude to Time row. Below we talk about the ten categories, and include a table of typical responses to each one. Read each section and complete the chart as you go. If you're unsure about the way you handle a particular category, put a cross in the middle squares. When you finish the chart, join the crosses with a line. It will trace a zig-zag path down the page.

The Personal Cultural Profile

Communication

1 COMMUNICATION STYLE

Direct											Indirect

2 WORKING STYLE

Formal											Informal

3 DISCUSSION STYLE

Fast-moving											Slow and measured

4 BUSINESS ATTITUDE

Progressive											Traditional

5 LEADERSHIP STYLE

Flat											Vertical

6 BUSINESS RELATIONSHIP

Relationship											Task

7 DECISION-MAKING STYLE

Individualistic											Collective

8 BASIS FOR DECISION-MAKING

Facts											Instincts

9 ATTITUDE TO TIME

Scheduled											Flexible

10 WORK/LIFE BALANCE

Live to work											Work to live

1 Communication Style

DIRECT	INDIRECT
Gets to the point	Encircles the point
Criticizes	Saves face
Faces disagreement	Avoids disagreement
Addresses issues directly	Addresses issues sideways-on

How much are you expected to read between the lines of what's going on in your own company or country, and how much is spelt out for you in detail? This is an area that's even more confusing for people from different cultures. A direct negotiation style means that you say what you mean and you're not particularly concerned whether people like it or not. Your primary concern is to state the truth or your opinion as you see it, and to get results and information. Germans, the British and Americans broadly think in this way.

However, there are differences between them. Americans find the British very indirect, especially their habit of retreating into generalities under tough questioning. But the British, and many other cultures, believe that there are times when politeness is more important than truth. They feel that speaking indirectly or giving people the response they want is an important way of keeping the situation calm and saving face. Indirect speakers try to preserve good relations by being polite and inferring rather than by asking direct questions. They also tend to give positive-sounding or vague answers rather than specific or clear statements. We discuss the different strategies for dealing with each style in Chapter 6 on communication.

2 Working Style

FORMAL	INFORMAL
Prefers business dress	Prefers 'dress-down'
Uses surnames and titles	Uses first names
Closed door	Open plan/open door
Prefers a more formal style of speech	Prefers a more familiar and intimate style of speech

Formal business people like to maintain a degree of distance from their colleagues and clients. They do this by using titles and qualifications and addressing people by their surnames. They avoid jokes and colloquial language and can come across as a bit stiff in business relationships. This is common in cultures whose languages distinguish between the formal and informal pronoun 'you', as does French (*tu* and *vous*) and German (*Du* and *Sie*), for example.

Informal people, on the other hand, want to sweep aside anything that gets in the way of business. They see titles, qualifications and surnames as an unnecessary barrier to communication. A colloquial, even jokey, style is quite common among such people, but they're often perceived by more formal types to be over-familiar and flippant. The British and North Americans use this informal approach, as can the Dutch.

INFORMAL vs FORMAL

Gareth, a zippy, lippy 27-year-old accountant, was moving from south London to Zurich. He wanted to rent an apartment from an elderly German-speaking Swiss, an agent consultant called Heinz Jacob. They negotiated in English, but Gareth noted that his colloquial, "Hi Heinz, how's it hanging?" street-smart style wasn't getting the friendly reaction that he was used to in London.

This wasn't a problem until Gareth ran into legal difficulties. Gradually, he got the message. He called Jacob one morning and changed his approach. "Good morning, Herr Jacob," he said. "Sorry to take up your time, but I've got a problem with the documents that I need to sign before I can transfer the deposit on the flat to your account. I'm planning to fly over on Friday to deal with it."

Jacob's response? "Don't worry. We'll deal with it in January when you move in." Gareth was left wondering: what had prompted Jacob's cooperation? Was it that he had adopted a more respectful and, to Jacob's ears, a more professional tone? That's the difference between a formal and an informal approach, and an illustration of what can go wrong and how to put it right.

Do you prefer formality or informality in your business dealings? Are you an open-door or a closed-door manager? Do you structure your day so that you give fixed times to certain types of communication, such as answering emails or face-to-face meetings?

> **FORMAL OR INFORMAL**
>
> An informal colleague put her head round the door of her manager's office and said: "I have a small problem? Got a minute?" His reply shocked her. "Do we have a meeting scheduled?" he asked. "I can only take unscheduled meetings after 6 o'clock." Managers who run very structured days to deal with the pressure of work may be on the more formal side of business relations.

3 Discussion Style

FAST MOVING	SLOW AND MEASURED
Interrupts more	Never interrupts
Talks more and quickly	Prefers measured tone and pace
Conversation has to keep moving	Pauses are acceptable
Dislikes silence	Is tolerant of silence

Fast moving and slow and measured are two extremes of discussion style. Speakers who use one style can be extremely irritating to users of the other. Fast moving speakers talk faster. They interrupt, and overlap each other's conversation. They're often seen as insensitive and arrogant. Slow and measured speakers pause between sentences, listen carefully to what others have to say and never interrupt: if they do, they apologize. They regard themselves as measured and careful, but fast moving talkers may consider them slow and dull.

We attribute these two styles of speaking to individuals, but they are also largely true of cultures. Spaniards are noted for always talking across one another and speaking simultaneously. Germans and the British tend to be more slow and measured. Meetings in almost any environment usually start slowly but increase in intensity, when the discussion styles of the participants and their cultures will emerge. It's important to recognize whether you debate in a slow and measured or fast moving style, and make allowances when you come across the other one.

4 Business Attitude

PROGRESSIVE	TRADITIONAL
Embraces change	Needs change to be based in present practice
Likes new technology	Is cautious in adopting new technology
Seeks new organizational methods	Prefers 'tried and tested' solutions
Wants new people	Prefers loyal staff

Progressive managers embrace change enthusiastically. They like anything that is new and buzzy: they want to be the first with new ideas, new gizmos, new procedures, new technology and new blood. Giving responsibility to fresh young people is part of their brief. They're often a company's young tigers, the trailblazers. But they can also be extremely irritating and unsettling, and can appear brash and rash.

Traditional managers are more cautious. They believe that if something ain't broke, don't fix it: tried and trusted is best. In some cultures, such as Japan, parts of India and, some would say, the UK, a cycle of change exists and innovation can't be hurried. They believe that traditional ways work and must be respected. This style of manager may seem old-fashioned and over-cautious to the young tigers.

Both approaches have a place, and it is important to recognize your own style. Most of us are a mixture of both. Ask yourself: when push comes to shove, which one do you tend to choose? That's your real comfort zone.

5 Leadership Style

FLAT	VERTICAL
Communicates directly	Communicates through hierarchy
Community decision	Leader decision (often after consultation)
Two-way feedback	Top-down feedback
Strict line management reporting	Dotted line matrix reporting

Different cultures respect different groups of people, for a variety of reasons. In some regions (Asia and Russia among them), respect for older people and seniority is institutionalized: it is granted automatically and almost without question. In others, such as North America and the UK, respect is functional – it has to be earned, every time. The British and American saying, "You're only as good as your last job," is a sign of their attitude.

The way that respect is displayed runs very deep in business structures. In what is known as a matrix management environment, you can get information from anywhere you wish in the company. There are few formal reporting procedures, and dotted communication lines dominate the organigram. But in a country where institutionalized respect prevails, such as Germany, strict reporting lines are in place. You don't go above the head of your line manager and you deal always through the same clearly defined channels.

RESPECT: INSTITUTIONALIZED VS FUNCTIONAL

Ullie was transferred from the Frankfurt branch to the London office of an international bank. "For the first few months I was a complete fish out of water," she said. "I was used to clear reporting lines and structures and suddenly there was literally no-one to talk to.

"Or rather, there was everyone to talk to, but the situation was totally confusing. I didn't know who was making decisions and I didn't feel I had the authority to take them myself. It really affected my productivity."

6 Business Relationship

RELATIONSHIP	TASK
Takes time building relationships	Focuses on getting the job done
Won't work with you unless he/she likes and trusts you	May begin with small-scale deals and then build up if original deal is successful
Takes an interest in understanding the people	Focuses on tasks rather than people
'My business colleague is my friend'	Business and friendships don't mix

This category highlights one of the most fundamental differences between cultures. Relationship-minded people like to do business with those they know and trust. Consequently, they invest time in getting to know their business partners and clients. This puts a premium on hospitality, wining and dining and establishing a good family and personal basis. It also demands frequent contact, and the investment of management time in building a good social rapport.

All this is good fun, but it tends to yield long-term rather than short-term profit, and can be frustratingly heavy on the travel and expenses budget. China and much of the Asia-Pacific region conform to this model. But for relationship-minded people, the establishment of warm personal feelings is the gateway to business.

The other side of the scale indicates whether you prefer to rely on task completion or systems in your business dealings. Sign the agreement, do the job as specified, pay on time – that's all you ask. If you do this regularly enough we may become friends over a period, but friendship is not essential to the relationship.

Many people find it difficult to decide if they are relationship- or task/ systems-minded. If you're in that position, ask yourself this: would you sacrifice a relationship to get the job done? If you would, you're task/systems-minded. The only question is, to what extent?

7 Decision-Making Style

INDIVIDUALISTIC	COLLECTIVE
Risk taking	Risk averse
Decides first then persuades others	Seeks consensus, then decides
Makes own decisions within budget and job description	Decisions and budgets are agreed with higher management
Is accountable for decision and implementation	Takes decision agreed by group or higher management and is accountable for implementation

What are you like as a decision-maker? If you take your own within your budget and responsibilities, know exactly what you can sign for and what you need to take to a higher level, then you're an individual decision-maker. You take more risks and can achieve dramatic success, but you could also get sacked. If, on the other hand, you research a problem and seek colleagues' opinions before you act, you're a collective decision-maker. The latter are more cautious and risk-averse, and tend to share the responsibility for making judgements. It works the same way with cultures as with individuals.

Once again, the Germans, British, Dutch, Americans, Canadians, Australians and New Zealanders tend to be individual decision-makers at middle management level, as do managers in top-down cultures, where the boss invariably has the final say. But in the Asia-Pacific region, collective decision-making is much more common, and there can be serious problems in a cross-border partnership if the two sides operate on opposing systems. We'll have more to say about this in Chapter 7 on leadership and decision-making.

8 Basis for Decision-Making

FACTS	INSTINCTS
Makes decisions on basis of data and figures	Makes decisions on instinct and intuition
Personal connections are not important in decision-making	Personal connections are an important factor in decision-making
Maintains a strict criteria-based system for decision-making	Prefers to work with existing contacts
Agreements are independent of hospitality or gift-giving	Agreements are usually accompanied by hospitality and gift- giving

Most managers are used to taking decisions based largely on facts and figures, the business plan and sales and market research data. However, others rely on instinct. Intuitional thinking is also widely used in the world of science. Einstein once said that a discovery is made on instinct and intuition, a leap of faith. Science then allows the discoverer to work back from that leap to find the evidence that supports it. In business, instinctive decision-makers are influenced by the kind of person they're dealing with. Building the relationship, recognizing a partner's potential and developing trust will be at least as important as the hard logical case. It may even sway the balance in deciding the awarding of contracts.

CASE STUDY

A South American telecoms company wanted to find a partner to handle its telecoms system. Two firms, one American and one European, were in final contention. The Europeans visited the country for three weeks, getting to know the people in the exchanges, understanding how the operation worked and the workforce's problems. The American team spent three days in the capital, meeting and presenting to the top brass. They offered a better specification system than the Europeans, at a lower price.

But the European firm won the contract: they had taken the trouble to spend time building confidence with the people on the ground. Instinctively, the South American client felt that the relationship was worth the extra money, and that the equipment could be upgraded later.

9 Attitude to Time

SCHEDULED	FLEXIBLE
Time conscious	Relaxed about time
Punctual	Late
Schedules by the clock	Schedules by activity
Meetings start and end on time	Completing the business is more important than the schedule

Scheduled managers run a very tight ship, and are often unforgiving of managers who 'run with the wind' and appear to be disorganized and unpunctual. Of course, people from a particular culture can show variations in their behaviour. I may work in a scheduled culture, yet be very flexible in my personal approach. The movie star Marilyn Monroe was American (scheduled), but was famous for keeping people waiting (flexible). What's your own style – scheduled or flexible?

10 Work/Life Balance

LIVE TO WORK	WORK TO LIVE
Overtime expected	Overtime unusual
Taking work home admired	Taking work home criticized
Out of hours phone contact tolerated	Out of hours phone contact unacceptable
Weekend working normal	Weekend working exceptional

Call a Japanese or Taiwanese company at midday British time, and you'll find someone still at the office, even though they're nine hours ahead. Continental Europeans sometimes feel irritated when communicating with Britain because they feel that they lose one to two productive hours a day in a business relationship. They start work between 8am and 8.30am, when they're already an hour ahead, while many Brits don't get to their desks until 9am or 9.30am. Koreans and Japanese often accuse British workers of not being 'diligent'. They mean that we're often not available when they need us, because of time differences and our desire to get home to see the kids before they go to bed. Germans are very protective of their free time and tend to work hard during business hours, but finish promptly. The switchboards of some large German firms close at 4pm, and most offices are empty by ten past five. The Japanese, on the other hand, work much longer hours but are not always very productive after, say, 5pm.

A live-to-work person routinely does overtime, stays late at the office, takes business-related phone calls at home, works at weekends and even cuts short holidays for business reasons. A work-to-live person performs well during business hours but rarely does overtime, rarely takes calls outside office hours, hardly ever works at weekends, may not even have a computer at home (except for the kids' homework and games) and certainly won't cut short holidays.

When the Japanese go on holiday they apologize to their workmates for the extra burden they cause by going away, and when they come back they thank their colleagues for taking responsibility. They have shorter holidays and rarely take all their allotted time. The British have the longest working week in Europe and like to boast about how many hours they put in and how early they're at their desks, despite starting late – by continental standards – at 9am or 9.30am. But Germans might see overtime and long hours as a sign of poor job specification or inefficiency. A British manager told me how he used to shoo German workers out of the office at five sharp in case one of them had an accident on the way home and sued the firm for keeping him/her on overtime and causing fatigue!

So which type are you – live-to-work or work-to-live?

Comparing cultures

You have just mapped your personal style. Now you can compare it with the culture you're dealing with. You don't have to know the culture well: what counts is your perception of it. Repeat the mapping process for the new culture. Put a cross in each square that you think matches its style and then, using a different coloured pen, join the crosses with a line.

You now have two lines on the chart, one mapping your personal style and one mapping your image of the other culture. In some cases the lines will be close together and in other areas they will be well separated. Now let's interpret what it means.

Interpreting your Personal Cultural Profile

Where your personal lines and your target culture lines are close together, you're probably not having a problem with the culture. Your perception is that your styles mesh. But where the lines diverge there may be something to investigate. In this case, ask yourself these questions:

1 IS THERE A PROBLEM?

If there isn't, then ignore the difference between the lines. But if you think the difference might cause communication problems or is already leading to them, you need to ask question 2.

2 DO I NEED TO CHANGE – OR DO THEY NEED TO CHANGE?

Usually the client demands changes from the seller. This is true not just of a commercial relationship but also of an in-company situation where the seller is the junior and the client is the boss. However, this isn't always the case. Often the more sensitive person will be the one who makes the change. Either way, if you need to modify your approach to the culture go to question 3.

3 HOW MUCH DO I NEED TO CHANGE?

No-one wants you to go native and mimic totally the ways of a new culture. It probably won't get the result you want, and may not be good for business practice or your image. This is where we invoke the 80/20 rule.

The 80/20 rule

Devised by the Italian economist Wilfredo Pareto in the early 1900s, the 80/20 rule noted that 20% of effort in any activity yields 80% of result. This was famously updated by Richard Koch in his recent book on the theory, *Living the 80/20 Way*, which observed that 20% of a company's business produces 80% of its profit. The 80/20 rule also applies in cultural relations. In other words, a 20% change in your behaviour will trigger an 80% difference in your respondent's attitude and actions.

To put it even more simply, if people see that you're making a bit of an effort, they will react much more positively. Remember the anecdote about Gareth the apartment-seeker earlier in this chapter, and you'll see that a touch of formality achieved a major change in the attitude of his landlord-to-be in Switzerland. The trick is to know which way to move – 20% more or 20% less.

Is it personal, procedural or cultural?

If you work in a globalized organisation with people of different nationalities, you'll tend to assume that any problems that arise are caused by national differences. But it isn't always so. Let's imagine you have difficulty dealing with a German sales rep. Is it because she is German? Before you decide, you must ask three more questions:

1 IS IT PERSONAL?

Do you just not get on? Maybe your personalities don't match, you don't click, you rub each other up the wrong way. The friction would still be there if she were British. In that case the issue is personal, not cultural.

2 IS IT PROCEDURAL?

In other words, is she lacking in job skills? She might need advice or training. Once again, if she were British, her behaviour in the same situation would be no different.

3 IS IT CULTURAL?

Is the problem due to the fact that she has a different attitude to the job because her approach corresponds to her German upbringing, education, training and experience? If this is the case, move to the next stage, and use your RADAR.

RADAR

RADAR is an acronym, like KISS (Keep it short and simple or Keep it simple, stupid) or SMART, when applied to objectives (specific, measurable, agreed, realistic and time-based). When you think you have a cultural problem, switch on your RADAR and go through these five steps:

1. **R** Recognize that you have a cultural communications problem.
2. **A** Analyze the problem. The simplest way to do this is to check your perception of the other person's cultural style using the Personal Cultural Profile. When you've completed the scores, you'll probably find three or four gaps in your perception of your cultural style and hers.

3 **D** Decide what to do. Change your behaviour (or ask the other person to change hers) by about 20%, depending on the situation.

4 **A** Act. Put what you have decided into action.

5 **R** Review the outcome. Did it work? If it did, continue. If it didn't, try something else. Remember that success is about doing more of what works and less of what doesn't, so if putting 20% more in doesn't work, try 20% less.

Like all acronyms RADAR sounds simplistic, but it works. Store it in your brain, apply the system when you have a cultural problem, and after three months it will become an automatic process.

An example

Talking of Germans, Klaus was an investment banker from Frankfurt who was moving to his company's New York office. He had excellent language and job skills, but encountered severe communication problems. His colleagues thought that he was very authoritarian (6 Institutional respect), very direct (8 Direct), and not very good at forming personal relationships (2 Formal). He was not close to his associates and lacked the authority to carry weight with them. But head office needed him to represent them strongly in New York, which was a more profitable division and acting too independently of the parent company.

Klaus did the Personal Cultural Profile exercise, and realized that he needed to change. We trained him to be much more hands-on and assertive: he began communicating more directly with his colleagues and discussing matters face-to-face rather than making them wait and receive decisions by email. After two days' training and two months' coaching, Klaus is now a fully integrated and effective international manager. He has made the step-change from working in a single-country environment, mainly with Germans, to operating in an international culture, a development that will enrich his entire career.

Personal qualities

Until now we've looked outwards: how do I as a national manager adapt or develop my skills to deal with the cultural issues raised when I work with another nationality? However, it's obvious that intercultural awareness also affects your own personality – an influence that is highly beneficial. There's a saying in Arabic: "Learn a new language and you become a new person." In the same way, if you become a culturally aware international manager your personality effectively changes. Some of your characteristics become enhanced and others reduced.

> **To do business worldwide it isn't enough just to understand and apply a universal business model. You have to understand the culture as well.**

What is it that allows some people to adapt to working with foreigners, while others struggle? There's nothing genetic about it, but there's no doubt that we feel more familiar with what we are used to. The problem is that as new economic opportunities are often located in Beijing, New Delhi and Moscow rather than Birmingham, New York and Manchester, the familiar is no longer an option.

Ian, an international sales manager, virtually lives on planes. In most places in the world he barely even thinks before he lands on foreign soil: he just slips into the cultural style of the country he's in. If he knows that unpunctuality is the thing, he relaxes and carries a good book or a laptop with him. If he knows that heavy entertaining is going to be the order of the day, he gets some rest, and snacks lightly first so he won't overeat or get drunk.

Above all, he mentally steps back and observes. "Never show frustration or anger," he says. "It suggests you've lost control. The problem arises when things get difficult. That's when you tend to fall back into your own cultural mindset, and start judging people and getting upset."

Milton Bennett is head of the Intercultural Communication Institute in Portland, Oregon, and a leading researcher and lecturer on cultural awareness issues. He believes that to blend into other cultures successfully, you have to change your mindset from what he calls an 'ethnocentric' viewpoint to an 'ethno-relative' one. In other words, stop seeing the world purely from the vantage point of your own culture and put yourself into the other person's shoes. Integrating your behaviour with that of your hosts is the ultimate display of cross-cultural courtesy, he says. But Bennett admits that it's a process of adaptation and can't be achieved in a single great leap. He identifies six stages in the evolution from an ethnocentric to an ethno-relative approach, and illustrates them in this diagram:

Ethnocentric — **Ethno-relative**

Denial — Defence — Minimization — Acceptance — Adaptation — Integration

Not everyone starts from the same baseline, but if you've travelled on business or lived or studied abroad, you'll probably recognize yourself in some of these profiles.

Denial

This can take two totally opposite forms, one probably more familiar than the other. The first form is to pretend that it's business as usual and to refuse to recognize that things are done differently in your new environment. If you take this approach – and most of us have done so at some point in our careers – you'll find that it can work initially with cultures similar to your own. But eventually it creates non-cooperation and resentment among your colleagues, in response to what they see as your insensitive behaviour. You're not deliberately being discourteous, just doing what comes naturally. But your behaviour cuts everyone else out unless they conform to your way of doing things.

The other form of denial is just as counter-productive, and even more embarrassing. This is the person who goes overboard in praising the country he or she is dealing with and constantly derides their own country. You may be making a sincere attempt to integrate, but it will look more like a misguided attempt to go native. Foreigners don't respect people who don't respect their own country. Russians, for example, believe that a love of one's country is a sign of self-esteem and self-respect in an individual. So 'my country right or wrong' or 'my country always wrong' are both causes of problems with foreigners, and are psychological responses to dealing with the unfamiliar – abroad.

Defence

As Milton Bennett describes it, this is the stage where we wake up and exclaim: "Oh my God, they're different!" We still don't fully accept the differences, but we're forced to face the fact that they exist, and we know we can't ignore them. The response to this awakening is invariably: "Circle the wagons and prepare to defend!" We dive into familiar procedures and apply them rigidly. This creates a real crisis: in this mode we can get very judgmental and criticize people for being lazy, disorganized or chaotic when they're simply approaching things in a different way. Britons who commit this error often become aggressive in meetings, and mutter jokes and insults among themselves to relieve their sense of frustration. This is extremely dangerous. Firstly, it reinforces a negative mindset. Secondly, someone always overhears you and they just know you're talking about them. The trick, and it isn't an easy one, is once again to stand back, observe, and don't get involved in your own emotional turmoil. The value of Milton Bennett's analysis is that it gives you a tool for exploring your own response. If you can say to yourself, "Yes, it's just a defence mechanism," you're well on the way to Stage 3 – minimization.

Minimization

You meet this reaction an awful lot in international business. People who use it are those who don't want to take culture on board. Heard these recently?

- "I take people as I find them".
- "People are people".
- "There's no difference ultimately. We've all got mortgages and families. Business is business, after all".

Yes, it is, but it doesn't hide the fact that how most Indians see relationships with their family and their bank is very different from the way most Britons or North Americans do. An Indian might have family responsibilities extending to more than 20 people, yet have no other assets than his monthly salary. He might still be living with his family at 36 years of age, and have to ask his father's permission to go out at night. His marriage may be arranged between his and his in-laws' families. Not all Indians live like this, and given the speed at which the Indian economy is developing, things will change fast. But it illustrates that even in the areas that we think make us similar, very different conditions may apply.

The three ethnocentric stages of denial, defence and minimization represent a situation known as unconscious incompetence. People at this level are unable to rise to the challenge of dealing with cultural differences, and even if they are aware that something isn't right, they don't know how to correct things.

Acceptance

People reach the acceptance stage when they begin to feel curious about other cultures. It's when we start asking questions.

But here again there's a danger: what questions can you ask without causing offence? Indians, among other nationalities, often ask what we Britons consider to be intrusive questions. Queries about family, income and health may be quite normal in one society, but over-familiar in another. The questioners think they're building a relationship: *we* feel they're doing the opposite.

On the other hand, Westerners often fall into the 'free speech' trap: they assume that any question about politics or society is acceptable. An innocent question to a Chinese about what happened in Tiananmen Square in 1989, the upheavals of the Cultural Revolution in the sixties and seventies, or relations between China and Tibet could open up huge political and social scars. Your curiosity may display, or rather betray, your cultural conditioning to your disadvantage. One question that went the rounds in a Japanese-owned chain of stores in the UK was posed by a manager from the Tokyo head office to a married shop assistant. "Tell me," he asked out of the blue. "Does your husband mind you working?" His query reflected his own cultural conditioning: dual-income families are more common than they used to be in Japan, but it is still normal for women to leave work when they marry and take on full-time responsibilities as a homemaker.

It's a sign of real progress when you arrive at the acceptance stage, but remember to temper your eagerness to learn about your new society. The great advantage of acceptance is that you have become conscious of your own incompetence. You are at a point where you can begin to adapt your behaviour to what the situation requires.

Adaptation

Adaptation is where positive action comes into its own. You investigate cultural differences, and begin to mould your behaviour to take them into account, or train others to adapt. Many US managers, for example, are transferred to the UK by their parent companies to 'lick the Brits into shape'; in other words, to get the British staff to conform to US work and productivity requirements.

This is a process that someone in the ethnocentric stages of intercultural development would do by blind imposition. But a manager skilled in cultural awareness would consider how to present new procedures and principles to achieve maximum buy-in by local staff. She would compare British and American practices and the personal styles of her team, and seek compromises. She would try to integrate her parent company's methods, while allowing the locals some flexibility. This is where intercultural training comes into its own: it is, to use the popular scale of the evolution of competencies, the stage of acquiring conscious competence.

Integration

Joanna is the HR manager of a charity and has worked in 22 countries on five continents. She jokes that you make your best friends abroad the week before you leave, and the moment you feel at home in a place, it's time to go. The good news is that the time she has spent developing sensitivity will never be wasted: people from different cultures will always respond well to her. Joanna is at the stage that in management terms we call unconscious competence. Tuning in to cultural sensitivity doesn't mean that she has all the answers, but she does know some of the questions.

One of the difficulties of moving through the six stages is that it is not a straight linear progression, although it is usually presented as one. People's backgrounds and experiences are varied, and they start at different points along the continuum. They may also step backwards in certain situations. It's possible to reach a degree of adaptation in some cross-cultural aspects, but to be right back at denial or defence in others. We're dealing with psychology and the emotions here, and it's less a game of Monopoly and more one of snakes and ladders.

The six personal characteristics of cross-cultural sensitivity

CILT is the National Centre for Languages in Britain. From its London base its mission is to encourage the British to learn foreign languages. It works closely with UK Trade and Investment, the government organization that helps companies to do business abroad, the British Chambers of Commerce and other state and private bodies. Two years ago, CILT received an EU grant to research the attributes of cultural awareness. "What", the EU asked, "are the characteristics of successful exporters who are culturally sensitive?" The research was carried out by Dr Michael Byram, Professor of Education at the University of Durham, and the results were published as the INCA (Intercultural Competence Assessment) project.

INCA offers definitions of the characteristics of intercultural sensitivity. They are:

1. Tolerance of ambiguity
2. Behavioural flexibility
3. Communicative awareness
4. Knowledge discovery
5. Respect for otherness
6. Empathy

How do they apply in business? INCA offers a skills profile at three levels for each characteristic.

1 Tolerance of ambiguity

This means not getting upset when you don't know the outcome of a situation. In flexible cultures, as we saw in Chapter 4, ambiguity is a fact of life. Things happen when they are meant to happen, regardless of your attempt to schedule them. Things simply don't happen in the time frame that you try to impose. A good international manager is constantly aware of the possibility of ambiguity; she does not get upset by it and learns to manage by adopting coping strategies. The obvious approach is to develop a good relationship with the person you're dealing with, maintain contact with them and make your own limits on flexibility clear. It's important not to be judgemental about the situation.

2 Behavioural flexibility

If you are used to working to precise schedules, deadlines and plans, it can be frustrating to work in environments where this is either not possible or not the norm. The important thing is to keep the vision clearly in mind (where you want to get to) while maintaining flexibility about routes. Once again, part of the skill is not getting upset if plans change suddenly or don't seem to be made far enough ahead. It's important to recognize that there may be different ways of reaching the same goal.

3 Communicative awareness

This is all about understanding your own communication style, and recognizing that different nationalities may have different ways of communicating and different expectations of your communication. This affects both your use of language and your communication and presentation style; we cover this in detail in Chapter 6.

4 Knowledge discovery

This is about building up knowledge of the business community you're dealing with through your personal experience, and what you learn from the experience of other visitors or residents or through research. It also includes the ability to understand your own culture as perceived by others and to modify your understanding of both your own culture and the one you're dealing with.

5 Respect for otherness

This is about recognizing and valuing diversity, ensuring equal consideration in the workplace and being able to deal sensitively with issues arising from different backgrounds or different orientation, especially in the areas of race, religion, respect for age, gender, disability and sexual orientation. To this list human rights is often added.

6 Empathy

This crucial skill involves being able to really listen to a member of another business community and to see things from their position. It is partly an intuitive skill, but also involves recognizing how other people may feel and respond because of their own culture.

Conclusion

Ultimately, in a globalizing economy, the key to communication success is to develop sensitivity to other cultures. The INCA skills suggest some of the characteristics you – as a culturally sensitive manager – need to adopt. It is a process that happens over time and experience. The first stage is to understand your own culture using the cultural style profile and then apply it to the culture you are dealing with. Developing this sensitivity will make you a better manager, not just internationally but also with your home team. It is to do with all-round personal development. The next five chapters will show how to apply this sensitivity in the areas of communication, leadership, team-working and motivation, meetings and negotiations and gift-giving and hospitality.

Key learning points

- Your feelings and perceptions of other cultures are important.
- The Personal Cultural Profile will help you understand your business cultural style.
- Use this to compare your style with the other business community you are dealing with.
- Use the RADAR system to see where you may need to adapt to the other culture, or them to you.
- Adaptation isn't instant. Expect a process of cultural adaptation to take place in dealing with another business community. Milton Bennett's scale shows the stages you go through.
- Cultural awareness is a process of personal development which will benefit both your work at home and with other business communities. The INCA project identifies the key qualities to develop.

SIX

Communication

SIX

Communication

We like to believe that in our 24/7 world, enabled by instant phone and email contact, we're good at communicating information and instructions. But what we often fail to consider is whether our messages are understood. Even in the UK and the USA, where English is the mother tongue and the majority of citizens are fluent in it, communication is often ambiguous, irrelevant, irritating, badly written and demotivating – just check your email inbox today. When we communicate across cultures, the opportunities for creating accidental misunderstanding are multiplied a thousand times.

Three things govern whether a message is successfully received:

- The language used;
- The style of communication;
- In a verbal communication, whether people are bothering to listen.

Two additional considerations affect international business communication:

- Virtual communication – the fact that we spend enormous amounts of time emailing, phoning and video-conferencing with people we don't know;
- The dominance of English as an international medium of communication.

Any or all of these factors can disrupt communication. Ironically, the fact that English tends to be the business world's language carries unexpected problems for native English speakers. The question is, do you want to be a part of the problem or the solution? If it's the latter, here's how. Let's take the English language first.

The English language

The English we use in the UK or the USA isn't the same as that used by foreigners. Take Christine: she's a Chinese university professor who was utterly confused on her first study visit to London. Why? She couldn't understand the English she heard. 'Did I study your language for twenty years for this?' she complained.

British and US business people must understand that foreigners learn a more structured and precise English in school (it's called English as a foreign language, or English as a second language in the UK), and that they are often bewildered by what they hear from their native-speaker counterparts. They have real difficulties with the wide range of idioms and slang that we use, as well as the variety of accents. The problem is the same for Britons and Americans who have learnt a foreign language: they can often express themselves well and understand and write business documents, but the pace and vernacular of everyday speech leaves them feeling stranded, frustrated and humiliated. So here are some things you can do to help your foreign counterparts understand you. If you follow these guidelines you'll also build much better relationships, as your foreign partners will appreciate the effort you are making.

1 Leave a beat when you speak

Listen to BBC radio and especially TV reporters: they leave a short pause between sentences and phrases when they speak. It's barely noticeable, but it allows the listener to mentally breathe, catch up and absorb meaning. Sometimes it's carried to extremes by young TV reporters, but the idea is a good one.

The British used to be told that.that if a foreigner asked you to repeat something, you should say it slowly. If they still don't understand, then say it slowly and loudly. But apart from being incredibly patronizing, this approach misses the problem. What confuses foreigners is not only the speed of delivery, but the lack of mini-pauses that allows their translating skills to catch up. By using the technique of slight breaks – you needn't make them obvious and condescending – between sentences and expressions, you can really help your partner to understand you better. This is absolutely vital in teleconferences and video conferences.

2 Avoid slang and idioms

In 2006 a *Financial Times* reporter claimed that one of the factors in the breakdown of talks between the British and German governments over BMW's investment in Rover, was the phrase used by the British ministers, 'It's five minutes to midnight.' They presumably meant that there was little time left to reach an agreement. But according to the *FT* writer, it confused and irritated the German side, who were too proud to ask what it meant.

A key question that we answered in a seminar that we recently conducted for German managers was: when you don't understand a term used by the British or the Americans, how do you ask for an explanation without sounding like an idiot? The expression in question was 'top whack', as in: 'That will cost a million Euros, top whack.' We suggested that the Germans use the phrase, 'That's a new one on me', to indicate lightly that clarification was needed.

Here's a verbatim report of a UK sales manager's astonishing reply in a phone conversation to his Spanish equivalent in Valencia, who had called him with a problem. It won't create problems for a British reader, but put yourself in the Spaniard's shoes:

'Haven't a clue, José, all Greek to me. Tell you what, leave it with me. Bear with me for a day or so. I'll bend the chief's ear over a jar and give you a bell.'

José's English is fluent, but not that fluent. Even an American would have had difficulty in understanding that stream of colloquial, clichéd English. If we'd been the manager in question we'd have said something like this:

'Sorry, José, I don't have the answer to that one. If you can wait for a couple of days, I'll ask the boss when he's free and call you back.'

The answer is learn to monitor your own speech. If you find yourself using an idiomatic or slang phrase, make sure you add an explanation in standard English. Better still, avoid slang completely and express yourself in standard English in the first place.

3 Explain acronyms and initials

Here's a test: what does UN stand for? United Nations, of course. But in French it's ONU – *l'Organisation des Nations Unies*. Now, imagine that someone uses an acronym or initials that you're not familiar with. Will you ask them to explain or will you feel embarrassed because you think you ought to know? Do your customer a favour: the first time you use an acronym or set of initials in conversation or in an email, spell out the full form the first time and then put the appropriate initials in brackets behind the phrase. Your customer or partner will appreciate your sensitivity.

4 Avoid jokes

Joking and banter is integral to British and US business. Americans like one-liners, and Britons love irony and sarcasm. Brits sometimes use this to establish balance between different levels of seniority and expertise. In a Japanese negotiation, the legal adviser from the UK team was delayed. Asked if they should wait, the British delegate suggested they proceed, adding as a throw-away joke, "He doesn't know much anyway." To the respectful Japanese, the joke fell flat and made them question the unity and reliability of the British team. We cannot stress this enough. When the British get uncomfortable, or too comfortable, they get jokey and sometimes make 'bolshie' remarks. Be careful: your irony and sarcasm may be taken literally or simply considered rude.

Germans make polite jokes to break the ice before a meeting or heartier jokes in the bar in the evening, but in the meeting itself, seriousness is appreciated so, if you can, avoid jokes. Good humour and charm will get you everywhere.

5 KISS (Keep it short and simple)

Business is complicated, so the language we use had better reflect that. In other words, we should use long, complex sentences to give our opinions a feeling of weight and seriousness. That's what many people believe about business communication, but they're wrong. Take a lesson from the American writer Ernest Hemingway, who had a major influence on the evolution of contemporary English. He used a very short, concrete and direct style of writing in his novels. Keep your own sentences short (15 to 25 words is fine), and don't run two thoughts together when you can express them as two separate sentences. If you still don't believe that this works, read *The Economist,* the internationally successful magazine of business and politics. It explains complex subjects in short but elegant sentences to a readership that is intelligent, but pressed for time – just like you. We hope that this book too is written in a form of English that makes it immediately accessible to any audience.

6 Keep it active

It's amazing how many people subconsciously switch to a pompous, bureaucratic style when they have to write a business document – a report, analysis, or proposal. They tend to use the passive voice rather than the active one, and it makes their writing dull and hard to read – especially for people who are working in English as a foreign language. What's the difference between the active and the passive? It's simple, as this example shows:

Passive	Active
The proposal to acquire HighFly Software Systems will be considered by the board next month	The board will consider the proposal to acquire HighFly Software Systems next month

In the active voice the subject of the sentence performs an action, but in the passive the subject *receives* an action. Notice how the active version is lighter and simpler in pace. Now imagine the effect of writing all your documentation mainly in the active voice. Your readers will absorb the message instead of half-understanding it, and you'll look like a contemporary, empathetic communicator. For final proof, just consider these two longer samples, one using the passive voice and the other expressed in the active:

Passive

In June last year an entry was made into the expanding mobile telephone market by HighFly Software Systems. A forecast was made that the company would capture 8% of the market for 15- to 22-year-old buyers within six months. However, unexpected growth in the market was rapidly noted by the project team, and production of phones was doubled. Profit projections for this year have therefore been increased by 42%, to $3.8 million.

72 words

Active

HighFly Software Systems entered the expanding mobile telephone market in June last year. It forecast that it would capture 8% of the market for 15- to 22-year-old buyers within six months. However, the project team rapidly noted unexpected growth in the market, and doubled production of phones. We now predict that we will earn profit of $3.8 million this year, a 42% increase.

63 words

Note how the active version feels vibrant, current and action-packed, compared with the cumbersome passive version, which reads like it was composed by a Victorian solicitor. The active paragraph is also almost 10% shorter. All business people are overloaded with documentation and emails, so the more concise you can keep your messages, the more you will be understood and valued.

7 Smile

In the 1980's, a survey of US high school students showed that what we register first about a person is not what they say or even how they look, but whether they appear friendly or unfriendly. A smile on your face puts a smile in your voice and ensures that you come across as friendly and warm. That's how you need to be to make a good impression on the phone or face-to-face. No wonder call centre trainers adopt the maxim, 'Smile when you dial.' It really works.

8 Put yourself in their shoes

It's obvious really: if you focus on the message or yourself, you forget about the receiver. So always keep the person you're talking to in mind. How will they understand and react to what you're saying? Are they getting it the way you mean it? Try to assess the experience, seniority and English skills of the person you're addressing. Try to relax them, too: a tense and nervous person will absorb far less of your message than one who feels confident that you are not mentally criticizing their language level or expecting too much of them.

9 Build empathy

Nothing irritates people more than the feeling that you're not listening to what they're saying. The feeling that you're just not 'there' in a conversation really destroys empathy, so build rapport by active listening.

Active listening involves really focusing on the speaker, who they are, what they have to say and how they're saying it. Nothing creates empathy more than the feeling that you are interested in me, and nothing destroys it faster than the feeling that you're distracted. It comes across as a lack of interest and commitment.

How do you develop active listening?

- Work on the skill. Spend time concentrating on what you hear: radio, TV, family conversations, anything. Don't assume that active listening is something that comes immediately. It's a communication skill, and you need to practise it.
- Focus on the speaker, her voice, and what she's saying, and don't think about what you want to say next. Working out your reply before you've heard the message is the commonest destroyer of empathy.
- Listen without making judgement. At this stage, don't approve or disapprove – you can make decisions later. Judgemental listening destroys empathy.
- Listen for background noise. On the phone it may be an electronic background (radio or TV), a baby crying or people talking. This gives you a sense of the receiver's environment and their degree of concentration. If you think they're having a problem focusing, ask if they're free to talk.
- Listen to the voice. Is it flat and unemotional (lack of interest)? Is it a bit rushed and irritated (no time to talk)? Is it snuffly and hoarse (a cold)? All these things affect a person's concentration. Don't be afraid to ask: the mere fact of enquiring if it's a convenient time to talk really improves their focus. If you have to reconnect later by phone or postpone a meeting, people will be much more open to you.
- If you have a problem, explain it so that your listener is aware of your situation.

Let's expand on that final point. The Frankfurt Book Fair is one of the world's biggest literary events, spread over 12 halls of the city's giant *Messe* (trade fair centre). Appointments often run late, especially as publishers and distributors arrange meetings in half-hour slots. We were running late in a meeting with a US distributor, and our eyes kept straying away from the stand to check for the approach of our next visitor. He was Japanese, it was his first time at the fair, and he wasn't sure how to find our stand. 'Do you have a problem?' asked our current appointment. Our active listening skills were clearly failing us. We explained that we had to keep an eye out for a person who might not recognize the stand. Our concentration improved and so did his. And yes, our next appointment found us without a problem. The lesson is simple: don't give confusing signals. If you're confused, say so. If you're thinking about something else, say so. It will make the communication and the atmosphere much better, and it will even improve your concentration.

You can practise active listening with a friend or your family. Spend a minute sitting down with someone and just listening, without distraction, without judgement, without thinking of your response: just accept the person as they are. People will say you're the best communicator ever.

Taking culture into account

Different cultures have different ways of communicating (we explored some of them in Chapter 5). If you understand them, you'll be in a strong position to create the trust and empathy that is at the root of this book. Remember the cultural triangle in Chapter 2: you build trust by establishing good relationships and credibility. Credibility means matching your communication style to your counterpart's. These six parameters control international communication styles:

1 Do you say what you mean?	Do I have to read between the lines?
2 Is truth more important than politeness?	Is politeness more important than truth?
3 Is it important to contain your emotions?	Is it important to show your human side?
4 Do you like a fast-moving discussion?	Do you prefer a measured pace?
5 Do you say what you want and then explain why?	Do you explain the background before you say what you want?
6 Do you like an informal way of speaking?	Do you prefer quite a formal way of speaking?

1 Say what you mean or read between the lines?

Hideyoshi is the general manager of a Japanese firm in London. One day he walked into the administrative staff's office and announced: 'Managing Director is arriving tomorrow. Very organized, very tidy man.' And he walked out. No further explanation was necessary. Immediately the staff stopped what they were doing and organized the office so that it looked spotless, with every file and piece of paper in place. That is an example of reading between the lines. Japanese executives are experts at it. Indeed, one of their cultural problems is that they often try to read between lines when there are none to read between! It's easy for European workers in Japanese companies to get caught out by this. If in doubt about whether you have received an instruction, always go back and seek clarification. 'Let me check that I've understood you. You want me to do this...', is a simple way of checking.

Reading between the lines is a speciality of the Asia-Pacific region. Paul Davies in his book, *What's This India Business?*, quotes an Indian company that uses the phrase, 'We've had the *neem*, now let us enjoy the *jaggery*,' when they've given the green light to a deal. The *neem* is a bitter herb in India, whereas *jaggery* is a sweet-tasting herb. The *neem* refers to the negotiation, the hard bit, and the *jaggery* to the implementation.

Every culture has its areas of 'high context', when we share common understanding about something without needing to spell out the details. But some cultures, as we've seen, rely on high-context communication more than others. Managers in the UK and the US are much more likely to explain the particulars of their requirements so there is no possibility of misunderstanding. This can slow things down (watch some Americans deciphering a railway ticket in London), but avoids confusion. However, it often loses some of the subtlety of the communication -- what we call 'low context'. What's important is to understand the difference and to recognize whether the culture that you're dealing with tends to communicate in high-context or low-context mode.

2 Truth versus politeness

India is known as a 'never say no' culture, and it can be frustrating for Westerners who are uncertain about a company's approach to delivery and performance. One reason for the Indians' approach is simply politeness. Another is that there is always someone else who can do the job. A third is pure competitive desire to get the business. So in India you say 'yes' first and worry about the details later. In many joint ventures, British and Indian managers are now developing a consensus in this area, linked by a determination to make things work. But again, in Asia-Pacific countries the wish to tell you what you want to hear (politeness) is frequently more important than telling you the truth about a situation. This means that truth is often hard to come by.

You can use various strategies to discover the reality of a situation. One is to find a friend in the organization that you're dealing with who understands Western priorities and will tell you what's really happening. Another is to ask how your colleague or partner will implement something they have agreed to. This will tell you whether they fully understand the process of your expectations of delivery. Above all, don't browbeat. Don't say, 'Repeat back to me the instruction I gave you.' Your partner will feel insulted. However, don't wait till the deadline has passed before you chase progress. People in 'never say no' societies often see progress chasing as a sign that you're taking an interest, and they can respond very positively.

All societies have coded ways of saying things. Cultures which have a reputation for relying on indirectness rather than directness are mainly to be found in Asian and Middle Eastern societies but countries like the UK also have a similar reputation for indirectness. However, it is important to remember that in all societies, immense individual differences exist in directness and indirectness and that even in predominantly indirect societies, a close relationship will often be the way to achieve directness.

More direct	More indirect
USA/Canada/Australia/New Zealand Germany/Scandinavia, Russia Central and Eastern Europe Southern Europe	Asia-Pacific Middle East Latin America

3 Show your human side

In societies such as India, Italy, Spain or Latin America, people are less interested in what you say (any fool knows that words can be manipulated) than in who you are. Therefore, containing your emotions and sticking strictly to the business in hand is not the way to progress. If I'm Italian, I want to know if you have family, what they are like, how the kids are doing at school. It tells me you have roots. I want to know that you have a beating heart. Eating and drinking together is an important part of getting to know your business partner as a person. Take into account people's personal aspirations, and not just their business or corporate goals.

Heinz is German, and a business manager for an international company. He learns that employees in one of his countries are doing deals below the firm's accepted rate. He also realizes that they could make more money if they used a different kind of relationship-management system. What does he do? Does he simply lay down the corporate law? No, he talks with each of his managers and shares their personal aspirations and his own. Then he shows them how they can realize their ambitions (and make more money – after all, this is a bank) by following the corporate policy. He can only make this work by demonstrating that he has their interests at heart and by sharing his own vision and feelings about his work and his life. That way he gains his colleagues' trust and confidence, and can make the changes needed.

4 Fast moving or measured?

Spaniards talk across each other all the time. Conversations are fast and furious, and it's easy for non-fluent foreigners to get lost. Germans, normally measured, can get into loud, intense discussions, and to outsiders it sounds like a fight's going on. Latins are known for fast, excitable speech, but Asians favour calm, measured discussion punctuated by silences. People tend to modify their communication style according to the communities they have worked in. If you work in Japan or Singapore and in parts of China, you will probably become more reflective and measured in your speech. If you operate in Latin America or Africa, your style is likely to become faster and more lively.

Of course, there are individual differences, and fast and slow speakers in every society. Nevertheless, distinct trends are apparent. The slogan on a mug in our office sums it up. 'I'm a New Yorker,' it says. 'Please speak faster!'

What do you do if you're a slow speaker in a fast society or a fast one in a slow-speaking society? Nothing. You recognize the difference and you don't get upset or impatient with it. It's just the cultural style.

5 Say what you want or tell them a story?

Nothing causes more irritation in international communication than people who waste your time telling you lots of stuff you don't want to know.

Your feet are twitching under the table, and your fingers are beginning to drum on the table top. And everything inside you is screaming, 'Get to the point!' The point is that the boring old f.... in front of you *is* getting there, but in his or her cultural way.

There are two dominant approaches to saying what you want. The one used by the British and Americans is, 'This is what I want and this is why I want it.' Or, 'This is what we want to achieve and this is how I think we should go about it.' Fine. Clear. Aims first, then reasons, and we can see what kind of decision to make. However, there is a whole swathe of the world that argues, 'How can you possibly understand what I want to achieve unless I tell you the background of why I want to achieve it?' So they start with the background and then tell you what they want. The problem is that sometimes there's a lot of background. I have seen normally polite Americans, irritated to the point of exhaustion, interjecting,' Is there a point at the end of this monologue?' as they often have no idea where the speaker is heading.

In 'culture speak' we call the UK/US style of presenting 'concise' and the other style 'expressive'. Much of the world is used to the 'expressive' style of making a case, including the Russians, Chinese, Japanese, Koreans, Indians and Brazilians. One of their cultural challenges is to learn the British, American, German, Dutch and Scandinavian preference for stating the point first and giving the reasons later.

The problem is that if you don't understand the other person's style, you'll consider the expressive presenter time-wasting and irrelevant, and they will consider you rude and inconsiderate because you haven't listened to what screenwriters call the back-story – the background to the request or business proposal.

What's the solution? Understand what's going on. Be patient, and if you really are pressed for time, say politely, 'We're short of time here. Can we move straight to the point?'

6 Formal or informal?

Remember the paper, stone and scissors game? Paper covers stone but scissors cut paper? Well in the formality-informality stakes, formality wins. Most British, American and Australian discussions take place in a relatively relaxed environment and in an informal style, with first names, minimum protocol and a preference for a direct, conversational style of speech. But much of the rest of the world feels that business is too important for informality and should be conducted with the seriousness it deserves. To do less brands you as a cowboy, in the bad sense of the word. Remember the story of Gareth and his Swiss soon-to-be-landlord in Chapter 5?

Italians often make a clear distinction between formal and informal environments, using surnames and a clear business protocol in the office, but being very friendly and intimate in entertaining outside it. The Chinese will negotiate harshly in a formal environment but still expect you to take part in friendly exchange over meals and the social side of the negotiation process.

The problem is that Britons and Americans often find it hard to switch codes between formal and informal, and prefer a relatively informal style throughout. The solution is to do your homework. Check out the style of the country you're dealing with (the country profiles at the back of this book will help you). If in doubt, curb your enthusiasm. A restrained, slightly more formal approach works better at first and helps establish your credentials as a serious player. You can warm up later when people get to know you.

Feel the people

Peter is a Finnish businessman working in IT. 'In Finland,' he says, 'you do three minutes small talk and then get down to business. In other countries (he was talking about France) you have to feel the people.' Sometimes we just want to cut to the chase and say, 'I haven't got time for all this.' Well, make time. In international business, feeling the people is what it's about, and the qualities you need are patience and commitment. Relax your schedule, allow for the fact that things will take a bit longer, especially in the earlier stages, and that you may have to invest more hours than you would like in monitoring activity and making sure things work. The pay-off in international business is often long- term loyalty and rewards rather than short-term gain.

Presentations

Presentations to colleagues, boards or groups of foreigners is an area of communication that most scares people. We are nervous about public speaking at the best of times, and presentation courses are still one of the most demanded forms of soft-skills training. There are rules about public speaking and we don't need to rehearse them here, except one: know your audience. Above all know your foreign audience. Different foreign audiences look for different things in a presentation.

Johnson and Co, a British firm, create adverts for sales directories. They're very good at it, and were recently pursuing some Spanish business. Accordingly they prepared a presentation to illustrate how successful they were. Facts, figures, pie charts and graphs were loaded with impeccable taste into the PowerPoint programme – until they talked to a Spanish marketing consultant. She told them that what Spaniards needed to know was what kind of people they were dealing with: figures can say just what people want them to say, but the eyes don't lie. So Johnson's modified their approach to include less formal get-to-know-you talks so that the Spanish company could feel out its potential partner. The environment for the meetings, the food, the hotel and the hospitality were all important in achieving this. As a result, Johnson's got the business. So before you make a presentation to a foreign group, ask these four questions:

1. How long are they prepared to listen? What's their attention span?
2. How much detail do they need?
3. What are they looking for? Facts and figures, a hard sell, a soft 'academic' sell, or do they just want to feel what kind of person you are?
4. What kind of feedback should you expect? Questions at the end, questions and comments in the middle, no response at all, hand-clapping, table-drumming (as the Germans do) or complete silence (common in Asia)?

Two contrasting cases illustrate the problem. In Germany, Christine's short, light, flip, jokey presentation with cartoons in her PowerPoint didn't go down well. The Germans expected to listen for up to an hour, and to see charts showing detailed product specifications and the benefits of what she was proposing. They needed to know that what she was selling was based on research and experience. They didn't want to know what she actually presented – that her company was a dynamic, young, innovative, fun organization to do business with.

In Japan, on the other hand, George was confused. He thought he'd got it exactly right in terms of length and level of detail, but was surprised when his presentation was followed by a total lack of reaction. When he asked someone for feedback he was asked why his PowerPoint slides were not fuller. He hadn't realized that for most Japanese, a presentation is a formal occasion. They would consider it rude to ask questions: that would suggest he hadn't been clear enough. Applause is also not what you do in Japan: reflective silence shows greater respect. Many Japanese are not confident about their ability to understand spoken English, and they prefer to see things written out. A handout is therefore a key piece of documentation for them. The visual nature of Japanese society also means that they like to see lots of information well presented on one screen rather than sparingly laid out over several. The Western advice not to have more than five points per screen is not the Japanese style. Most importantly, George needed to remember the maxim that in Japan it is better to say a few things three times in a different way each time, in order to get the message across.

Writing emails

If you are in international business, especially if you're coping with different time zones, you will rely on email even more so than when you're dealing with affairs in your home country. There's another major difference: your audience may well be working in English as a foreign language, and their speed of reading and comprehension will be slower than yours. So it is vital that you adopt a sympathetic policy when emailing. Here are some ideas:

1. Observe the rules we've already suggested for communication: keep it simple and concise, using short sentences, and avoid slang and idioms.
2. Use lists instead of dense paragraphs to make things clearer for your contact.
3. Be clear about what you want. The British are notorious for finding it embarrassing to express what they want other people to do. It's not aggressive or rude in business to make your needs or wishes plain.

You can find detailed guides on email usage just by keying 'email' into a search engine. Meanwhile, consider the right and wrong ways to write an email shown here, and model your messages accordingly.

Bad email

Dear Giorgio,
We agree that you should progress with the plan to set up a distribution centre to handle the company's entry into the Italian market. We have discussed this at length here at headquarters, and we would be pleased if you would consider several factors that would expedite the process. The building that you choose should be within 50 kilometers of Milan Malpensa airport to allow facilitation of export requirements. As for size, we were thinking in terms of something around 100,000 cubic metres in size, and in that there should be an office area for up to 20 people. Of course we're taking into consideration how easy – or not! – it might be to recruit local staff, so we would be grateful if you could take into account bus and train access to the area. There is also the question of the tax incentives apparently lobbed out by the Milan city authority – yes, we definitely want a slice of that pie! We don't want to pressure you, but it would be helpful if we could get from you a shortlist of up to six sites by April 20. Occupation by October 1 would be desirable.

If you have any queries or suggestions, please get back to me ASAP.

Ciao,
Simon

Clear email

Dear Giorgio,

We agree that you should progress with the plan to set up a distribution centre to handle the company's entry into the Italian market. Here is the brief that we would like you to consider:

- *It must be within 50 kilometres of Milan Malpensa airport;*
- *It must be around 100,000 cubic metres in size, with an office area for up to 20 people;*

- *Bus and train access must be excellent to help staff recruitment;*
- *It must be within the tax-incentive zone set up by the Milan city authority;*
- *We would like you to submit a shortlist of up to six sites by April 20;*
- *The sites must be available for occupation by October 1.*

If you have any queries or suggestions, please let me know within 48 hours.

Ciao,
Simon

Note the bits of pompous, ugly English in the bad version, the nervousness about making reasonable business requests, the inclusion of slang, clumsy attempts at humour and an abbreviation that would probably not be familiar to a foreigner. The fact that everything is contained in one slab of text is also off-putting.

Conclusion

In this chapter we've explored some of the reasons why people don't receive our messages as we communicate them. We've looked at the use of English, the importance of building empathy through active listening, and the different styles of communication and how they apply to presentations.

In the country profiles at the back of the book you'll learn what different nationalities look for in presentations. If you're doing business abroad, do your homework and find out what's expected before you start. You'll probably need to change your communication approach to ensure that your message is received. It all comes down to having respect for your audience. How much respect you should show is part of the next chapter on leadership.

Key learning points

- A message isn't communicated until it's received.
- Adapt your native English style to the needs of people working in English as a foreign language.
- Active listening builds empathy.
- What annoys you about someone else's communication style may simply be due to their cultural background.
- Communication with other cultures demands patience and time – but the results are worth it.
- Find out what your audience expects before you deliver. Remember the four presentation questions above.

SEVEN

Leadership and decision-making

SEVEN

Leadership and decision-making

Sarah, a US management consultant, was on an internal flight from Krakow to Warsaw in Poland. As the plane taxied she saw the man in the window seat across the aisle still on his mobile (against all airline regulations). Next to him was his obviously Polish assistant. "Excuse me," Sarah said, "can you ask him to turn it off. We're about to take off." "I can't," was the reply. "He's my boss."

One of the stereotypes of intercultural communication is that the further south you go the more authoritarian the boss is. There's some truth in this, but so-called top-down approaches extend pretty far north, and business styles are much more dependent on an individual's personality than on some of the other cultural factors we have considered. Nevertheless, you can usually identify a common leadership style in any regional or national community, although how the style is applied may vary according to whether the company is a family-run SME or a large conglomerate.

The key issues are likely to be these:

1. Is the management style top-down or egalitarian?
2. How reliable is the company organigram, if there is one?
3. What is the degree of delegation in the company? Who has the power to decide what?
4. How important is hierarchy in the company? Is the reporting structure matrix or vertical?
5. Are decisions reached by seeking consensus or by individuals?
6. Who do you refer to in order to speed things up or if things go wrong?
7. What happens if you break ranks and jump the chain of command?
8. How important is status in the company? Is it team-based, or is communication limited to managers at the same level and above?

1 Top-down or egalitarian?

In a top-down management structure all major decisions must be referred to or authorized by the boss. Depending on the organization, this can vary from major purchasing or investment decisions to ordering office stationery. In Central European countries such as Poland, and in Spain, Italy, Portugal and anywhere where family-based firms form a significant part of the economy, the boss is the boss is the boss. All initial discussions and all management decisions will be taken at the top. This means that your first significant meeting will be with the company chief, although you may work operationally with a middle manager at your level and with a responsibility equal to yours.

Don Julio Jimenes is the founder and director of a large SME in Spain. His daughter, who will take over when he retires, is responsible for some of the company operations, but ultimately it is her father who controls. When he needs to, he brings in a relevant operational manager, but decision-making rests with Don Julio, as everyone calls him.

Michael, on the other hand, is the sales manager of an SME in the UK. He has a reasonably clear job description, operational budget and decision-making power within his responsibilities, and he knows pretty well what he can sign off and what needs escalating to a higher level. His approach is to do exactly the same with managers in other business communities – look for the decision-maker at his level. Unfortunately, two things get in Michael's way. First, his opposite number may have the same title but not the same executive powers. Secondly, that person's middle management level may deny him access to the real decision-maker. Michael's counterpart will only be able to make decisions if he has his CEO with him, at least during the meetings establishing the relationship between the two companies.

In a business run on top-down management styles, decisions will not be taken if the boss isn't there; lower managers may champion your proposal, but they cannot decide. This inevitably causes delays, and your strategy needs to take account of this. It's really important not to assume that another company's working methods are the same as yours. Instead, find out what their structure is and how it works. The question is not, "How much can you sign off?" but "Who makes strategic and project decisions?"

2 Company organigrams: are they reliable?

Understanding who is responsible for what, who can sign for what, who decides and who implements is usually pretty clear in the UK. Managers have job descriptions and budgets, and they know at what point they have to escalate matters higher up the food chain.

Just don't expect it to be like that in other countries. Julian was an international sales manager. His first request in dealing with any new company was to ask for its organigram so that he could note the names and positions of all the managers. This worked fine until he dealt with an Italian company. Its organigram listed the position and name of the sales director but the actual decision-making power belonged to the supply-chain manager. Why? Because he was personally close to the company president. The sales director was simply an implementation manager.

In the Italian army, Massimo was a person of enormous power and influence, although he was only a captain. The reason was that he was aide-de-camp to a full general. His influence, he explained, was because he had spotted the general's talent early on and had harnessed his career to that potential. As a result, although Massimo's rank hadn't increased, his power and influence had.

In India, organigrams are a useful indication of who used to do what: they're not always reliable guides to who will be doing what when you visit a company. Indian business can move very fast, with managers extending or adapting their responsibilities and job descriptions to match the organization's changing needs. One of the first things you should do with an Indian corporate organigram is to sit down with a senior manager and update it. And be aware that it may change again before your next visit.

3 Taking ownership and delegation

Delegation is an important leadership skill. If you fail to delegate, how can you progress in your career? Delegation leaves you free to take up higher responsibilities, at least in theory.

We have already seen that with a top-down management style, middle managers are delegated to. But they themselves do not delegate. When they 'delegate' to junior staff, they are simply giving orders and not allocating responsibility. So you should establish in the early stages of working with a new company exactly who has executive responsibility and who is just carrying out orders. Because there is less delegation and more giving of commands, managers may be reluctant to take ownership of a piece of work or a project.

UK and US managers working with Indian IT firms have noticed that their opposite numbers often show less initiative and challenge decisions less than they themselves are used to doing. Nothing in the Indian's organizational structure or education encourages them to do so. They are perfectly aware of the issues involved, but do not feel they have the authority to speak up.

Managers in Central and Eastern Europe are equally reluctant to take ownership: acting beyond their strict responsibility level could get them into trouble. Carol ran into this problem in Poland. She would delegate what she thought was responsibility for a piece of work, only to find out when the deadline had passed that nothing had happened. Why? The manager concerned had not thought that he had the authority to carry out the task, or had questioned it personally but not felt able to challenge her. She was left dissatisfied and suspicious, and the local manager was left confused by what he felt was an unclear order.

This is a difficult situation to deal with, but it happens a lot. Carol's solution was a good one. What she did was to approach a senior manager who she knew and trusted and explained the problem to him. He agreed to take ownership of the work and make sure it was done. He talked to the manager concerned and resolved the difficulty. He also kept an eye on the situation to make sure the task was completed. It was, although because of the misunderstanding it was still two weeks late.

The lesson? Don't assume that delegation is the answer. Don't assume that the manager delegated to will have the authority to take ownership of the task in hand. Check with senior decision-makers and ask them to give the appropriate instructions and, if necessary, monitor the work to be done.

4 Hierarchy

German managers working in the UK or US face a common problem: they're used to a vertical structure with direct reporting to their line manager. Faced with a dotted line matrix structure, or what's even worse for them, a liaison rather than a clear reporting responsibility, they can feel bewildered. German organizations are changing, but they still have a preference for strong hierarchies, with clear reporting structures.

German managers are also used to receiving precise instructions and having clear responsibilities, and then getting on with the job and delivering on time. They don't take kindly to being micromanaged by British or American colleagues wishing to keep on top of things. They may also feel angry and suspicious when British or US managers buck the hierarchy.

Waltraud is the HR manager of an international bank in Berlin, and reports to a director there. Howard, a new HR manager from London, is flying over for a visit, and she is asked to attend a meeting with him. Waltraud suspects that Howard is about to take up global responsibility in the company and, if that happens, she would report to him. She is told that during his Berlin visit Howard also wants to chat to two employees, but without her or her manager present. Oddly, he is not scheduled to meet her German HR director.

As a result of all this, Waltraud is on high alert. She feels that Howard's arrangements are discourteous, and show a lack of respect for the German hierarchy. She is suspicious about his motives, her mood is uncooperative, and she is getting mildly paranoid about the whole thing.

Is she right? There is a management view that says, "Only the paranoid survive." But Howard may only be doing a quick fact-finding tour to help him to understand the overall structure of his new multinational organization. What could he have done to ensure cooperation? Obviously, he should have explained to Waltraud, either by email or phone or both, the aims of his visit. He should have said why he wanted to talk to the employees in Germany, and he needed to schedule at least a courtesy few minutes with the HR director in Germany. Basically, he applied British lack of formality and protocol to the German situation – a mistake. Germans need a clear system, and this involves a degree of protocol. Britons prefer a transparent process, which involves consultation and explanation. In this case, neither happened.

The lesson? You don't have to approve of another company's hierarchy, but you do have to recognize that it exists. Understand how it works, and then decide how you want to deal with it. If you fail to take hierarchy into account, you'll experience problems of communication and cooperation.

Sri Lanka provides another example of the need to understand hierarchy. Managers there will always try to deal with their equivalents of the same level and responsibility. This may be difficult to achieve when foreign managers visit the country, as PA's try to match job descriptions and degrees of authority from business cards and letters. Richard was an operations manager for a major British company seeking business in Sri Lanka, but he could not access the local decision-makers: they were above his level. Not until he took his CEO to Colombo did he get the meetings he needed. His experience again shows that checking how the hierarchy works can save time, frustration and expense.

5 Consensus or individually driven decision-making

Andrea was seriously frustrated by her Japanese colleagues. Extracting decisions from her head office in Osaka was like getting blood from a stone. For her, as a British manager, the issue was simple. How much could she sign for? What decisions did she have to escalate upwards? Why couldn't her Japanese equals do the same?

Andrea hadn't realized the importance of *nemawashi* and *ringi-sho* in Japan. *Nemawashi* describes the process of collective negotiation. It means that before a decision is made and communicated, everyone in the management loop must be consulted. And *ringi-sho* means that everyone must agree. This condemns Japanese management to a lengthy process of decision-making, although once they have reached agreement they implement matters quickly. British and US business people often worry that opportunities might be lost in this way, but the Japanese say: "It is better to be second now and first later." They criticize other cultures for taking fast decisions but implementing them slowly. For the Japanese, making the decision and ensuring that resources are in place to implement it are part of the same process.

Japanese managers recognize the problem that *nemawashi* and *ringi-sho* can cause, and in high-level negotiations will often employ a senior retired manager to act as unofficial liaison on the state of play of negotiations. This may be the UK manager's original Japanese contact (see Chapter 9).

Nordic and German companies also work on achieving consensus within the team. In Germany, the importance of a company's works council means that all major decisions must be the basis of detailed consultation at all levels and commitment by all parties. In Britain, too, it is important to be seen to consult and achieve buy-in from stakeholders, but the process is less all-embracing and much quicker than in the countries mentioned earlier. British managers often chafe at the slowness of other nations' decision-making: they know what they can delegate, and when to escalate a problem to a higher level.

But even in communities that arrive at decisions by seeking consensus, there can be exceptions. Carlos Ghosn, president of Renault, took over the ailing Nissan brand after the French manufacturer bought a stake in the Japanese company in 1999. The Brazilian-born Ghosn is the perfect example of a corporate executive whose multicultural experiences have taught him the importance of combining various cultural perspectives. Within a few years he had turned Nissan around. Did he employ *nemawashi* and *ringi-sho*? No, he used French charismatic personal leadership and a detailed knowledge of production and market information. And did the Japanese hate him for defiling their leadership values? Not at all. They respected his seniority as managing director and went along with his management style. Why? Because he was successful. Had he not been, it might have been a different story.

The lesson? You can break the rules – as long as you're successful.

6 Speeding up decision-making

A group of German managers working in an international Japanese company were angry. A long-term, high-volume customer had requested a 10% discount on his next order. The German manager wanted to comply, but he couldn't: he had to relay the request to Tokyo. He'd already advised the customer that he might have to wait ten days for a decision. But it took three weeks to arrive, and the offered discount was just 3%. To keep his customer happy, the German had to concede the other 7% and hide it in his costs. We asked a Japanese manager how he dealt with this kind of situation. He thought for a while and then said: "*Nemawashi!*" In other words, there is no solution. You have to go through the process.

But what if you have to make a fast decision and don't have time to go through the chain of command in your own company? If you're working in a multinational, your manager might be based in Sydney, Delhi, Toronto or Tokyo. What strategies, if any, can you use to speed up decision-making?

Tony had a new job at his bank, liaising between corporate headquarters and investment centres in London, Frankfurt and New York. He knew that investment relied on initiative to get new business. He also knew that the corporate side of banking is more about systems, record-keeping and risk control. His strategy was simple but labour- and phone-intensive: contact and close consultation.

He never missed an opportunity to talk to colleagues in all three centres in person or on the phone, and to take them to lunch or dinner when they were in town. He wanted to build the kind of relationship that would allow him to call people at short notice when he needed a rapid decision, even out of office hours. He even made sure that the German team visited London for face-to-face contact with their counterparts to ensure that relationships and understanding were good. Why? Tony reasoned that routine business doesn't need close contact, but when everything is slightly out of the norm you have to rely on each other, and you can only do that by establishing good relationships and trust. The lesson? Create trust beforehand by building good personal contacts by phone, visits and hospitality with members of the distant team. Emails just don't hack it.

7 Breaking the chain of command

Here's how we lost a business relationship in Germany. We were working on a project in a number of German *Laendër*, or states, with a manager in the organization who was championing the plan to the other states. He was to address a meeting of all the *Laendër* when it would be discussed. To aid the process, we independently sent background information to all the state heads prior to the conference. But the scheme was not adopted, either by our champion or anybody else, and we never heard from him again. We had broken the rules by going over his head.

The rule is, when you come across a vertical hierarchy, it's risky to break the chain of command. You could make an enemy of your own manager and embarrass everyone else. Be careful before you do it: if you do feel a need to break this rule in a vertical structure, it should only be done informally and not in writing. Be sure that the manager you are dealing with accepts the situation, and be clear that at some point you will need to revert to dealing with your own boss.

The importance of observing a clear vertical command structure can be a problem in a matrix or dotted-line structure where managers feel free to get advice and consult anywhere within the organization, and may even try to play one manager off against another in order to get ahead. Witness 'vanity mails' – the sending of inessential copies of emails to senior people 'for information'. It's blatant creeping (there are less polite phrases for it). We know one American CEO who never opens emails that are copied to him, or those from anyone he doesn't know. It's the only way he knows to keep his mailbox under control.

Showing respect is also important in top-down companies. Letting your senior manager know what's happening is an important way of displaying consideration and maintaining cooperation. We recently got caught out by failing to observe this rule. The Arabic-speaking head of a department queried a split-second decision we had made about a flier advertising a conference which bore his department's name. We'd obtained approval to release the leaflet from another source but why, he wanted to know, hadn't we approached him and – more to the point – why hadn't he been invited? Respect and protocol had been ignored. We quickly apologized, explained the short notice we had faced and sent him a formal invitation. Honour was satisfied (and predictably, he didn't turn up).

The lesson? Shooting from the hip may seem like excitingly fast decision-making and may sometimes be necessary, but try and observe the consultation protocol. The more top-down the management structure, the more important it is.

8 Maintaining status

"How did you get on at lunch?" we asked a university colleague at a conference. We'd spotted him sharing a table with an older man with the slightly scruffy air of a boffin or a professor. "OK," he said, "but he wasn't interested in me because I wasn't a vice-chancellor." The scientist he was sharing a table with was a university vice-chancellor and didn't want to waste time talking to a humble senior lecturer at another university. You have to recognize that even in informal egalitarian-ish Britain, status can be a real issue. Vice-chancellors run universities: some are friendly and egalitarian, others not.

An events manager we know had a hard time at a conference in Germany. He wanted to provide identical suites and Mercedes-Benz cars for two departmental managers. But the conference village, a spa in Bavaria, had only one five-star hotel, which had only one presidential suite. Hiring the two identical-model Mercedes was no problem, but the suite? The events manager had a bright idea. The hotel had two identically-priced executive suites. Unfortunately, advised the events manager, the presidential suite was unavailable, so would the departmental directors accept the executive accommodation instead? They would: problem solved!

Older style German managers will deal with people at their level or higher, and will not expect to communicate with junior managers outside the strictly office environment. The Danes are far more egalitarian with managers, PA's and executives all lunching together in the staff canteen.

When you visit an international office, or the local office of a multinational company, look at two things. Note how the staff greet the receptionist and are greeted by him or her: this is often a good indicator of the relationships and degree of formality within the company. And secondly, observe the canteen ritual. Who sits with whom? British managers tend to lunch with their mates, who may also be colleagues. Germans eat with other managers at their level, but not necessarily from the same department. French and Spanish managers may go home for lunch or eat with friends. Japanese managers won't lunch, but will go out with their team from seven to nine in the evening once or twice a week before the commute home. And Americans, we are told, don't lunch at all. As Gordon Gecko, the corporate raider character in Oliver Stone's film *Wall Street* notoriously said: "Lunch is for wimps."

Lessons on status? By and large British and US managers are reasonably egalitarian in their behaviour. More vertical management structures are more status-conscious and will put a black mark against you if you cross the line. Check their status and what kind of person they are before you greet people, and double check that you're welcome before you sit and break bread.

Conclusion

A key difference in world business is between communities that adopt a vertical structure and those that operate a matrix management plan. Some industries tend to favour one or the other: the IT world is much more relaxed than the legal profession or banking, for example. Understand the type of structure you are dealing with and be prepared to adapt. In particular, note who takes decisions and whether decisions are reached by consensus or by individual managers, and above all how reporting lines operate and how status is maintained. This will impact on the discussion of team-working, meetings and negotiations in the next two chapters.

Key learning points

- Distinguish between vertical top-down and matrix management structures; each requires different treatment.
- The organigram doesn't necessarily represent the power structure in an organization.
- Check if the decision-making process is consensus driven or individually driven and adapt accordingly.
- Check the reporting line and adapt.
- Check the status distinctions and decide whether to adapt or buck it. But remember, rebellion may cost.

EIGHT

Teams, motivation and feedback

EIGHT
Teams, motivation and feedback

You could almost excuse Valentino Rossi if he were a petulant prima donna. The Italian is a multiple world champion in MotoGP, motorcycling's equivalent of Formula 1, regularly features in the Forbes Top 100 Celebrities list, and is said to earn between $25 and $30 million a year. He also has to cope with the stresses of riding a motorcycle at up to 215mph just centimetres from other hotbloods eager to grab the glory and the adrenalin rush of finishing first.

So when the engine of Rossi's Camel Yamaha motorcycle broke when he was leading the 2006 French Grand Prix at Le Mans just seven laps away from an easy win, you might have expected him to splash just a little blame on someone else: Yamaha, his engineers, the designers – anyone in the line of fire, really.

But Rossi breezed into his post-race press conference and announced: "The good news is that we now have a great-handling bike!"

Yes, he regretted the fact that his engine had failed and cost him valuable points, but here he was focusing on a positive that the team had achieved that day. Unlike many Formula 1 stars, he declined to lash out at others: no recriminations, no accusations, no sulking.

One of the reasons that Rossi has become an icon to millions of fans worldwide is that he doesn't whinge when things go wrong. He's a team player, spending long testing days with his mechanics to solve problems, keeping morale buoyant and accepting the bad days along with the good ones.

Scandinavia is noted for its team culture and egalitarian management structure. The chief chemist in a Danish glass-making firm was in no doubt about what to do if a batch of products was sub-standard. "I just go down to the factory floor and ask the foreman. He knows exactly what's wrong," he says. That's a part of teamwork: working together, exchanging information and ideas.

But it doesn't always work like that. An international banker in Bangkok became aware that information about clients was not circulating within his team. It took him a while to realize that two of his local hires came from rival clans and to them, not sharing information with the 'enemy' was more important than the team's goals.

People who share a culture generally share a team ethic. But when you work with another culture you play by different rules. To find out what they are, check the following:

- How is the team selected?
- Who leads it and how?
- What is its team-working process?
- What is the role of the individual in the team?
- What are the motivational factors in the team?
- How do team meetings run?
- What constitutes team results?
- How do you give team feedback?

Management theorists identify two essential elements in creating a successful team. First, you should include different psychological types, as proposed by the Belbin analysis of personalities. And the team must be allowed to experience the four stages of evolution known as forming, storming, norming, and reforming. In other words the team will assemble, decide how it will function, go through a process of adjustment as people get used to working with each other, and finally reform as they establish new norms. All teams, the theory says, go through this process to achieve success. But in international and multinational teams an additional set of factors comes into play.

Two types of team

There are generally two kinds of team in international business:

- Multinational teams
- Virtual distributed teams (VDTs)

Multinationals

Ten employees of a UK pharmaceutical company are meeting on an away-day in a hotel by the river Thames near London. Their department runs clinical trials on drugs that will be marketed if the tests are successful, and what is interesting about the group is that they come from seven different nationalities. The team leader is American, there are two Australians, three Brits, a Swede, a Colombian, a German and a Frenchman, and each has a different management background and level of international experience.

VDTs

Members of the HR department in an international law company meet just once a year, at an annual conference in Texas. The six are based in Toronto, London, Moscow, Delhi, Hong Kong and Sydney. Their common language is English, but two are Americans, and there is one Canadian, Russian, Chinese and Indian. They communicate electronically, using Skype internet-based phone calls, emails and phone and video conferencing.

Both types of team share two characteristics: different nationalities and different management backgrounds. How do they manage to get on? Celia, who co-ordinates the VDT, is clear. "Never assume that people come at things the same way," she says. "You've got to find out how each team member approaches the task and then mould them into a common agreed method of working."

Team selection

Business communities generally rely on four criteria to select teams, but weight them in different ways. The criteria are:

1 Technical expertise

Technocratic business communities such as the Nordic countries, Germany and France will look for the right technical specialists.

2 Seniority

Other communities, especially those with top-down management systems, may feel that it's more important to have teams with the right degree of seniority, and that technical expertise can be assumed or brought in as required.

3 Longevity

Other communities may place the highest value on experience and loyalty to the company. Team members chosen in this way may be more senior, but they are not necessarily there because they run things or have detailed technical knowledge.

4 The generalist

Anglo-Saxon companies often introduce a wild card into the pack, a generalist. This is an all-rounder, a person of general skills whose quality is that he or she can keep things moving forward, get results and trouble-shoot problems regardless of seniority or technical expertise. The difficulty for this kind of person is that their position and value may not be recognized by team members chosen on the grounds of seniority, loyalty or technical expertise.

People appointed to an international team often assume that *their* country's selection method has been used, and can be disagreeably surprised when they discover that different criteria have been in play. The job of an international team leader is to understand these different selection criteria, take them into account and ensure that the positive qualities of each individual are emphasized. The leader must also understand how each team member sees their function. Failure to do this may be a key factor in destroying cohesion when the group first starts working together. Specialists and generalists may be sceptical about one another; both may question the authority of team members selected by seniority, and the value of people chosen on grounds of longevity and experience in the company.

Team leadership

Different business communities see team leadership in different ways, and this can also cause conflict at the group's formative stage. In some cultures the most senior member becomes team leader, but in others the honour goes to the one with the best technical qualifications. In others, loyalty and longevity will decide the choice. Generalists are rarely appointed team leader as they're usually not close enough to the company hierarchy and lack technical expertise. Team members often question the rationale behind the appointment of their leader, but you can now see that it may be grounded in the culture of the community that made the decision. You may not agree with it, but you should at least try to understand the motives.

How leadership is exercised will depend how the leader views his or her role. An American or Briton may deliberately diminish his authority in order to encourage input from others, but a French, Spanish or Italian leader may impose his authority and dominate discussions, controlling who contributes and how. Scandinavians and to some extent the Germans, like the British and Americans, prefer to allow everyone to contribute in order to seek a consensus, and do not lead the discussion until the time comes to summarize. If you're working in an international group it's important to understand these issues. If you're the leader, you should explain your style and what is expected of team members at the beginning of the project.

The process of team-working

One of the highest compliments that you can offer a European or an American is to say that she or he shows initiative. The equivalent in Japan is to congratulate someone on being a good team player. To stress their commitment to the team, Japanese executives will often refer to themselves as 'we', to identify closely with the firm. They may even introduce themselves by company and department position before they give you their own name. To Western minds the Japanese desire for team identity can be unsettling. The Japanese have a saying: "The nail that sticks up must be hammered down," implying that individualism must be crushed and frustrated. This isn't so – individual effort and initiative are appreciated in Japanese business – but they need to be coordinated in a team effort. This means that a lot of time is spent in collective discussion, and decisions are made through the process known as *nemawashi* (binding the roots).

Team-working means talking and often delaying decisions until you reach consensus. If you're on the outside waiting for a decision, this can be seriously annoying, but for those on the team it makes sense. "We can't move forward quickly unless we are all of the same mind," says one Japanese manager.

Within limits, the Germans and the Scandinavians agree. They are also consensus-driven communities where the aim is to listen to all appropriate views, and to reach decisions acceptable to all parties.

Rob Martin, a British manager seconded to a German company, provides a good example of someone who experienced difficulties by offering an inappropriate viewpoint in the wrong place. In the egalitarian style of his country, he was used to expressing his opinions about any subject under discussion. But he came unstuck in a meeting in Germany. In a discussion about changing production procedures, he opened in classic British style. "I'm not in production," he said, "but speaking as..." only to be cut off in mid-flight by the German production director, who said, "So you are now a production expert, Mr Martin?" "Get back in your box," was the real message. In German business you speak in your professional capacity and keep your feelings about matters outside your specialist competence to yourself, or at least outside the meeting.

Sarah Lyons, who worked in the UK in the marketing division of a Swedish company, had a similar problem. She is what she terms 'feisty', and feels no embarrassment in saying exactly what she means in no uncertain terms. Swedes, on the other hand, try to avoid confrontation: they believe that reasoned argument is best and that disagreements are best sorted out before the meeting, or at least outside it. Sarah's impatience and frustration in meetings, and her colleagues' discomfort at her outspokenness, was one of the reasons she left the firm quite rapidly.

The lesson is: in a consensus-driven environment, leave your guns at the door. Disagreements and strongly expressed arguments are best dealt with outside.

In Asia-Pacific, a united front in a team meeting is essential. Internal disharmony or people who constantly try to emphasize their own individuality stand out and weaken, not strengthen, the team. In Australia, for reasons of egalitarianism, a saying reminds you that 'the tall poppies get cut down first'. The conclusion: do nothing, even in jest, which even hints at friction or a less than united front and, above all, don't push yourself as the superstar above your team leader. It may have quite the opposite effect.

In Britain, as in countries such as Poland, team members retain their individual identities and accept a majority viewpoint rather than a decision reached by consensus. British team members protect fiercely their right to be consulted. However, they do on the whole accept that if the majority disagrees, the majority's desires will prevail. In France or in Italy, the team's main function is to carry out the boss' decision. Team members may input their views and exert influence, but ultimately the team's role is to implement strategies and not to make policy.

What, how and why cultures?

A team's job is to complete a task on time and within budget, and to predict and resolve problems that arise. But business communities vary in the way they troubleshoot issues, and this affects how multinational teams operate. American and British teams usually recognize difficulties very quickly, and their concern is then to search for solutions. It makes for fast, action-oriented teamwork, as long as the problem has been correctly identified. These we call *how* problem-solving cultures.

However, in more cautious environments people often feel that more time needs to be spent discussing the problem. They believe that once you have identified the difficulty, the solution becomes clear. These countries – and Germany is a prime example -- we call *what* cultures. Their prime concern is to identify what the issue is. However, the discussions can be very protracted and can lead to what is often labelled analysis paralysis: Britons would call it not seeing the wood for the trees.

The French tend to be a special case. Their insistence on logic and background understanding often leads them to speculate on why the problem has occurred in the first place. We call them *why* cultures, which generally means that team meetings become longer and more involved, and tempers can get frayed, when the French are involved. For them, it is important to establish the principle, and once that is done, action follows quickly.

Imagine a multinational team leader in a European Union committee, faced with why, what and how cultures all jostling to establish their methodology. If you don't know the different approaches adopted by different cultural groups to troubleshooting problems, you have a recipe for chaos and a fast-track to failure.

The way that these three cultures tackle tasks and troubleshooting problems affects team communication. For the French, Germans and *what* and *how* cultures generally, the talking takes place at the beginning of the process. Once the principle has been established and the problem identified, team members go off and do their individual work. However, that's when the *how* cultures want to continue talking, to discuss and probe different solutions. We've seen the irritation and frustration caused to Germans when Brits or Americans start tossing new ideas into a project at this stage. "Why didn't they introduce this at the beginning?" the Germans complain to one another.

Team motivation

Apart from the operational aspects of project management, the leader of a multinational team also has to work out how to motivate the group. Do you stress cooperation and team results, individual success and esteem, or competition?

Anjna runs a team of Japanese, Americans and Brits. They work in a Japanese company, so her job is to motivate the Japanese by appealing to teamwork and team results, and to educate the Americans and British in these values. But if the company were American, the group would focus on beating the competition and achieving personal aspirations. Similar triggers might be used in a British organization, although status and position in the company would also be emphasized.

People are generally motivated by five core factors, but the importance of each one will vary according to your cultural background. A skilful manager will learn what matters most to her team members in order to get the best from each of them. The five factors are:

- **Money** is especially important in communities that lack social security and pensions systems. Indians will tell you that money is the most vital consideration to them, as they need it to look after families and dependents. It's literally all they have to fall back on.
- **Status** is a major issue in Germany, France and the UK, where how you are seen and whether you receive equal status to your colleagues matters greatly. In Asia-Pacific, status is expressed in terms of gaining or losing face, and your growing awareness of how to achieve that is a major business strength. Acquiring face in these societies is such a subtle art that it really can only be achieved by experience. The Chinese like to say that they know foreigners will make mistakes, but that they are a tolerant people. However, many Asians will avoid Westerners who they think might put them unwittingly in difficult positions.
- **Security** is another factor in war-torn or economically unstable countries where having a job – any job – and hanging on to it for dear life is a major pre-occupation. This means that the people you deal with will be disinclined to take risks or move outside their narrowly defined area of authority. Clear instructions and no incentive to think beyond the limits of their authority suit these people, so don't expect

them to challenge statements by authorities or experts. These are features of many managers in the former Soviet bloc, and you will also find it in India, although there it is more likely to be due to respect for age and seniority.

- **Power** is often more important than status in many countries, because it determines what you can do: with it comes money and status. Russia tends to be a power country, as do Spain and Portugal and Latin American countries.
- **Fun** is a peculiar category, but it can be an important motivator in communities where job security and social support are adequate. People in these countries may be content to remain in steady but fairly low-paid jobs because they find there are opportunities to learn (professional development), the work is interesting or the conditions and relationships with colleagues (the general working environment) are attractive. Many Britons are content in these situations, and when you ask them why they're not more ambitious, they say: "We have a laugh." In other words, we enjoy the work, but we might not do so in a more testing environment.

It's clearly important to recognize which factors are most valued in your team or company. In mergers and acquisitions, for example, taking over a company and changing the culture from one of a good working environment to a colder one based on competition and bonuses may actually reduce productivity in the short run and lead to substantial attrition in the key workforce.

The lesson? As part of due diligence, analyze the company culture and pay special attention to the motivational factors. If you wish to change them, gently does it. It's no accident that Carlos Ghosn, the Renault boss whom we referred to earlier, went to live in Japan when he took over Nissan in order to understand the local culture and maximize team spirit.

Feedback

How do you give feedback to your team? This again varies between business communities. For instance, do you offer feedback behind closed doors or in the open office, by email or face-to-face? To do it in the right way earns respect and improved performance, but to handle it in the wrong way causes disaffection and demotivation. There's a general rule here: if in doubt, in private, face-to-face and behind closed doors is best.

You must also decide on the appropriate style of feedback. Do you tell a person straight out that their performance needs improving or do you, in American and British style, ask how they felt about a particular task or situation and encourage them to evaluate their own performance? If you are less than direct, will they miss the point in a top-down management structure? Will they feel there is nothing to improve and carry on as normal?

Once again, when giving feedback, what do you appeal to? Team spirit is the key in Asia-Pacific, but in North America you should consider the individual's personal aims and aspirations: you'll have to demonstrate that if they perform better they will earn more and get promotion. In the UK, the appeal is to improve individual performance within the context of team goals.

So far we've talked about feedback from a superior to a subordinate, but what about managing your manager? In a London bank, foreign associates wonder what to do when they think the boss has got it wrong, and how to express this. Here the issue is empathy. Put yourself in your manager's shoes. How will she take it if you criticize her? Show appreciation, show respect and, in the UK, be indirect. The British ask permission to ask questions: "Could I make a suggestion?" "This is excellent but if we...", can be a successful strategy.

The lessons on feedback? Before you offer it to a foreign manager, find out what style of feedback they're used to and use that. You'll achieve better results, cooperation and respect.

Virtual distributed teams

How do you create a team out of individuals from different nationalities, separated by thousands of miles and with different local and international reporting structures? That was Jennifer's problem. As the leader of an international HR team, her job was to co-ordinate policy and institute best practice across six training managers in London, Houston, Toronto, Cape Town, Tokyo and Mumbai. As well as dealing with several countries and cultures she also had to communicate between time zones. To get all seven together for a conference call was a struggle, but even when she did so, at least once a month, it was difficult to ensure successful communication. The

London-Houston-Toronto axis tended to dominate, as they spoke English the most fluently. The South African was responsive but felt inhibited by her English. And for cultural and linguistic reasons the Indian and Japanese team members tended to stay quiet and listen. After the first two or three slightly lame video-conferences, Jennifer realized there was no alternative to putting management time into ensuring that team communication worked. First she organized a six-monthly live meeting on HR issues and rotated it between the different centres. That way everyone had a chance to get a sense of each other's working environment; thereafter they visibly relaxed in the video-conferences. Each three-day meeting allowed her team members two days in a hotel to get to know one another, with a programme of seminars and visiting speakers, and another day at the office to meet local staff and acquaint themselves with the culture.

Before every video-conference, Jennifer phoned individual team members to ensure that she knew the issues that were affecting them, and that she focused on them during the conference. This gave the Tokyo, Mumbai and Cape Town representatives the confidence to participate more fully. She made the calls every two weeks and always in the week before the monthly video session. By combining the frequent phone conversations with the video-conferences and a twice-yearly face-to-face session, she built a dynamic interactive team. Although it rarely met, members felt involved with each other and with the central office.

Jennifer's lesson? Long-distance communication means putting in extra personal effort to make it work. The problem? You have to budget in the extra hours you have to contribute to make sure the system works. If you're a hands-off type of manager, distance communication, although it may sound ideal, is not for you. With virtual teams there is no alternative to getting your hands dirty.

Conclusion

A leading international organization appraises its overseas employees yearly on a number of indices. The one they score lowest on is intercultural working. In other words they have problems working in international teams. When you have a multinational or an international group, and especially a virtual distributed team, a whole new set of variables comes into play. To be successful you have to take them into account.

Key learning points

- Three types of cross-cultural teams exist: multinationals within a company, international teams across a group, and virtual distributed teams. The latter rarely meet and communicate mainly by phone, video-conferencing and email.
- When dealing with international teams, ways of working are influenced by community communication style, hierarchy and decision-making.
- Key issues are team selection criteria, team leadership, team contributions and team results. These need to be examined within the context of the nationalities of the different team members.
- Team communication and organization, motivation and feedback all vary according to national and community styles.
- Virtual distributed teams demand a 'hands-on' approach from team leaders in order to work successfully.

NINE

Meetings and negotiations

NINE

Meetings and negotiations

The meeting was tense. The British team handling due diligence in the takeover of a French company were trying to sort their way through the agenda. The French team were discussing everything under the sun under every agenda point. Eventually, tempers frayed. "Look, can't we at least keep to the agenda?" one of the Brits said. 'But that's not the way we do things," replied his French counterpart. "Everything is linked to everything else." "Do you mean to say you only prepare agendas for us?" challenged the Brit. The Frenchman said nothing, just smiled.

If you assume that meetings work in similar ways the world over, think again. Different communities have different procedures, covering matters such as the location of meetings, the type of meetings there should be and who attends them, the function and role of agendas and orders of business, ways of working and the role of minutes and action points. If you understand these, you can get the best results and avoid a lot of frustration.

Where are meetings held?

There are generally three types of location: the meeting room, the private office and the hotel restaurant or bar. Where you prefer to meet is obviously a personal decision, but it remains true that in relationship-oriented cultures the key discussions often happen during hospitality sessions. The decisions are then ratified in an official meeting. In systems-oriented cultures the crucial debates usually take place in a meeting room. There may also be preliminary talks in private offices, as in Scandinavia, and the agreements reached will then be brought to the table in the meeting room for formal approval. It's important to be flexible about meeting venues and to focus on the result, not on where you feel most comfortable.

Who attends?

Japanese business tends to hunt in packs. Many people attend meetings, as opposed to the minimal numbers in the UK or the US. The Japanese believe that everyone who is in the loop should know what is going on. A number of junior executives may be in the room, but their job is to listen rather than contribute. Be careful you don't spend your time talking to the junior staff member just because he appears to be paying rapt attention. Jack Howard, a former senior lecturer at Birmingham University, once gave us an invaluable piece of advice. "How do you know who is the senior person in a Japanese meeting?" he asked. "See who is served the tea first."

In Spanish meetings you talk to the top person, possibly accompanied by his or her deputy. Other managers are on standby, and they will be brought into the discussion as necessary. This is your signal that all decisions go through the boss, and he will attend or keep a close eye on any policy meeting.

The Germans, like the British, tend to have a minimum number of people present, but they will include both policy and implementation personnel required for the task. If you're dealing with a manufacturing project, representatives from the works committee will also participate to ensure that the employees' legal requirements are looked after.

It's often difficult to find out in advance who is attending a meeting, but it's always worth asking. It's also important to identify the key decision-maker, as it may not always be immediately obvious.

How are meetings arranged?

Once again, relationship-oriented societies may appear far more casual about setting up meetings than systems-oriented ones. Gatherings may be convened at short notice by telephone or brief email. No attendance list may be considered necessary and no agenda circulated. In contrast, in Germany, Austria, and the Nordic countries, full details will be circulated up to six to eight weeks beforehand. The British and Americans are somewhat more relaxed about this, but clear notice will still be given.

Expectations of meetings

"Why do we go to meetings?" grumbled the sales manager of an international French firm. "To be told what to do, of course," he continued. The distribution of information is often the function of a gathering in a top-down management system. Objectives are laid down, and the details of any changes in organization and working methods explained; negotiations take place in private offices outside the main meeting. If you hear about a change in the working environment at a French meeting, it's probably too late to influence it.

Many German firms, on the other hand, make a clear distinction between information meetings, action meetings and brainstorming sessions. An information meeting is just that: it gives instructions. An action-point meeting is expected to achieve minuted decisions for implementation, while a brainstorm gathering comes up with ideas for dealing with a particular problem or project.

In Italy, all meetings are aimed at eliciting ideas and gathering the mood of the participants. Decisions are then taken outside the meeting. In Japan, the principle of *nemawashi* means that all meetings must end in the agreement of all participants. Collective agreement and collective commitment are the order of the day.

These examples indicate how different business communities have their own expectations of meetings. The lesson? Don't assume that your assumptions about a meeting and its outcome will be the same as everyone else's. In a multinational or virtual distributed team, find out what others – and particularly the group leaders – will be thinking.

An agenda or not?

British and US meetings tend to run on agendas. Even in an informal meeting someone will ask, "What do we want to cover?" and a rough agenda or order of business will be drawn up. If an agenda is distributed beforehand, the order of business might be amended according to how the discussion flows, but if an item of business isn't covered in its original order, it will usually be dealt with before the end of the meeting.

Other business communities have very different attitudes to agendas. Some see an agenda as more of a wish list of things to cover, rather than a detailed order of business. For the French, for whom everything is connected, keeping to the strict order of an agenda seems unnatural, while for the Germans and Swiss the order is sacred, and you only go back over a topic if there is time at the end of the meeting.

We once got a surprise when we circulated a British-style agenda before an international gathering, with the usual Any Other Business line tacked on the end. It caused an eruption: colleagues from some countries saw it as an invitation to potential chaos. We thought it was totally innocuous, but for those who liked to control meetings from beginning to end, the phrase 'AOB' seemed like a minefield, the equivalent of a supplementary questions session at Prime Minister's Question Time in the House of Commons. This is not to say that you shouldn't include 'AOB' on any agenda that you circulate in an international environment, but be aware that it may not be seen as a way of tidying up loose ends that the British use it for.

Lessons? Remember that agendas are not routine for everyone and, when they are used, are not always rigidly followed. Don't insist on drawing up an agenda if one isn't produced at a meeting that you attend, and don't insist on your way of doing things without checking other people's views. Consideration for others is everything.

Meetings etiquette

International meetings can be a minefield of frustrated expectations. Do they start late? Yes, in Italy and the Arab world. Do they finish late? Probably, if you're in France. Do people feel that it's OK to answer their mobile phones and indulge in long conversations round the table, oblivious to everyone else? They do in Central and Eastern Europe. Are meetings interrupted by foreign phone calls or personal visitors while you sit there helpless? Frequently, in Arab countries. Do meetings begin with long involved speeches by the chairperson, extolling their education or explaining in detail the story so far? Yes, in Spain and Latin America. Do participants get up while you're making your presentation, help themselves to coffee and biscuits and stand there chatting while you sit there, your concentration totally distracted? It's not unknown in France or the USA.

These are all things that we've regularly encountered in international get-togethers. British people's response is often to lapse into ironic humour and ask barbed questions such as, "Is my meeting interrupting your conversation?" But avoid that approach at all costs. The fact is that all of these incidents were seen as normal meetings etiquette by the people involved.

On the other hand, we arrived in Nicosia late for a meeting after a delayed flight. We raced to the venue, walked in, said 'Hello', and – still hyped up from the journey – launched into the reason for our visit. Our host listened quietly for a few minutes and then said, "Wouldn't you like a cup of coffee first?" We'd committed a major sin by forgetting a Mediterranean custom: people first, business second. In the Arab world, and also in Japan, it's considered polite to wait for your host to introduce the business. To march in and open discussions is seen as discourteous.

The lesson? Check the meetings etiquette before you start, so that there are no surprises.

Results and outcomes

What's the ideal outcome of a good meeting? Everyone emerges knowing the project's objectives, their responsibilities and the time frames, and everything will be recorded in the minutes or action points, right? Not necessarily. A meeting can simply be held to gather opinions: decision-making comes later. Or it might be about a simple statement of aims or values, and any action planning will be done somewhere else. In a German 'action' meeting, plans, responsibilities and time frames for delivery are clearly defined. However, in one German company we know, minutes are circulated not only to those who were present, but to everyone else involved in the operation, who then have the right to alter or add to the minutes. A British manager involved with this firm said that it felt as though another meeting that he hadn't attended had been superimposed on top of the original one, and that completely different decisions had been taken. Result? Confusion and demotivation.

The lesson: team members from other countries may see the British and American practice of agreeing the outcome with action planning, time frames and allocation of duties very differently. In an international environment, check your understanding of procedures, and in your own team make clear what you expect and why.

Negotiating

In any negotiation you must know two things: your walk-away point and what concessions you are prepared to make. However, as with meetings, negotiation styles are subject to cultural variation, and it is important to identify those differences before you start discussions. This section will identify the key areas where differences generally occur.

Who do I negotiate with?

The Chinese and Japanese negotiate with individuals, not companies. Therefore your initial contact in an organization from one of those countries will probably remain in the discussions, even if he changes his responsibilities within the firm before an agreement is reached. He will probably continue to attend meetings, even at a high level, until the deal is completed: the Chinese and Japanese feel that this adds confidence to the relationship. If there is a change in your key contact, however, handle your initial communication with him or her formally and carefully: a casual phone call or email won't do.

We've already noted that in countries such as Spain or Italy, you negotiate with the top person, with others being brought in to arrange implementation. The negotiator's first aim will be to establish trust and a working relationship, and then to decide prices and logistics. Without the first, the second is unlikely.

In Nordic countries, as in Britain or the USA, negotiation will be with a manager at the appropriate level, and debate will quickly centre on the contract and the price. A British negotiating team will usually make an opening bid, after which there is discussion and a response by the other side. If the bargaining becomes aggressive, the British are well known for withdrawing and seeming to appear quite vague before repackaging the deal in some form of acceptable compromise. Whether you recognize your tactics in that description or not, it's the way foreigners usually view the British. They also think that Britons like to 'sleep on a deal' to be sure they are comfortable with it, and that Brits are capable of changing their minds and renegotiating some points the following day.

There are three stages in a negotiation:

- Opening bids
- Bargaining
- Close

The British and Americans like to state quite early in the proceedings what they want to achieve. Americans are often quite firm about this and put the deal 'on the table'. When alternative bids are made, they will then respond with: 'But that wasn't on the table!' The French, on the other hand, like to listen to the other person's offer and put forward their proposals in the light of what the other side is saying. This can cause friction with Americans, in particular.

Germans and Scandinavians tend to know what they believe is a fair price in a contract, and get upset at what they feel is a British tendency to start at too high a level and then move down to a lower figure. Italians, on the other hand, are quite happy with that process, and will worry away at each aspect of a deal until they bring the price down to their satisfaction.

The lessons are clear:

- Know absolutely what your final situation is and never deviate from it.
- Never assume that the other nationality's approach to negotiating is the same as yours. Learn anything you can about their style so that you have some idea of what to expect.
- Remember that cultures like the Indians, Chinese and Arabs have been negotiating and haggling successfully for thousands of years and have developed their own approaches.

In his fascinating book on the call-centre industry, *What's This India Business?*, Paul Davies goes into detail on the Indian style of negotiation. When you first mention your price, he explains, you will be met with shock and horror. Take no notice, he advises: repeat your position exactly as you did the first time. Indians will then try and wear you down. It's acceptable for you to leave the room; they will wait, expecting you to come back and restart the negotiations.

Simultaneously, you're building a relationship with them and a kind of trust. Finally, he says, the green light may come not in the office but somewhere else entirely, such as over dinner.

The Chinese seek agreements that will not cause political problems and can lead to a sincere partnership. If they see you behaving dishonestly, they will feel free to be less than frank with you. Their concern is balance: if they take something, they feel that it's important to be seen to give something back.

Be aware of the danger of flattery in China. An 'old friend' is expected to offer better terms. Also, be wary of introducing lawyers too early – it may be seen as a sign of mistrust. Never lose your temper – although the Chinese may sometimes use anger as a pressure tactic.

Russians treat negotiation like a game of chess. They plan several moves ahead, and it is important to think carefully about the consequences before you respond. A well-known Russian tactic is to tough things out and to regard compromise as a sign of weakness. Concessions are exchanged for concessions. Therefore it is important to have a number of throwaway positions at your disposal. Ultimately, however, what is important to Russians is that you show your human side: understand Russian difficulties – layers of hierarchy and the need for government approval – don't hide your own problems, and be direct and straightforward. Russians combine hard-nosed negotiating skills with the personal touch: you need to be able to do the same.

In the Arab world, negotiators combine requests for favours and concessions on price as an important part of the process. In his book *Cross-Cultural Business Behaviour*, Richard Gesteland writes: "Some Arab businessmen measure their success at the bargaining table by how far they are able to move you away from your opening offer. They think of negotiating as a challenging contest, a competitive sport." Negotiations in these circumstances can be a long process, and you should build in wide margins. Visitors to Arab markets always comment on how bargaining is almost like a game, and how sellers are disappointed if you don't enter into the pleasure of haggling. Business negotiation is not dissimilar, with each concession reluctantly offered, and only on condition that something is given in return. Don't rush, and write everything down.

Finally, to Brazil. In Brazilian negotiations, socializing and bargaining go together, often in the same space. For a polite social people, Brazilians can be quite blunt. This is less a pressure tactic than simple directness: they like you to know where they stand. Once again, allow time for negotiations and build substantial margins into your offer to provide for concessions. Be prepared for them to ask for favours in other areas, which you should try to help with as it will tend to cement the relationship.

Conclusion

These and other examples stress the need to do your homework in dealing with another country or someone from another business community. Understanding the negotiating style and what brings your bargaining partner to the table and keeps him or her there is a vital part of business negotiation. You will do yourself no favours by ignoring this: they will probably have studied your culture's style.

Key learning points

- In relationship-oriented societies, small talk and hospitality are vital to successful meetings.
- Agendas aren't for everyone – don't insist on them if they're not a normal part of the meetings process.
- Find out if the meeting is for general discussion, information or to take action.
- Familiarize yourself with where business is done, who attends meetings, who chairs the session and the way business is conducted.
- Check the anticipated outcome of a meeting – it may not be minutes and action points.
- Familiarize yourself with your counterpart's approach to opening bids, negotiation and close.
- Be certain of your walk-away point and don't deviate from it.
- Be careful how you price your opening bid. Leave a margin for concessions, but remember the German, Dutch and Nordic preference for the concept of a fair price.
- Remember that high-pressure bargaining and haggling may not get in the way of warm hospitality.

TEN

Gift-giving and hospitality

TEN

Gift-giving and hospitality

George, a lecturer at an English university, was visiting a university in Uzbekistan. The weather was hot and his host, Maliko, offered him a cup of green tea. George declined and asked her for black tea with milk, the usual British choice. Maliko looked despondent, but served the black tea.

George is a sensitive man. Later he asked a colleague if he'd done something wrong. "Maliko is a newly married bride," his colleague said, "and green tea brings you luck. When a newly married bride offers green tea it's an offering of the greatest good luck. And you turned it down."

You can't go back and apologize for this kind of slip, but the moral is obvious: if you're offered food or drink, accept gracefully and taste it. Then, if you want, ask for something else.

We arrived in Genoa in Italy after a late-evening flight to be greeted by our potential business partner. Asked if we'd eaten, we explained that we'd had a bite on the plane and were going straight to the hotel to be fresh for the following morning. Once again, the long face. This time we recovered fast. "But we'd love to eat with you first," we added. His face brightened and our host took us to a seafood restaurant that he'd frequented since childhood. He considered it an honour to invite us there, and we enjoyed delicious food and wine and found that we'd virtually accomplished the hard part almost before we'd even started the visit. If we hadn't accepted the invitation, we'd have had to work far harder the next day to seal the deal.

The lesson? If you're offered food or a drink in Italy, take it. It's an opportunity to move the business relationship forward. To refuse might be seen as an insult.

In China you've had a hard negotiating session. You never want to see these people again, you just want to get some time to yourself and rest. Then their negotiator says: "We'll see you at dinner then." For the Chinese, the difficulty of negotiation must never spill over into bad social relations. For Westerners, however, the strain of business discussions can easily affect social relations.

Once again, when you're working internationally there is no such thing as downtime. Gift-giving, hospitality and entertaining all affect the impression you create with your hosts or business partners, or that they make on you.

Gift-giving

You're going to a meeting in a foreign country or receiving a visitor. Do they expect gifts? If so, what kind of gift? When should you give it? Who should you offer it to? Should they open it immediately? Should the gift involve odd numbers or even numbers? Should gifts be offered wrapped or unwrapped? Gift-giving protocol is immensely varied, and the better you understand it, the better the impression you'll make. Let's take the issues one by one.

When do you give gifts?

Gifts are a way of building a personal business relationship. They are not a bribe or a sweetener, but a personal statement that you value the relationship, actual or future, with that person. But you need to be sure that your gifts are acceptable. Singapore business contacts are wary of accepting anything due to their country's draconian anti-corruption laws. And what's acceptable at one point in time may not be in another. One of us once offered a large bottle of vodka to a Russian at the time of President Gorbachev's crackdown on drinking. "Don't you know?" he exploded. "It's against the law to drink vodka right now!" In dealing with a new country it's always worth checking what the gift-giving limits might be.

On the whole, relationship-oriented countries both appreciate giving and receiving gifts. In systems-oriented countries, they are not seen to be necessary, although a personal gift may be much appreciated.

Who gives? Who receives?

HSBC's witty advertising campaign that highlights cultural differences has become famous worldwide. The scene for one of the TV ads was a golf match in Japan. If you get a hole in one in the UK or the USA, your fellow players congratulate you by buying you drinks in the bar (the 19th hole). In Japan on the other hand, *you* buy your partners expensive presents. In the ad, a low-handicap golfer is easily beating the other members of the four-ball round.

He drives off at a tee, and the ball veers off towards the rough. Then it bounces off a tree – and rolls onto the green to score a hole-in-one. He was trying to avoid just such a scenario, and paying for the gifts that go with it, but fate took a hold and decided differently.

Korean golfers also celebrate a hole in one with expensive presents – a Rolex watch, for example. In gift-giving in Asia-Pacific there is generally no need to go to such lengths, but the brand is important. Welcome gifts for a Japanese, Korean or Chinese business contact might be a box of good-quality golf balls or a golfing towel from a famous club. Most items from world-class brands are well received, as are gifts that relate to the receiver's personal interests, or those that reflect a country's heritage, such as Scottish shortbread or malt whisky.

When it's your birthday in the UK or US your workmates might buy you a card and a cake or chocolates, which are handed round the office. In Germany it's the other way round – you buy the goodies, and you also declare open house and invite your colleagues and neighbours to celebrate at your home.

Wrapped or unwrapped?

Many businesses keep a cupboard of corporate gifts for Japanese, Chinese and Korean visitors, as do they in turn for their European counterparts. The important thing about these gifts is that they need to be tasteful and professionally wrapped. The wrapping is as important as the gift: it shows care and consideration.

In contrast, in Germany there's a superstition that you should always give flowers unwrapped, and that you should never carry them in wrapping across the threshold. Professor Mittendorfer turned up at a leaving do for his PA, who was retiring, and handed over a bunch of unwrapped flowers. They looked like he'd just pulled them from a neighbourhood garden on the way to her home, but that's the way things are done in Germany. Once again, you demonstrate your cultural know-how and sensitivity by observing local conventions where you can.

Gift-giving shows you care

I was travelling to Poland on a business trip to Warsaw. As I trooped through the airport my travelling companion, a Bulgarian, persuaded me into the duty-free shop. Our haul? Six tins of shortbread, two bars of Cadbury's milk chocolate, four bottles of single malt whisky and two of those little china models of thatched English cottages. The cost? Over £60. Explain that to your sales manager when you submit your expenses. Value? Inestimable.

You hear many stories about 'mean' Brits and Americans who never offer gifts. This is seen as demonstrating a lack of interest and commitment. Even in Russia, where the days of giving away *Vogue* magazine and blue jeans are now thirty years back, a small present still means that you care.

Taboo gifts

If you're entertaining Chinese, Japanese or Korean people, provide a photo opportunity. A framed picture recording the occasion of the visit will be a really important souvenir. But as in all cultures, certain gifts are less than acceptable. Alice and her group were from a prestigious Chinese university on a study visit to the UK. Things had not proceeded in the Chinese way, and we worked hard to make it up to them by providing a meal, an official reception and, yes, a photo op. We also gave the Chinese some presents and for Alice, as one of the group leaders, there was a special gift. When she came in the next morning she was laughing. Why? We'd given her a clock – to Chinese eyes a symbol that we wished her dead, or at least desired the end of the relationship! Luckily, she was used to Western ignorance and accepted the clock as the useful present that it was intended to be, without any negative connotations. As the Chinese say: "We are very tolerant."

The lesson? If you're going to give gifts to foreign visitors or hosts it's worth checking the taboos that are associated with their culture. Ask people who know the country, and you can also Google 'international superstitions'.

Open or closed?

You may have noticed that Alice didn't tell us about the clock until the following morning. Didn't she open the gift immediately? In the UK or US, you open the present immediately and share your pleasure with the giver. But in Asia-Pacific it's exactly the opposite. You thank the giver and put the present aside to open in private. Why? Because if you display a lack of pleasure, however skilfully you try to hide your feelings, it would cause the giver to lose face. Westerners often embarrass their Eastern counterparts by insisting they open presents on the spot.

Odd or even?

Americans and Britons give flowers in half dozens or dozens, and money in even units. But this is not the case internationally. For the Japanese it's preferable to use odd numbers, whereas in China, even numbers are better. In Europe, Germans also prefer odd numbers, but a gift of 13 flowers would stick in the throat of Brits or Americans.

Colours

The key thing in choosing colours for presents is to avoid those associated with funerals and death rituals. Red and gold are lucky in China, but blue and white are linked with funerals. White chrysanthemums are associated with funerals in Japan, but purple is a funeral colour in Mexico. The *Hong Bao* is a present given to employees at the Chinese New Year. It is usually cash, in even denominations, and is always in a red envelope, perhaps with gold writing.

If all this feels like a minefield, don't worry. The key is sensitivity, not whether the gift is entirely appropriate. If you're sensitive to these issues you'll always succeed, even if your present isn't ideal or ideally presented.

The key things to watch out for are:

- What are acceptable presents?
- When do you give them?
- Do you open them on receipt?
- What colours and numbers are appropriate?

Danger occurs when a relationship is starting or going through a rocky patch. A demonstration of inappropriate gift-giving can then be a nail in the coffin rather than the cementing of goodwill.

Hospitality

It starts with a good meal

A highly successful British company wanted to expand its business in Spain. It had identified a potential Spanish partner and invited some of its managers to their UK headquarters to see the centre of operations. The plan for the day was to greet the visitors at the premises, show them round, and give them a series of PowerPoint presentations. Oh, and they'd take the Spanish out for lunch. Everything was geared to demonstrating how successful the company was and what a good partner it would make. In our view there was no question that the Spaniards would go on their way impressed, but they would probably not be committed. And commitment was what the British company wanted.

This is a fairly common approach in British organizations. It's basically, "Turn up and we'll look after you." After we had discussed things a little they began to change their approach. Here's what the new programme looked like.

- Arrange hotel accommodation for the visiting managers;
- Meet them on the evening of their arrival for a get-to-know-you dinner at the most interesting restaurant in town;
- Pick up the visiting managers from their hotel in the morning, or arrange taxis to bring them to the office;
- Make a brief presentation of the company in the boardroom and tour the factory, allowing time for discussion with key people;
- Arrange lunch offsite, allowing plenty of time for the two management teams to get to know one another personally;
- Have a final meeting after lunch, with the opportunity for further informal conversation.

Basically, the programme was re-arranged not around the business side of the proceedings but around the social side. It was also much more labour intensive by putting the stress on building personal relations. The British managers would have to invest out-of-hours time away from their families, but it would ensure that the business relationship progressed more positively. Above all, it would create the personal commitment to make the venture work.

What would matter mainly to the Spanish managers was what kind of people their British counterparts were. Were they sincere? Above all, were they committed? That could only be established by sitting down, breaking bread and discussing each other's aims and aspirations. As any Spaniard will tell you, PowerPoints, like statistics, can lie. It's people you trust, not computers.

Any relationship-oriented organization will look for similar qualities in its business partners. The opportunity to spend time talking to them and understanding their human side is crucial. They need to feel that there is a commitment to life, not just to the work. They also take into account not just facts and figures, but also the character of the managers they will work with, and their sense of the community and environment they live in. That is the basis for a long-term business relationship.

Here's another example. Remember how our Genoese business partners took us to dinner off the plane? Well, they came to London. The father, who owned the family company, spoke only Italian; the son Italian, English and French. How to look after them? At the time, the musical *Miss Saigon* was on in London. It is the Puccini opera *Madame Butterfly* adapted to the Vietnam War and the fall of Saigon, but the story is immediately identifiable. So we booked that, and we had dinner at one of London's most venerable Italian restaurants. We then invited a couple of Italian friends to join us. The father loved the show, and enjoyed speaking Italian at dinner. What he said afterwards is something we won't forget. "I always thought the British were cold and mechanical," he reflected. "Now I know that isn't true." A long-term business relationship was born.

Never underestimate the power of a good lunch

What goes for Italians and Spanish, also applies to Greeks, Portuguese, French, and to people south of the Mediterranean and to Latin America. Where your partner's prime concern is to find out what kind of person you are, the time and thought you put into the 'not strictly business' side of your relationship indicates commitment and thought, and that's what your new counterpart is looking for.

In Spain, an indication that a meeting has gone well is an invitation to lunch. A hint that it has gone badly is when such an offer is not extended. In France, an hour and a half for lunch is normal. It's hard for the French to understand how you could possibly get by on a sandwich at your desk. These are not the outdated customs of a more leisurely business era, but symbols of a civilized life. Even if you only nibble on salad, the time you spend out of the office provides an opportunity to breathe and to create good relationships with business colleagues.

Cathy is the HR manager of a firm that has outsourced some operations to India. The relationship is in its early days, and performance issues have cropped up. How best to deal with them? India is a hands-on culture. Things happen when you are there, so we advised her to fly out and meet the relevant managers face-to-face to discuss issues and how to resolve them.

We also advised her of the best way to make this happen. She stayed in one of the excellent five-star hotels run by India's own Tata and Oberoi groups. On her first evening she invited the Indian company's senior managers to an informal chat at the hotel. This way she was able to catch up on local news, raise issues in a relaxed session, and agree an action plan and a timetable for discussion. The hotel environment increased the level of trust, and displayed her confidence in the managers. The following days went smoothly, and the performance difficulties were resolved and mechanisms for resolution agreed. On the final day she arranged lunch on the terrace by the pool, and gave a small present to each team member.

Job done: Indian outsourced operations need to feel part of the outsourcing company's family. They work better, like the rest of us, when they feel involved. Unnecessary waste of time and resources? No: necessary input into ensuring loyalty and commitment to performance and to the company. Of course, the problems didn't disappear overnight, but resolving them from a distance by emails and phone became much easier and more successful.

Can we eat now?

One of the hazards of cross-border meetings is mealtimes. Your stomach has been conditioned by years of practice to expect refuelling at certain times of day. But just because you're British or American and expect to eat at a particular time, it doesn't mean that everyone else has to. Spaniards have lunch at two. Even worse, they often don't have supper till nine or ten: getting to bed after midnight on a full stomach is no joke. In Poland they can go right through the day without food until four or five o'clock, by which time their British colleagues are almost fainting for lack of nourishment. Nordics, on the other hand, eat early at noon or even at 11.30am, so that they can finish work at four.

These three rules will help you to avoid food fatigue:

1. Don't assume their mealtimes are the same as yours. Check the local custom beforehand.
2. Have a good breakfast if your host country lunches late. It will ensure that you don't waver at a time when you need your greatest concentration.
3. If necessary, take some fruit or bottled water from the hotel for refreshment during the day.

"I'm not eating this foreign muck"

It's not a joke: we've heard British executives faced with unfamiliar and slightly dubious-looking dishes use this phrase, with a look of disgust on their face. They forget the key cultural advice: you don't have to eat everything you're offered. If you don't like the look of it, pronounce it excellent and move on to something more palatable. Your foreign hosts may have gone to a lot of trouble to think about your tastes or to give you the opportunity to taste national or special dishes. Don't insult them by refusing to give it the time of day.

One dish stumped us, however. La Orotava is a volcano high above the beaches of Tenerife in the Canary Islands, and we were invited to enjoy a national dish of calamari at a well known local restaurant. We all know calamari from the menus of Greek restaurants: neat, deep-fried circles of squid. But this was different – the whole octopus was sitting up on the table, its head and beak looking at us, with the tentacles and suckers spread out across the plate. "Wonderful," said our host, digging his fork into the sac to release the black inky substance secreted by octopi. "Now this is really special," he said as he sawed off a tentacle, complete with suckers. We looked on, aghast. We still aren't sure if the whole thing wasn't a practical joke.

Table etiquette

In her novel *The Joy Luck Club*, Amy Tan depicts a memorable evening when the heroine, Waverley, a Chinese American, invites her white American boyfriend, Rich, to meet her parents. At the table everything goes wrong. He drinks a full glass of wine and then pours another for himself and makes the first toast. The Chinese normally just have a sip to taste, and the host would make the first toast. Then Rich helps himself to a large portion of food. Normally, the Chinese try a little of each dish and go back for second and third helpings. No wonder that Waverley's mother observes: "He has good appetite." Finally, Rich insults Waverley's mother's cooking. She serves her best dish but apologizes for it, saying it has no flavour. The Chinese would normally taste a little and then praise her to the skies. Rich, on the other hand, takes her at her word and pours soy over the whole dish. The scene is beautifully dramatized in Ang Lee's film of the novel.

Chinese hosts usually provide Westerners with a fork or spoon, but will be delighted to show you how to use chopsticks. In Japan, Korea and China you usually pour each other's drinks. If you've had enough, never empty your glass. An empty glass is never a sign that you're full, but an indication that you want some more. The same goes for food.

Another well known HSBC TV ad shows a British businessman being served a huge dish of eels by his Chinese hosts. The Brit doesn't like the dish much, but valiantly he eats for England and his plate is soon clear. Delighted, his Chinese hosts order up another plate. Not wanting to appear impolite, he maintains the great Western tradition of clearing his plate, and his relief turns to horror as the Chinese desperately source more eels for their guest to devour. The lesson? Always leave something on your plate to show you've had enough.

Knife and fork, right hand or left hand?

Good manners in one country can be bad manners in another. At the end of a meal, where do you put your knife and fork, or chopsticks? In a Chinese, Japanese or Korean household or restaurant there's usually a chopstick rest to the right of your plate. Don't leave your chopsticks on your plate, and definitely don't leave them crossed, anymore than you would your knife and fork.

In countries such as India, or regions such as the Middle East, you may be invited to eat with your hands. If so, you must always use your right hand. Your left hand is judged to be unclean, and to take food from a communal plate with it means that no-one else will touch that plate. You need to be careful how you deal with this, as it can cause considerable embarrassment to your hosts.

In most countries with taboos about using the left hand to eat or take food, left-handed children are trained to be ambidextrous. This is more difficult for visiting adults, so if in doubt explain that you're left-handed but try and use your right hand wherever possible. You may find that your hosts will be eager to serve you, using forks and spoons so as to save you embarrassment.

To toast or not to toast?

"The VP gambei'd me twice!" said Nick after a Chinese banquet in which he'd been honoured by the host by being twice toasted in the Chinese fashion. *Gambei* is the Chinese word for 'Cheers', and literally means 'Bottoms up' (you're supposed to empty your glass in one go). In many countries, toasting is not just a way of showing community spirit but a means of recognizing and building relationships. Foreigners are often amused at the throwaway spirit of British and American toasting.

A particularly excruciating toast for reserved Brits occurs in Denmark (and other Nordic countries), where you look at the other person for up to a full minute (it can feel like an eternity) before saying '*Skol*!' Russia is famous for its toasting rituals, and even though vodka doesn't have the status it once had, especially in professional circles, it's still worth having a few appropriate phrases prepared to answer the frequent toasts as glasses are refilled.

One of us had a problem as the honoured guest at a dinner in Denmark. We knew at some point that we would probably have to propose a toast to thank our hosts, but the whole thing was done in Danish and we didn't understand what was going on. We ended up bobbing up and down every time we heard our name mentioned: embarrassing for us and amusing for our Danish friends.

Once again, forewarned is forearmed. Take the trouble to check if there is a toasting ritual and how it is applied. Find out the following information:

1. What is the appropriate expression? In Central and Eastern Europe, it can be confusing, as various versions of *Nastroviye* – the Russian equivalent of 'cheers' – are used.
2. When are toasts given and who starts the process? In China the host will always make the first toast.
3. What is the appropriate body language? Do you stand up, sit down, make prolonged eye contact or what?
4. Do you drain your glass or take only a sip?
5. Do you not touch your glass until the first toast is proposed?

Official dinners can be scary occasions, where you can make a good or bad impression. Therefore it's worth checking the local procedure before you go in. However, remember one thing, especially in the Asia-Pacific region: where formality rules in business meetings, the hospitality is an opportunity for officials to let their hair down just a little and be a bit more personal.

When to arrive, where to sit and when to leave

These are all areas that can create difficulties for guests. In India, if you are invited to a party at 9pm and you arrive on time there's a fair chance that you'll be the only one there: most of the local people won't turn up until an hour or two later. In Nigeria, we were once invited to dinner by a German. Observing Nigerian time, we turned up half an hour (well, maybe an hour) late to find that he had eaten and cleared up: he was still keeping to German time. Always check when you're expected to arrive.

In some business communities, depending on the occasion, the seating arrangements may be random or pre-planned. Again, you should never just sit down, but check with your host what is expected. Does he or she want you to sit on their left or right, opposite them, somewhere else, or even at a different table? Never assume the protocol. In the same way, always check when to leave. Do you leave when you're ready, or when the host gets up and says the meal is over? In China the host ends the meal.

A habit in Saudi surprised us. In Britain and many other countries you might arrive at 7.30pm for 8pm, have a cocktail for half an hour or so, move to the table and enjoy dinner, and probably sit around talking for a while before dispersing. But in the Arab world, people talk for an hour or an hour and a half before the meal is prepared, and leave immediately after eating. Expecting to chat leisurely with those we'd met afterwards, we were discomfited to find they'd all gone.

Dealing with honoured guests

In Indonesia if a VIP is attending a dinner, you should expect to meet him or her at their car on arrival and escort them inside. No-one eats until they appear, and you personally take them round the food (usually a buffet) and help them choose their meal. At the end of the meal they expect you to walk with them to their car.

It's important not to forget about protocol with VIPs. For most Brits and Americans the important thing is to provide a pleasant environment and sufficient good food and drink but, in Asia-Pacific, the tradition of courtesy and hospitality goes far deeper. This leads us to the final area we need to consider – reciprocating hospitality.

Reciprocation

If your foreign host invites you to lunch or dinner, it's normal to return the courtesy if you're staying long enough. There's only one rule here: reciprocation should be at the level at which hospitality was offered. A good idea is to arrange a reciprocal invitation through your hotel, which will understand the protocols involved. An alternative suggestion is to approach the PA of the person you wish to entertain and seek their advice, or ask her discreetly to ask your host. Don't stint on hospitality, but don't go over the top either: be careful not to be seen to outdo your host.

This horror story comes from north Germany a few years ago and illustrates the last point perfectly. A British engineering firm in the Midlands secured a contract with a local company. At the end of the key meeting a celebration was arranged in the local bar or *weinstube*. Flushed with success and generosity, the British CEO did the equivalent of 'the drinks are on me!' The following day, back in his office, he received an email to the effect that the agreement had been cancelled. Horrified, he telephoned his opposite number in Germany to find out why. The German said that his president had been so shocked by the Brit's behaviour that he couldn't do business with him. Apparently the British CEO hadn't asked if it would be OK to stand his staff drinks. Unacceptable *lèse- majesté*!

Germans would consider their countryman's behaviour extreme, but it makes a point. There is room for spontaneity in international business hospitality and entertaining, but check that your gestures fit before you leap into action.

Home entertainment

British and American business people quite like to entertain at home, but most other nations prefer to entertain out. An invitation to someone's house in these countries is therefore an honour, and needs to be treated as such. Once again, the usual rules apply. Check arrival and departure times and the likely dress code (this might be influenced by whether you are the only guest). Always take something (or apologize if you can't), but not wine to homes in wine-producing countries: you may be implying that they don't know their own wine culture. If you do take alcohol, go for Scotch, a liqueur from your own country or an expensive wine from theirs. People can be quite nationalistic about wine, so don't take a bottle from another country unless it's a really special one.

Britons and Americans often like to show people around their houses, but in most other countries, stay where you're put. In homes in continental Europe, for example, there is a clear distinction between public (yours) and private spaces. The private space may include the kitchen, so the customary British courtesy of offering to help or to clear the dishes may not be appropriate. Enjoy the meal and the company, don't outstay your welcome and always phone or send a note to say how much you enjoyed their hospitality and how much you look forward to reciprocating it.

Conclusion

Gift-giving, hospitality and entertaining are as much a part of the international business process as all the factors we've discussed in previous chapters, and need thought and care. Especially in relationship-oriented business communities, people want to see your human side and to know what kind of person you are. They also want to feel that you're an educated and cultivated person to deal with. Therefore your knowledge of social etiquette, or at least your willingness to learn, is important.

Key learning points

Gift-giving

- Check what gifts are acceptable, when they should be given, and whether they should be wrapped or unwrapped. You may also want to check colours and numbers.
- Don't assume that presents should be opened in front of you, as insisting on this might cause embarrassment.

Hospitality

- Never refuse appropriate hospitality. It's a way of deepening the business relationship.
- Check times of arrival, seating arrangements, and when to leave.

- Don't refuse food. Taste and move on.
- Find out about drinking and toasting conventions.
- Reciprocation, even if not immediate, is important. Even if you can't reciprocate, never forget to thank your host.

Home entertaining

- This is a privilege – don't turn it down.
- Check out the dress code with your host, and arrival and leaving times with someone else.
- Take something, but preferably not wine in wine-producing countries. They know better.
- Stay where you're put – don't wander round the house.
- Always send a note or phone to show that you appreciated the invitation.

ELEVEN

The top ten countries in 2050

Doing business in China

Doing business in China

Five Ways to Succeed	Five Ways to Fail
Be sincere: it's the quality most prized by the Chinese	Expect quick results
Do favours: it's a great way to build relationships and they will be returned	Lose your temper or get impatient – it shows a lack of control
Show respect to senior people and older people	Fail to keep regular contact
Spend time building the relationship	Be extravagant or immodest in your dress, behaviour or personal habits
Reciprocate: if someone asks for your help, help them	Ignore Chinese social etiquette – especially at mealtimes

Overview

When China began to reform its economy in the late 1970s, few could have foreseen the transformation and paradoxes that would sweep over the country in only three decades. China now exports more IT products and services than the USA, but poverty is rife in rural areas. It is the world's most populous country, but is also one of the most rapidly ageing, a partial consequence of its one-child policy introduced in 1979. It is ruled by a communist government, yet only a third of the economy is now directly state-controlled.

China is now attempting to achieve a more balanced pattern of economic growth and fairer rewards for more of its population, and will have to address some of the severe pollution issues caused by its surging expansion. But that rampant growth will continue, given a nudge by Beijing's staging of the Olympic Games in 2008, and business opportunities for foreign companies will continue to flourish.

A key organizing principle in Chinese society is Confucianism, the code established by the sixth century BC philosopher Confucius. He preached that the family is the basic unit of society, and praised the virtues of hierarchy and filial piety. Daoism is another strong force in China: it lays down a system of natural justice first propounded by Lao Tse in 570 BC. Even 30 minutes absorbing the ideas of these two movements would benefit visitors to China.

Although reciprocity is an important principle in Chinese society (if you receive something, you give something back), companies investing in China need to ensure that potential partners are fully aware of the issue of intellectual property rights.

Values and attitudes

For centuries, China's civilization was more advanced in the arts and sciences compared with the West, so it's not surprising that its people continue to believe in their superiority, despite the social and military problems that afflicted the country in the 19th and early 20th centuries. The Chinese admire the work ethic, Confucian tenets, the power of the extended family and sincerity. They appreciate patience, soft-spokenness, adaptability, humility and perseverance. They don't appreciate boisterousness, impetuousness or anger, and they also dislike losing face, immodesty, disrespect towards elders and extravagance. They practice *guanxi* – gratitude for favours – and rely on the *danwei* unit, which regulates much of its members' working, social and community lives.

Duty, self-sacrifice, gentleness and wisdom are other traits admired by the Chinese. They consider that relationships are more important than tasks, and that the quest for virtue is more important than the search for truth. The Chinese do business with people rather than companies, so personal contact and loyalty are important. They value sincerity above all other qualities.

Cultural style

Chinese business is based on the development of good personal relationships over time, from which the business will grow. They are formal and quite ritualistic in business behaviour, although this is changing with the return of US-educated managers and the emergence of younger people in the workplace. The Chinese are punctual at work and for social engagements, and cancellation or lateness may be seen as insulting unless good reasons are given. They are quite reserved, and separate emotions from business.

China/UK cultural styles – a comparison

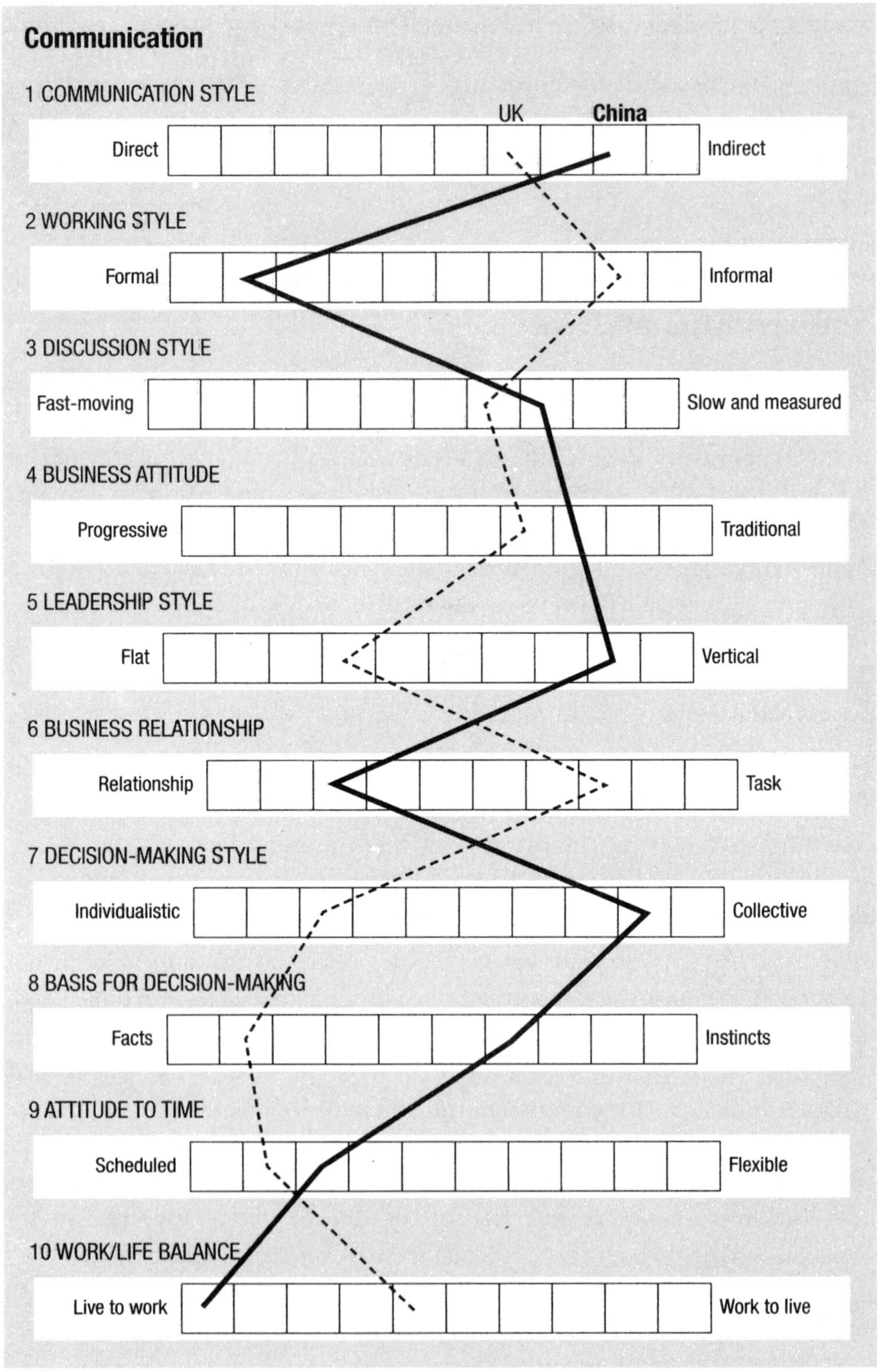

Communication

Introductions in China are courteous and formal, so expect to take a fair amount of time over them on your first visit. The highest-ranking member of your group should lead the way. You might be greeted by applause from your hosts, in which case the polite response is to applaud back. The Chinese are sensitive to titles, so use them whenever possible (e.g. Director, Engineer). Don't address a Chinese person with the word 'comrade', a privilege reserved for Communist Party members. If you don't know a person's title, use Mr, Mrs or Miss until you're advised otherwise. In China the surname comes first and the given names second. So Mao Tsedong was known as Chairman Mao, not Chairman Tsedong.

The Chinese don't use gestures and strong facial expressions, and are not tactile, so it's not surprising that they are often said to be inscrutable. They appreciate conservative suits and ties, and dislike loud colours. Women tend to wear high-necked blouses and low heels.

Interpreters are often used in discussions, but never make the mistake of addressing the interpreter and not the boss. In discussions with the Chinese, check whether they're talking about today, tomorrow or several generations in the past or future. Unlike Indo-European languages, Chinese does not use verb tenses to differentiate between the past, present and future, so a Chinese person might say, "I eat chicken yesterday," rather than "I ate chicken yesterday." Time is indicated by the context of the sentence or by specific references, so Western visitors must ensure that they clarify times and dates for appointments and in contracts.

Allow for a moderate attention span of about 30 minutes when presenting. Stress the benefits of your proposal for China and for the bottom line. Remember that the Chinese rarely say 'no'. Instead they will hint at difficulties, so be sensitive to this. Show commitment and enthusiasm to your project, and repeat your key points several times. Don't assume that silence means acceptance, and avoid asking personal opinions.

Organization

China is a bureaucratic country, so things are unlikely to happen fast. Don't show impatience or anger: this is seen as a serious character flaw. Keep your schedule light to allow for long meetings. Office hours tend to be 9am-5pm with a half day on Saturday, although a five-day working week is becoming more common . The key break is between noon and 2 pm, when there is a general lull in the working day. Many offices are closed in the week before and after the Chinese New Year, whose date varies from late January to mid-February.

Meetings and negotiations

Agendas are adhered to in China, but expect slow, repetitious dealings: patience is essential. The Chinese like to establish general principles before moving onto detailed discussion. They also take the long view – sometimes extending over several generations. Be prepared to discuss problems at length to achieve total agreement, and be ready to understand their difficulties – these may be linked more to social matters or relationships than to the business. Don't push for information, and despite any irritation that you might feel internally, maintain a flexible but firm negotiation style. Your aim is to develop mutual trust in the long-term.

Be aware that 'Yes' in China means 'I hear you' and not 'I agree.' A Chinese may also say 'yes' where Britons or North Americans would say 'no'. 'Is it ready?' Englishman: 'No, it isn't.' Chinese: 'Yes, it isn't.' Check what's really being said.

Subordinates in your team should not interrupt in business meetings. Other tips: don't assume that a smile equals satisfaction, or that agreement equals understanding. Business cards are important, and it can be useful to have yours printed in Chinese on the back.

Team-working

Chinese teams are groups of specialists working under a leader, who may not himself be a specialist but will have links to the head of the company. Show respect to him and refer issues to him in the first place. Any one-to-one contact between members of your team and the Chinese should be authorized by the team leader first.

The Chinese like to experience harmony and consultation. Team members like to see their view expressed in the outcome of a project, although implicit obedience to the team leader is also expected. There is a strict hierarchy and a clear chain of command in Chinese businesses. The working pace tends to be slow and methodological, and deadlines are regarded as flexible. Give praise, and make your instructions clear (but in a courteous way), and check the team's progress regularly. Emphasize the moral and social aims of the project.

If there is disagreement, manage the problem in private, and always use an impersonal approach. Say, "Our partner was disappointed that the deadline was missed," not, "You missed a deadline and now our partner is angry." Stress harmony: "Yesterday we won four new clients," not, "Yesterday I negotiated deals with four new clients."

Leadership and decision-making

Organizational structures in China are vertical. A manager will seek consensus from his team, but will take personal responsibility for decisions. One potential difficulty for visitors is that a manager's authority is often based on his wealth and family background, rather than purely on his competence at the job. Personal connections will also influence decisions. All of this, together with language difficulties, makes it hard for visitors to read meetings and negotiations accurately. In addition, family businesses tend to belong to trade groups, which will also exert pressures.

Decisions are made slowly in China, but will have a long-term effect. Unlike many Western organizations, the Chinese are not obsessed by achieving short-term successes that may look impressive, but have not been fully thought through. Be prepared to invest time and money in visiting the decision-makers regularly. Be patient, and allow your hosts plenty of time for reflection. You'll find a difference in leadership style between older and newer organizations: the latter will tend to move faster and be less formal. Even so, don't be too forceful, and be careful not to express too many differences of opinion in public.

Women in business

The position of women in Chinese society has improved dramatically since the advent of Communism in 1949, but they still hold only a few senior seats in government and business. Women visitors to China therefore receive special respect by virtue of being foreign.

It's important for a visiting woman to establish her credentials and expertise. One way might be to send an agenda, with brief biographies of your team members, before meetings. Dress conservatively – trouser suits are acceptable – and be prepared to be stared at – you're unusual. There will also be some unintentional rudeness in the form of cigarette smoke, or a door slamming in your face.

Moderation is expected of women in China, so it might be best to avoid alcohol, or drink very little (many Chinese women abstain). The principle of respect in China means that women may be polite to senior men, which may be seen as sexist by some Westerners. Don't react to this: Chinese women have considerable authority at home, in politics and in commerce.

Socializing and gift-giving

The Chinese tend to get up early and go to bed early, so expect to eat lunch around noon and dinner at about 6pm for around two hours. Hospitality is an important tradition in China, and sharing the bill is unknown. You must reciprocate, however. Tea is always served in mugs with lids: never refuse.

You'll probably be honoured with at least one banquet during your visit. Start by eating lightly – there may be a dozen courses. Your host may serve the tastiest food directly to your plate, but don't reciprocate. There will be no dessert, but fresh fruit might be served. Rice at the end of a meal is intended as a filler: you don't have to empty your plate. Use chopsticks, not your fingers, if you need to remove food from your mouth.

The host will sit opposite the door, the honoured guest to his right. Speeches and toasts will happen. *Ganbei!* is the equivalent of 'cheers!' and literally means 'to dry the glass', but just drink the quantity that you're comfortable with. The evening will end when the host stands, usually soon after the last course. It is important to reciprocate with a return banquet if you have time during your stay. The Chinese like to invite visitors to their homes, even though the conditions are unlikely to match your own domestic circumstances.

Gifts are important, as is the wrapping. Gold and red are good colours, but avoid black, white or blue (they're associated with funerals). Offer gifts with both hands and don't open any that you receive in the presence of the giver. Make it clear that the gift is from your company to their company. Post-visit gifts – calendars, cards, etc – are also appreciated. Unless you are invited to do so, don't take partners to business entertainment.

Great gifts: Company pens, ashtrays, paperweights, books, whisky

Avoid giving: Flowers, chocolates and especially knives or clocks, which represent death or the end of a relationship. Money should be given in even numbers.

Conversation topics

Ice-breakers	**Ice-makers**
Plans for the 2008 Olympic Games in Beijing	China's carbon emissions
China's economic boom	'I have to make my feelings known about Tibet'
More schools in the UK are teaching Mandarin Chinese	Tiananmen Square 1989, when the Chinese army shot dead several hundred protesters

Doing business in the USA

Doing business in the USA

Five Ways to Succeed	Five Ways to Fail
Be positive and clear about what you do and who you are	Use British understatement and sarcastic humour
Network and be visible	Make un-PC comments about sex, race and religion
Deliver on time and on budget	Suggest that Americans lack a sense of humour
Adopt a relaxed and friendly approach	Fail to advise of slippage in the project
Be supportive: modify proposals, don't reject them	Slip out for a beer at lunchtime

Overview

It should be so easy for Britons and Americans to do business easily and immediately. Sometimes it is. But often there's a real clash of misunderstandings, made even more confusing by the fact that the two countries speak the same language. Why can't we all get on better?

The problems start in part with the fact that Britain is an old country, and America is still new and shiny. Britons, like many Europeans, carry a touch of cynical world-weariness about them. Their country is over-crowded and over-expensive, the infrastructure creaks, and for much of the year the weather is chilly and depressingly grey. The British also have characteristics – admirable in some circumstances – that Americans just don't get. Among these are self-effacement, understatement and an acidly sardonic line in humour. Britons hoping to make an impact with Americans should bin – to use an American expression now current in British English – all three.

So, to do business with Americans it's a case of: chest out, shoulders back, head up and stand tall. Be proud of who you are and what you do. Think positive and optimistically. Say what you mean plainly and clearly, and delete from your speech pattern that wickedly corrosive Brit humour – it will only lead to blank faces, and possibly downright irritation.

Things have become more complicated post 9/11. America's leadership and foreign policy have won it few admirers around the world (although neither has Britain's), and there is an undeniable – if often unspoken – anti-American sentiment in the air. Whatever your feelings about this, remember that American people themselves are extraordinarily generous and open-hearted – and they really have a soft spot for Brits.

Values and attitudes

Despite the difficulties that the country has suffered in recent times, Americans continue to believe fervently in the American dream. They believe in their legendary 'can do' attitude – though this can lead to huge errors, as the bursting of the dot.com bubble in 2000 vividly demonstrated – and they believe that individuals can transform their lives by hard work. They like to think big, and are impressed by statistics that suggest that a project will be the biggest ever of its kind, or the first, or the finest.

Many more Americans than Europeans – especially Britons – express religious feelings and attend church. So visiting Brits should edit out of their speech the mild religious profanities and the swear words that pass as acceptable in the UK, at least until you're sure of usages within the group you're working with. Remember, too, that the USA is a nation of immigrants – these days more a salad bowl of races and cultures than a melting pot. At around 40 million, the Hispanic population recently overtook the black population in numbers.

Cultural style

Broadly speaking, the US and the UK share the same behaviour profile. Both societies focus on systems and tasks, are informal, strict on time and don't believe that showing your feelings has a place in business. Differences between the two cultures are really a question of degree, not style. The US believes that for Britain time is important whereas for them it's important and urgent! They can be more informal than many Brits and they consider themselves to be more target focused. One thing is true. Americans will share personal confidences with you more readily if they think it will give them an edge.

US/UK cultural styles – a comparison

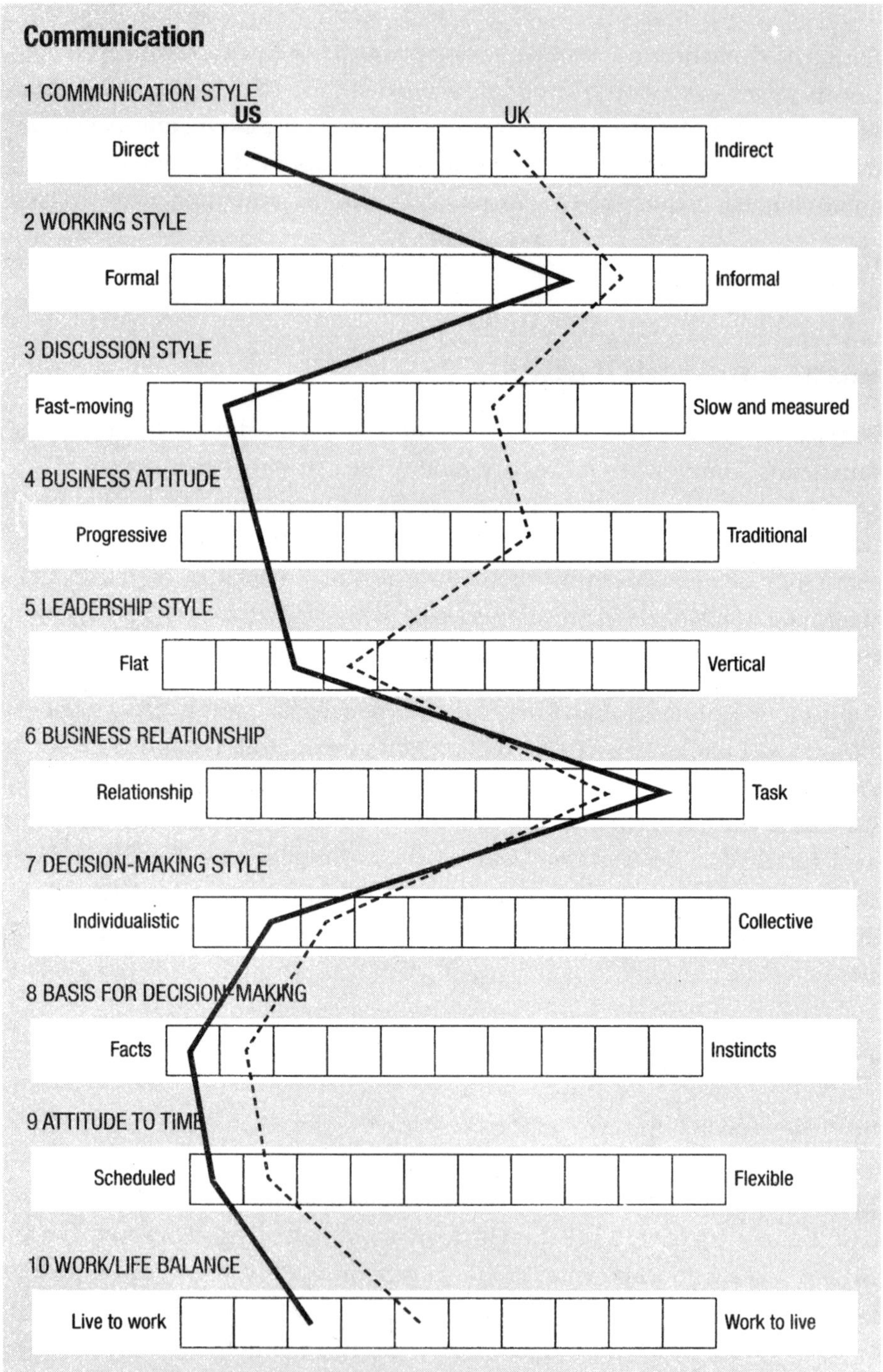

Communication

Americans can appear so damned self-confident to many Europeans. They tend to speak louder than Europeans – very much louder, in some cases – use exaggerated body language, and manage to sound almost jarringly optimistic. They also talk in phrases that create mini-pictures: 'He's right behind the eight ball' (he's on top of his job or project), or 'I'm not going down that route' (I'm not going to talk about that, or pursue that course of action).

If you try to imitate American characteristics, you'll end up looking and sounding like the worst kind of mid-Atlantic European. But you should project your voice confidently, address *all* the people in a meeting or group instead of mumbling to the chairperson, and sound positive about what you're proposing.

Americans may use first names almost immediately, even from the first handshake. But don't be deceived: this will not prevent them from subjecting your proposals to hard questioning. Focus on the bottom line – American business is very much systems-oriented, and always wants to see how much money can be made, and when. You will often hear the phrase, 'Are you hitting your numbers?' – are you achieving budget? The numbers are sacrosanct in the USA, and those who don't hit them might experience a rapid farewell – still with that confident eye contact and the use of your first name as you are given that final handshake.

Allow for a moderate attention span of 30-45 minutes in a presentation, and build in plenty of time for debate. Americans appreciate an informal style and humour, but make sure that your jokes and light-hearted asides don't drift into that area of dark Brit humour that can provoke blank stares. Relevance is very important – use simple, direct expressions, conveyed quickly with short pauses. If your pitch is going down well, expect categorical responses: 'Absolutely! 'Definitely!', 'Fantastic!', all of which reflect their can-do, achievement-focused attitude. If you're fortunate enough to have the kind of personality that allows you to entertain your audience while delivering a winning proposition, they will appreciate that even more.

Although Americans can often seem very direct, to the point of appearing rude, remember that their use of language is just different to that of British English. When an American says, 'Pass that file!' it's just her way of saying, 'Could I trouble you to just pass me that file, please?' They're not being discourteous: Dutch, Scandinavians and German people tend to have the same speech patterns.

First names, informality and humour are valued in the USA, although the terms 'Sir' and 'Madam' are often used with strangers as a mark of courtesy. Handshaking is common when Americans arrive at work or enter a room at the start of a meeting, and a friendly approach in general is considered important. It's part of America's 'Have a nice day' culture.

Organization

Punctuality is regarded as crucial in the USA, because time is equated to money. Start and complete tasks quickly and respond to emails and voicemail messages promptly – certainly within 24 hours. If they are out late, many Americans often check emails before going to bed – a practice that stress management experts would not recommend as a means of achieving a good night's sleep. They tend to take short holiday breaks, and fewer of them than Europeans. Even then, they will often check emails every couple of days.

Office hours in the USA are from around 8am-5pm, although this varies according to the industry you're dealing with. Eating lunch at the desk is a common practice: the two-hour cocktail-fuelled lunch break is a feature of the distant past in most professions in the USA.

Meetings and negotiations

Meetings in America are for making decisions, rather than for gathering views or simply sounding out people. The pace is brisk – 'Time is money' – and you should be open about your aims from the start. People are not always well prepared for meetings, and papers are not always read beforehand, but this won't stop them from commenting on your proposals. The dress code and seating are usually informal, and the discussion will follow the agenda.

Argument and debate are considered constructive and are highly valued. A tough negotiating style is often used, which can appear rude to non-Americans. Americans are willing to express disagreement frankly – 'You must be kidding!' – but it's part of what can be a rough and tumble atmosphere. Show humour, say what *you* think (even in front of seniors), and be ready to forget everything and start again if you lose the debate.

Try not to appear old-fashioned or slow, or get into too much detail. Negotiations are usually finalized quite quickly, and will often centre on figures. Concessions may be agreed when time is running out, whereas in other cultures there would be a break for reflection and a subsequent meeting to try and reach a conclusion. Equally, decisions may initially be made on principles, with everyone happy to settle the details later.

Team-working

Teams in the USA are usually selected on the basis of an individual's competence, his passion for trying new things, and a reputation for getting results. There is also an emphasis on equality of opportunity regardless of age, gender or race. Team members themselves often place their personal goals first, but they align these to the company's aims. Competition within the team is encouraged because it is said to release creative tension. Team members expect to be consulted and to have their views influence the outcome. Deadlines are regarded as fixed, and overtime to complete a project on time is common.

You'll be expected to work long and hard, show energy and enthusiasm and volunteer for anything that you feel you can complete. Understand the aims and motivation of other team members, but be there and fight your corner, and make sure that your individual contribution is recognized in this highly competitive environment. Being overly modest or submissive doesn't work in the USA.

Leadership and decision-making

American managers are expected to lead in a way that generates confidence in the workforce. Tough leaders who get results are particularly admired. On the other hand, managers are expected to arrive at decisions only after consulting their teams and colleagues, and to convince them by logic rather than by feelings or intuition. An autocratic style is not liked: inspirational is what really wins followers.

Executives are usually focused on goals, action and the bottom line, which can lead to short-term-ism. Failure doesn't automatically carry a stigma if the manager was seen to be acting boldly, perhaps in an untried market or with new processes. Consistent failure to deliver will surely lead to dismissal, however.

Set high targets for yourself and others, and give clear orders and opinions: Americans feel very uncomfortable with what they see as British timidity in telling people what they need to do or in expressing disagreement. Don't be pessimistic or hesitant. Take responsibility for initiating implementation, be prepared to disregard everything and start again, and be open about mistakes, failures and delays.

In the US there is no formal bar to the advancement of women in any trade or profession, and the two sexes receive equal pay for equal work. There are many women executives, especially in fashion, cosmetics, arts and the media. The US is very sensitive to sexist language, including the use of the masculine pronouns – 'he' and 'him' – when you're referring to both men and women. So if you were writing a business plan to target air travellers, for example, you would write: "He or she makes an average of six journeys per year," rather than just "He makes..." It can be cumbersome, but it's best to observe the etiquette. It's illegal in the US to ask the age, marital status or number of children of a potential employee, and endearments such as 'Honey' are not acceptable.

Socializing and gift-giving

Like many other aspects of American life, business entertaining and socializing is often informal. Americans tend to eat early, with lunch at around noon and dinner at six. The 'two-Perrier' lunch is increasingly the norm, and working lunches over sandwiches in the office are common. Heavy or enthusiastic drinking is frowned on amongst Americans, but tolerated in visiting Britons. If you smoke, you will increasingly feel like a pariah: if you need to, join those who step outside, or ask if it's OK if you're at all unsure. Dress will be smart-casual or informal, especially on the more laid-back West Coast.

Americans are quick to invite you to their homes. Arrive on time, as you should for all appointments in the US, and have the host's phone number in case you're running late or get lost. Think about leaving by 10pm: many Americans go to bed early and rise early.

Great gifts: Wine, flowers. A good Scotch used to be appreciated, but many Americans now drink less, or prefer lighter spirits.

Avoid giving: Most things are acceptable.

Conversation topics

Ice-breakers	Ice-makers
The glory of their huge country, kindness of American people	Start a debate about American foreign policy
British history and the Royal Family: most Americans love both	Mock the Vietnam war (around 60,000 Americans died in it)
American TV and movie hits in the UK	Sexual jokes and innuendo

Doing business in India

Doing business in India

Five Ways to Succeed	Five Ways to Fail
Spend time building the relationship	Keep your human side hidden
Do things on the phone or face-to-face when you can	Be patronizing – India ceased being a part of the British Empire more than 60 years ago
Check performance and delivery – but with courtesy	Show intolerance if things don't happen exactly the way you expect
Be more relaxed about time and schedules	Show impatience if things don't happen in your timescale
Build a basic knowledge of India's religions and dietary customs	Fail to adapt to local business customs and adapt them to your needs

Overview

India is a South Asian nation with the world's second largest population of 1.1 billion people after China's 1.3 billion. There is already a sizeable and increasing middle class of some 250 million, and India will have the third largest economy by 2050 after China and the USA, according to Goldman Sachs. Indians are proud of the huge variety of their country, which includes the six metros (metropolitan cities) of Delhi, Mumbai, Hyderabad, Bangalore, Kolkata and Chennai, 28 states, more than 20 official languages and seven major religions (Hinduism, Islam, Buddhism, Sikhism, Parseeism, Jainism and Christianity). They are also deeply aware of the poverty and wealth that exists side by side in India, and in the contrast between the cities and the rural areas.

Hindi is the official language, and the majority of Indians (80%) are Hindus. But English is the country's lingua franca, although Indians speak a particular variety of English, which differs in some respects from English used internationally.

The famous caste system, which divided Hindus into four groups, Brahmins (priests), Kshatriyas (warriors), Vaishyas (merchants) and Sudras (clerks), together with the Dalits (untouchables) was outlawed in 1950 but still has some social values. India won independence from British rule in 1947 and became a republic in 1950. Many Indians settled in Kenya and Uganda, but came to Britain in the early 60's.

India and the UK share many superficial similarities in the way they conduct business. Legal, banking and administration systems have many synergies with British procedures. This is not surprising, as many Indian business practices originated during the Raj, the era of British colonial domination that endured from the eighteenth century to 1947. However, these apparent similarities mask significant cultural differences.

Indians think the British are much more formal than we really are, which accounts for their sometimes old-fashioned approach to us and the use of what has been called 'dictionary' English. Equally, Britons must be careful not to patronize. This is all too easy to do after the decades of *Carry On* films that caricatured Indian speech and mannerisms. The Indians you deal with will probably be highly qualified, and many have wide experience in a number of industries. Show respect for their abilities and point of view.

Values and attitudes

An Indian's prime concern is his family. Indians recognize a wide variety of relatives as immediate family, and it is common for different generations to share a property. The father is the absolute head of the household. Foreigners are often unaware of the domestic, religious and environmental (such as the monsoon) issues that bear on Indian working life, so don't assume that someone who is occasionally late at work or requests time off is slacking. They usually make up for this in other ways, but if there are persistent problems, be prepared to sit down and talk with people.

India is a relationship business culture, while the UK is, by and large, systems-oriented. Indians appreciate a family atmosphere at work, so take time to learn names – it's a sign that you care – and expect them to ask you a lot of personal questions. Indians are emotional, and they appreciate seeing the human side of the people they deal with: kindness and empathy are the keys to success in dealing with them. They display great courtesy and consideration to guests and foreigners, and what may seem like exaggerated politeness and deference is in some cases simply a sign of respect.

Indians are devout, and are likely to observe the traditions of their different religions. Hindus reject beef and venerate the cow, Muslims will not touch pork or ham, and Sikh men wear long hair under a turban and carry a ceremonial knife. Followers of Jain eat no root vegetables, such as onions, garlic and potatoes, and most Indians follow a mainly vegetarian diet with meat eaten occasionally. They believe in karma – your destiny as shaped by your actions in previous existences – and fatalism.

However, they also appreciate the profit motive, creativity, and the importance of seeking compromises that will benefit all parties. They cherish democracy – India is the world's largest democratic state – and hate any suggestion of exploitation by Europeans or Americans. Impiety, loss of face and personal criticism are also offensive to them.

Indians respect authority, which means that in the workplace they may be unwilling to take decisions beyond their immediate responsibility, challenge instructions or contradict a manager – even if he is wrong.

Cultural style

British business behaviour tends to be informal, but unemotional and focused on tasks and time schedules. The environment in Indian business is more formal, more relationship-based, and flexible in its treatment of time.

India/UK cultural styles – a comparison

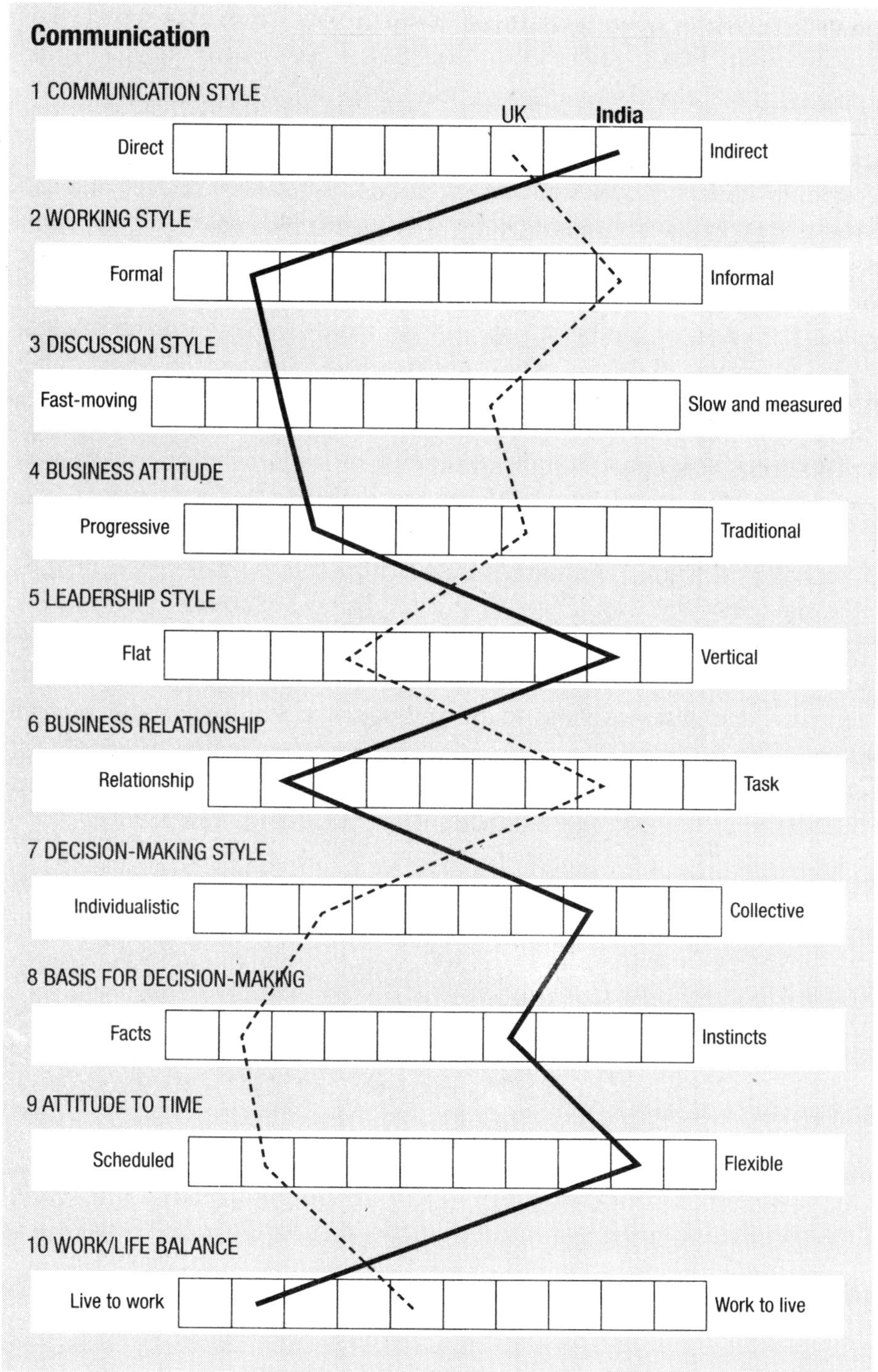

Communication

Regular contact by phone and email backed up with frequent personal visits are important when you're doing business with Indians. If you try to communicate simply by sending occasional formal emails, no matter how detailed and clear they might be, you won't build the kind of relationship they prize so much.

Flattery and compliments are an important way of putting them at ease when you're developing the relationship. Beware, though, that this inevitably means that Indians may say what they think you want to hear rather than objective truths. The word 'no' has harsh implications. Evasive refusals are more polite, so say something like, 'I'll try,' instead. Learn to develop a tolerance for ambiguity in conversation.

Indians value eloquence in spoken communication, which can lead to long speeches delivered with passion. They normally present the reasons for doing something first and the conclusions afterwards, which may conflict with American and British approaches. The British and the Americans tend to work the other way round – they say what they want and then explain the reasons. Indians may not always understand Western humour, but they appreciate charm and laughter, so rely on those approaches to get you through. Politeness and praise are important, and people often use 'we' rather than 'I'. Indian body language is expressive and important to communication – but don't be confused by the nodding of heads when people are listening to you. It means, 'We are paying attention', not 'We agree with you.'

Oral agreements are very important in India, and the phone is a vital communications medium. Voicemail systems are often seen as impersonal, and may not be responded to.

Organization

Indians are masters of improvisation and flexibility, and their attitude to time reflects this. They believe in cycles – the equivalent of the saying, 'What goes around, comes around.' Adaptability is therefore a necessary skill for visitors doing business. Your pre-planning may not be acted on until you arrive, but when you do get there, it will be put into practice fast.

So although the overall process of business is quite time consuming and demands patience, individual actions will be accomplished very fast. Some say it's easier to see the CEO of an Indian company at three hours' notice than at three months'. Company organigrams are not fixed, and people may be given additional internal responsibilities in your absence or be transferred to you without notice. Be prepared for change when you arrive and maintain a relaxed attitude. Keep in regular contact with colleagues to stay up to date with changes in personnel responsibilities and job movements. Indian managers believe that the prime factors in winning promotion are connections, education and hard work.

Meetings and negotiations

Indian business is unhurried, and people take time to discuss the finer points of a project. But implementation can move extremely fast. So expect negotiations to take longer than you are used to: what you see as efficient time management may be viewed as aggressiveness or greed in India. Time spent at the beginning discussing all the points of the relationship will save time later. There will be a difference between managers who are used to working in the old family-run businesses and those who have experience of multinational companies. The latter will behave much more in ways that you are used to.

Indians are open to being persuaded. They appreciate eloquent speech and elaborate description, and it's also useful to outline your education, expertise and experience. Your audience will want to give feedback: allow time for this when you are presenting, and indicate when you will accept questions.

Respect for education and formality means that Indians use titles and surnames when they first meet you. Don't use first names unless you are asked to, although the younger generation gets on first-name terms much faster. Don't offer to shake hands unless your Indian counterpart does. You don't normally shake hands with women in India, but Westernised women will sometimes offer their hand.

Agendas are not strictly adhered to. The broad aims of a negotiation will be revealed early in a discussion, but the specific objectives may not be divulged till later. They may say what they want to achieve in general terms but the details may take time to emerge. Indians are usually flexible, patient negotiators, and they often use personalized and sometimes emotional arguments. They are usually willing to compromise, especially in the interests of forming good long-term relations.

Negotiations often involve large groups, although individuals may be given the responsibility to pursue discussions beyond initial meetings. Remember that contracts are often considered as statements of intent, which can be modified, an approach that can be confusing to Westerners. This is because the first and foremost aim of an Indian negotiation is to achieve an agreement on which the relationship can be built. The details can be managed later. Indians tend to see contracts as the beginning of a negotiation, not the end. But anything written will be held to and will be scrutinized carefully.

Team-working

Indians often feel happier working together on tasks that Westerners would normally do on their own. For example, emails are often not acted on, as people feel more confident talking things through face-to-face, so be prepared to follow up requests with a phone call to discuss issues.

A team is usually headed by a charismatic leader, who will often have family or trade group connections; remember that these may influence his decisions. Team members will usually be selected on the grounds of seniority, experience and education. Decisions are reached by consultation, and team members will expect to see their viewpoint reflected in the outcome. The working pace tends to be slow, and deadlines are flexible. Although consultation is important, the team leader makes decisions, the most powerful ones with or without consultation. Try not to put the team under too much pressure, or be too openly competitive or ambitious. Don't attach personal blame: if something goes wrong, it's karma.

Leadership and decision-making

Indian companies operate a top-down system of management and all major decisions will be taken at the top of the company, so make your approaches at this level. Indians prefer established processes, and new ideas will have to be sold convincingly to your new colleagues. Persistent persuasion and appeals to emotion are often more successful than hard logic or fact. Remember, too, that Indians appreciate a win-win situation, and compromise is therefore acceptable to them.

Listen carefully to proposed solutions. They may seem illogical to you, but will usually work in the Indian context. People do not express disagreement directly. Disagreements may be expressed in writing or face-to-face. Women can occupy senior positions in business and administration in India. However, Indians generally are not accustomed to women in authority and may feel awkward dealing with senior foreign women.

Socializing and gift-giving

Don't refuse refreshment – it's an insult. It is customary to decline the first offer, but you should accept the second or third. Business lunches are preferred to dinners. Most Indian meals are vegetarian with a little meat on the side, but remember that Hindus do not eat beef and Muslims do not eat pork. People drink water (only from sealed bottles), soft drinks or beer. Evening entertaining is quite often done at home: if you are invited, arrive 15 to 30 minutes late. Wash your hands after a meal.

Gift-giving is common, but if you receive one, don't open it in front of your visitor. Green, red and yellow are seen as lucky colours, but black and white as unlucky. Traditionally the head and the ears are viewed as sacred and the feet as dirty, so don't point your feet or touch another with your shoes (if you do so, apologize). Don't pat a child on the head, which is seen as the seat of the soul.

Great gifts: Chocolates, flowers (but not frangipani – associated with funerals).

Avoid giving: Leather products, dog toys or pictures (to Muslims, dogs are unclean).

Conversation topics

Ice-breakers	Ice-makers
Ask about their family, describe yours	Politics, particularly Kashmir and China
Show interest in what state they come from and what it is like	Be patronizing about Indian culture and the colonial period
India's economic progress	Moan about call centres and Indian accents

Doing business in Japan

Doing business in Japan

Five Ways to Succeed	Five Ways to Fail
Spend time building a good relationship	Try and stand out as an individual in a land of consensus
Work hard and earn trust	Cause a Japanese person to lose face in front of others
Socialize – sing in a karaoke session even if you've got a lousy voice	Try to rush people into an agreement
Stress team achievement, not individual achievement	Ignore Japanese protocol and customs
Study Japanese business protocol – correct process is as important as a good result	Talk loudly, gesticulate extravagantly

Overview

Two factors have heavily influenced the development of Japanese society: population density and isolation. In Japan's islands, 3% of the world's population lives in just 0.3% of the world's landmass. Moreover, three-quarters of the country is mountainous and two-thirds forested, so only about 3% is habitable. Japan therefore has one of the world's highest population densities.

For two centuries, from 1648 to 1853, Japan was cut off from Western and other Asian trends. This isolation, together with crowded living conditions, has produced a society with carefully evolved social rituals marked by high degrees of politeness and consideration. After Japan began to modernize, a strong work ethic, a mastery of high technology and a comparatively small defense allocation (1% of GDP) helped it advance with extraordinary rapidity from 1955-89. Then its bubble burst, and stock market and property prices slumped. Since then economic growth has recovered, but now Japan faces similar problems to those of Western European countries: a contracting workforce (estimated to fall by 20% in the next two decades), and heavy expenditure on pensions and healthcare. The country remains, however, the second most technologically powerful in the world, and a giant in economic terms.

Values and attitudes

Japanese thought is based on the principles of Confucius, the Chinese philosopher who taught that the family was the basic unit of society and that the father was its leader. From this developed a social model which includes these values:

- *We are members of a group, not individuals;*
- *The father is the leader, and relationships are unequal;*
- *Save, stay calm, avoid extremes and shun indulgence – maintain moderation in all things.*

The Japanese respect age and experience. Listeners are careful not to disagree with teachers or presenters, and the relationship between a mentoring manager, or *senpai*, and the learner, the *kohai*, is important in Japanese business.

Gaman is the quality of endurance, of which the Japanese have great amounts. It implies following orders without question, not complaining but 'gritting it out' and getting on with the job. It is this quality in the workplace that explains why the Japanese will work long hours, remain late, and stay up all night if necessary to complete projects and sacrifice themselves for the group. An interesting manifestation of *gaman* is the *Endurance* TV series that Japan is famous for.

The Japanese have a dread of losing face, which to them implies that you cannot be trusted. Extravagant gestures, loud voices and aggressive behaviour are signs of a lack of control and can lead to this situation. Much Japanese reticence with foreigners is due to the fear of them losing face through Western unawareness of their culture. If you yourself lose face by failing on a task or deadline, simply apologize: explaining the reasons is seen as making excuses. Accept responsibility, and work hard not to repeat it.

Cultural style

Japan is relationship-focused, formal, very time conscious and reserved, whereas the UK is more task-focused and more informal. British business people need to spend time building the relationship with Japanese colleagues and partners, and need to be more formal in their public business dealings.

Japan/UK cultural styles – a comparison

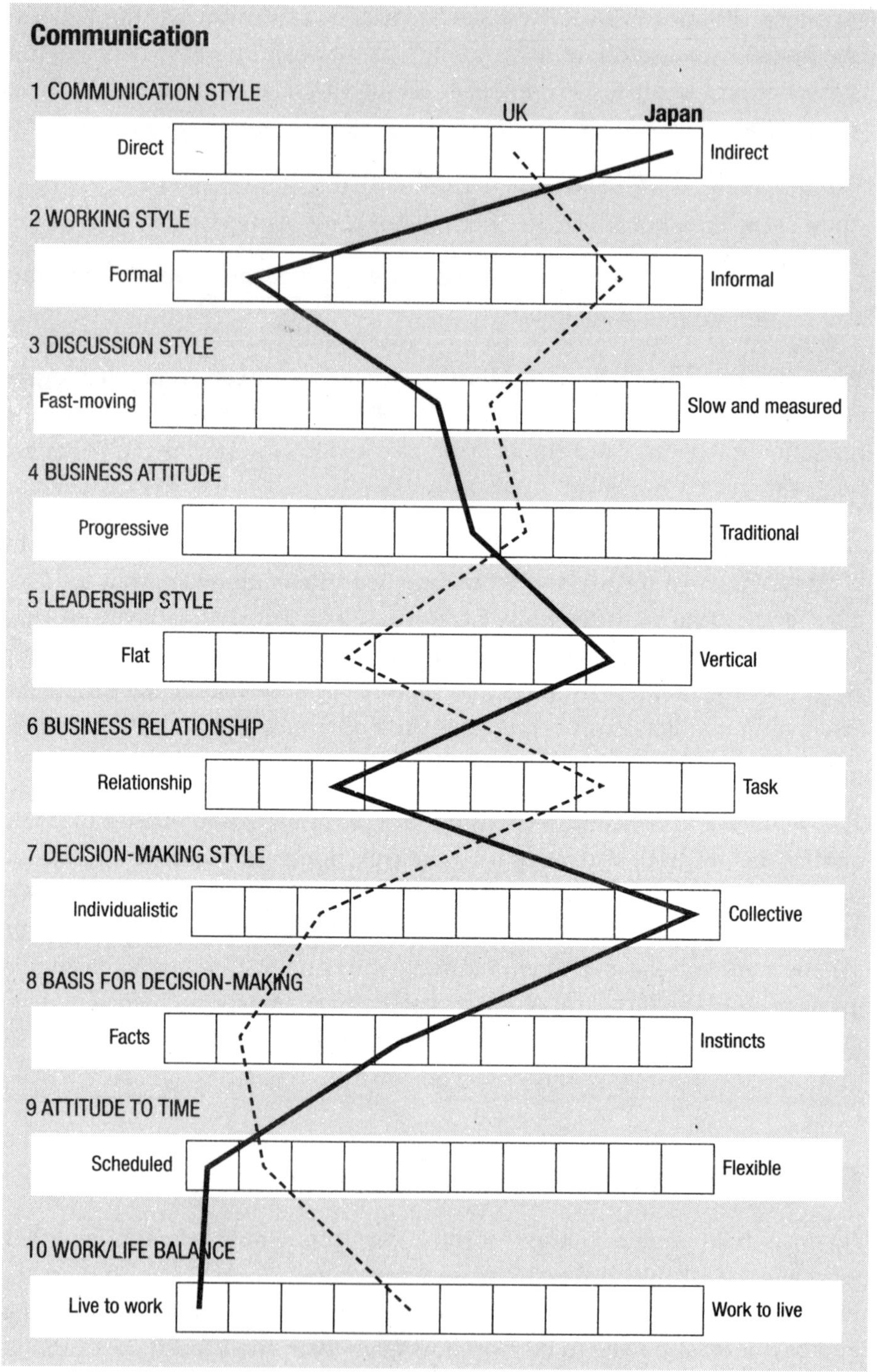

Communication

Communication in Japan is subtle and much is left unspoken, although it is perfectly understood by the Japanese. It's easy for Westerners to cause offence where none is intended, so until you are attuned to Japanese nuances always check that you've clearly understood instructions.

The Japanese think it is wrong to get emotional or lose your temper. Rather than saying 'No' outright, they will convey disagreement through silence, hesitation, or responses such as, 'Yes, but ...' or 'The situation is delicate'. They often refuse by saying, 'Thank you. We'll study that.'

Their presentation style tends to be quiet, and the presenter should be soberly dressed. The Japanese are polite and attentive listeners. They avoid steady eye contact, and maintain an impassive expression. Some may adopt a posture of deep concentration, and may appear to be asleep, although they're not. They prefer hard facts, visually presented, rather than emotional persuasion. The Japanese take time to consider and are comfortable with silence for reflection, which can unnerve Western visitors. If the room falls quiet, resist the urge to burst into speech. Signal any questions you wish to ask before you ask them.

The Japanese can usually read and write English, but can't always speak it or understand spoken English. Try to help them unobtrusively to understand you by giving them more than one opportunity to grasp your message by using different ways to say the same thing, and always support any oral presentation with written backup.

Japanese managers often introduce themselves by identifying their company, their department and finally their name. This is because they think of themselves as a 'we' society and not an 'I' society. They have a strong group mentality, which shows in their collective decision-making and in the way they get together after work. So use 'We' and not 'I' when talking about your own department or company, and socialize with your Japanese colleagues after work when you can.

Contrary to a widely-believed myth, bowing is not necessary for foreigners, but the business card ritual is. Offer your card so that the receiver can read it, study his card, keep it on the table while you're talking, and then put it in a business card holder, not your pocket. Your card should carry your company's name, your name, your job title and department. It should be in Japanese as well as in your own language.

Organization

The Japanese value hard work and long hours. Business hours are from 8am-6pm, and although Saturday duties don't exist everywhere, many executives go in then to get themselves noticed. It is considered respectful to leave the office after the boss. Executives usually have a one- or two-hour commute, and often don't see their children until the weekend. Punctuality is essential in Japanese culture, and suggests organization and respect. Office dress is quite formal, usually a dark suit, white shirt and dark tie. Women tend to wear dresses or a suit.

Japanese women tend to have separate lifestyles to men, and control the household. It is still usual for them to give up work on marriage, and promotion for them is therefore restricted as they are not expected to stay in the workforce. This may change with the younger generation adopting more of an American lifestyle, and the end of the job-for-life 'salaryman' tradition in Japanese business, which may lead to a greater need for double-income families.

Japanese offices are quieter than British and continental ones. The Japanese are happy with silence, so just remain aware and soak in what's happening. Seek 'adoption' by senior Japanese managers to get your ideas accepted. In a hierarchical structure such as theirs, it's important to address questions and suggestions to the next level of management, who will then direct them to the appropriate sources.

Meetings and negotiations

The Japanese are less concerned with what you say (they can read that) than with who you are. As a result they set a high value on *haragei* (belly talk), the art of reading feelings through silent meditation and observation. Senior Japanese managers sit in on meetings but rarely speak, preferring to feel what's going on and listening in a state of deep concentration. *Ishin-denshin,* heart-to-heart communication, and *harage*i are important in revealing the internal state of partners, expressed through tone of voice, facial expression and posture. They will hear one thing (the content), but understand two, (content and your feelings).

As in many countries, there is a difference between reality and façade. *Tatemae,* the art of diplomacy, indirectness and avoiding controversy and conflict, refers to the façade. As the Japanese get to know and trust you, they will reveal their real feelings – *honne* – and be more direct and honest. *Honne* often happens not in the office, but in social events. It's important to take every opportunity to attend these. Next you can practise *shinyo* – consistency in thought and action by doing what you say and showing loyalty and respect – to build still more trust.

Before you enter a meeting, prepare a short introductory statement explaining why you're in Japan and how long you'll be there, the sort of people you're seeing, and your previous contact with the country. Decide on the five or six crucial points you want to make, and repeat them at each encounter. The Japanese believe that everyone who is in the loop needs to be at meetings, so they can be quite large. The most senior person may say little, but to learn who that figure is, note who is served tea first!

The amount of time spent on a meeting is less important than the procedure, so expect these sessions to be quite long. Formality and the sequence of events matter. Don't use first names unless you're asked to. Use the suffix *san* for both men and women (e.g. *Suzuki-san*). Don't seek final decisions in meetings – they're for gathering information or stating positions. And don't expect instant feedback: the Japanese prefer to question and clarify. Check what is verbally agreed, and follow it up with a written minute.

The Japanese negotiating style is impersonal and unemotional. But emotion lurks just below the surface, and logic alone will not work – the Japanese manager must like and trust you. It is important for the Japanese to establish the status of the person they are dealing with in order to know how to talk. This means that they may ask personal questions about your job, your responsibilities and your reporting structure. The exchange of business cards at the beginning of meetings is an important way of establishing this status for the Japanese, and should be carried out with proper respect.

Team-working

A Japanese team is a group of individuals who work together for the wider good of the company. The group is therefore superior to individual wishes. Harmony is crucial: avoid open confrontation, or criticizing superiors or subordinates. Allow all parties to save face, and reject nothing bluntly.

The team leader will make decisions, but will not act independently without internal support. The process tends to be slow to allow for consensus to emerge, and team members will be modest and self-effacing. It's important to keep to schedules, but deadlines can be extended if necessary.

Wa, the preservation of harmony, is another feature of Japanese office life. The Japanese are extremely sensitive to what others think of them, are obsessively polite and will shower you with compliments. You can return the gesture by being polite and respectful to them, especially in the early stages of a relationship. If Japanese colleagues get drunk in evening social sessions, no mention is made of it the next day.

Leadership and decision-making

The Japanese consult at all levels within a group before they reach the decision-making stage: this is called *nemawashi.* They then seek universal consensus –*ringi-sho* – to arrive at a decision. Japanese managers like to understand the background and reasons for decisions and proposals. Be patient – *nemawashi* and *ringi-sho* mean that they may be slow to decide, but once they do you can expect fast implementation.

Japanese managers rarely give direct orders: they hint at what is needed instead. Courtesy for the other person controls all their dealings. They use polite, indirect forms of English such as the passive voice: 'The company has decided', rather than, 'We have decided.' They also rely on impersonal forms of speech: 'It has been found necessary to cancel...', rather than, 'We are cancelling...'

The Japanese desire to save face becomes evident when they deliberate carefully and avoid taking risks in their statements and actions. Be patient in trying to get decisions: even routine issues may be subject to extensive discussion. Look for a contact who can keep you up to date informally on progress.

Socializing and gift-giving

Evening hospitality offers an opportunity for personal revelation and more relaxed conversation, when you can discuss things off the record and reach decisions. Karaoke nights are important in team-building: grit your teeth and go for it, and have a popular song ready to perform if you're up for it. You might also be invited to expensive restaurants, and if you're the MD of a reasonably-sized company, you'll be expected to reciprocate. Entertaining usually takes place immediately after work. Midweek entertainment may stop at around 9pm to allow for the long commute home. Keep alcohol under control: the Japanese may get drunk to let off steam, but they don't expect it of Westerners.

Giri – gift-giving and the creating and resolving of obligations – is an important consideration. Gifts should be carefully wrapped and will often show the brand name. These are practical examples of *giri*, which manifests itself at a much deeper level between people as a debt of honour for favours received.

Great gifts: good quality branded goods especially to do with local drink, whisky and golf. The packaging is as important as the gift.

Avoid giving: White chrysanthemums (funeral), even numbers.

Conversation topics

Ice-breakers	Ice-makers
Silence, when your Japanese counterparts are being silent	Home and household – until you get to know people well
Japanese culture and food	World War Two and Japan's role
Sport, including baseball – big in Japan	Any criticism of a Japanese company or Japanese lifestyle

Doing business in Brazil

Doing business in Brazil

Five Ways to Succeed	Five Ways to Fail
Build the relationship	Avoid mentioning Portuguese or Argentinian superiority in any area
Dress your best – good clothes and accessories, clean and pressed	Insist on bringing up the disparity of wealth in Brazil
In all-male company, compliment the beauty of Braziiian women	Decline social invitations
Brazilians are very house proud: accept if they invite you for dinner or just a drink	Be inflexible, stiff and formal
Stay in good hotels – style matters	Ask to see the *favelas*, Brazil's shanty towns where guns and drugs are frequent

Overview

Nearly everything about Brazil is vast. It has the largest economy in South America and the most advanced industrial sector in Latin America, and it is the world's fifth biggest country in terms of land area and population. The Amazon basin covers some 60% of the country's surface, and contains 20% of the world's fresh water supply and the world's largest rain forest. Some 20 million people live in greater Sao Paulo, the largest city in the southern hemisphere. According to Goldman Sachs, by 2050 Brazil will be the world's fifth largest economy, thanks largely to its offshore oil and gas reserves.

But not all of Brazil's statistics are so impressive. It is one of the world's most unequal societies, 5% of the population owning 85% of the wealth. And its economic growth rates have been weak compared to those of many Asian countries. Barriers to growth include poor infrastructure, low quality public services, corruption, social conflicts and government bureaucracy, while deforestation in the Amazon remains an environmental controversy. But Brazil also has vast natural resources and strong manufacturing and service sectors, and in recent years President Luiz Inacio Lula da Silva has had some success in redressing the country's imbalances.

Portuguese is the official language of Brazil, making it one of the few Latin American countries where Spanish is not the main tongue. It has historical links with the UK, which was an early supporter of Brazil's independence (declared in 1822), helped the country to build a railway system, and encouraged it to abolish slavery. Some three to four million African slaves were transported to Brazil during its colonial period, seven times the number taken to the US.

Brazil is a racially mixed country with large mulatto (Portuguese-African) and mameluco (Portuguese-Amerindian) communities. However, divisions in Brazilian society are between rich and poor. It remains a class-based society and coming from a 'good family' is respected.

Values and attitudes

Personal contacts are the way of doing business in Brazil: the time you spend socializing will greatly contribute to your success there. Brazilians respect social class, family and education rather than personal achievements, and will value your personal style, emotion and commitment.

Dress well: Brazilians are fashion conscious. In Rio, even if someone is dressed casually, their jeans and shirt will be fashionable and perfectly pressed. Businesswomen wear sandals with 'city heels' and often no tights. Men wear designer ties, good shoes and a good leather belt; a short-sleeved shirt with a tie will make you a figure of fun. You will also enhance your status by showing a lively interest in intellectual pursuits – some knowledge of Brazilian history, writers and music will help – and by stylish entertaining.

The Brazilian sense of time can be erratic. It is more important to complete what you are doing than to observe a pre-arranged timetable. Events often begin fifteen to thirty minutes late, and it's important not to take offence at this and to accept this is the way things are done there. In a business environment it is important to state clearly when you need people to turn up: stress that you mean American time, not Brazilian time, but say it with a smile. Failure to do so may mean a long wait. Equally, it would be impolite to arrive bang on time for a dinner invitation.

Brazilians are happy to stand close to each other – much closer than the British are happy with – and they can be tactile and extrovert: touching, back-patting and kissing are normal greetings. Don't initiate it, but don't respond stiffly.

For Brazilians a warm friendly approach is important. Stiffness and formality are disliked. Even in companies, the top-down management approach is often muted by the use of informal greetings, and Brazilian Portuguese makes a lot of use of diminutives to convey emotions. An important unofficial concept in Brazilian business is the *jetinho* – the little way – which gets round obstacles and makes life run more smoothly, especially when tackling the country's bureaucracy. Finding loopholes to get through difficulties is part of the Brazilian way of life.

This means that Brazilian society is quite individualistic. This is partly due to the lack of a welfare state, and means that the key unit of loyalty and support is your family. There are many family businesses in Brazil, run by both men and by women. The head of the family is the father and this has led to a tradition of looking upwards to a father figure for leadership in society at large. It is also felt to be important in Brazil to know your place in society, although with increasing upward mobility, this is changing.

Saudade, the Portuguese or Brazilian soul, expresses a sense of nostalgia or longing for things you miss. Untranslatable in English, it is at the root of the Portuguese *fado* song tradition and is a popular theme in much of Brazilian music. For Brazilians and Portuguese alike, *saudade* is never far from their thoughts, despite the joyful exuberance they display.

Brazilians feel good about Brazil; its size, its potential, its variety and its beauty. They feel they can accommodate and absorb new ideas and structures without damaging their social fabric and are very future-oriented. Be inspiring and positive with your ideas and don't criticize the country, even if they do.

Cultural style

Brazilian society is very much relationship-based, quite formal at first although it moves towards informality fast as rapport is established. It is relaxed about time (but less so in the big commercial city of Sao Paulo), and Brazilians like to see the human side of the people they deal with.

Brazil/UK cultural styles – a comparison

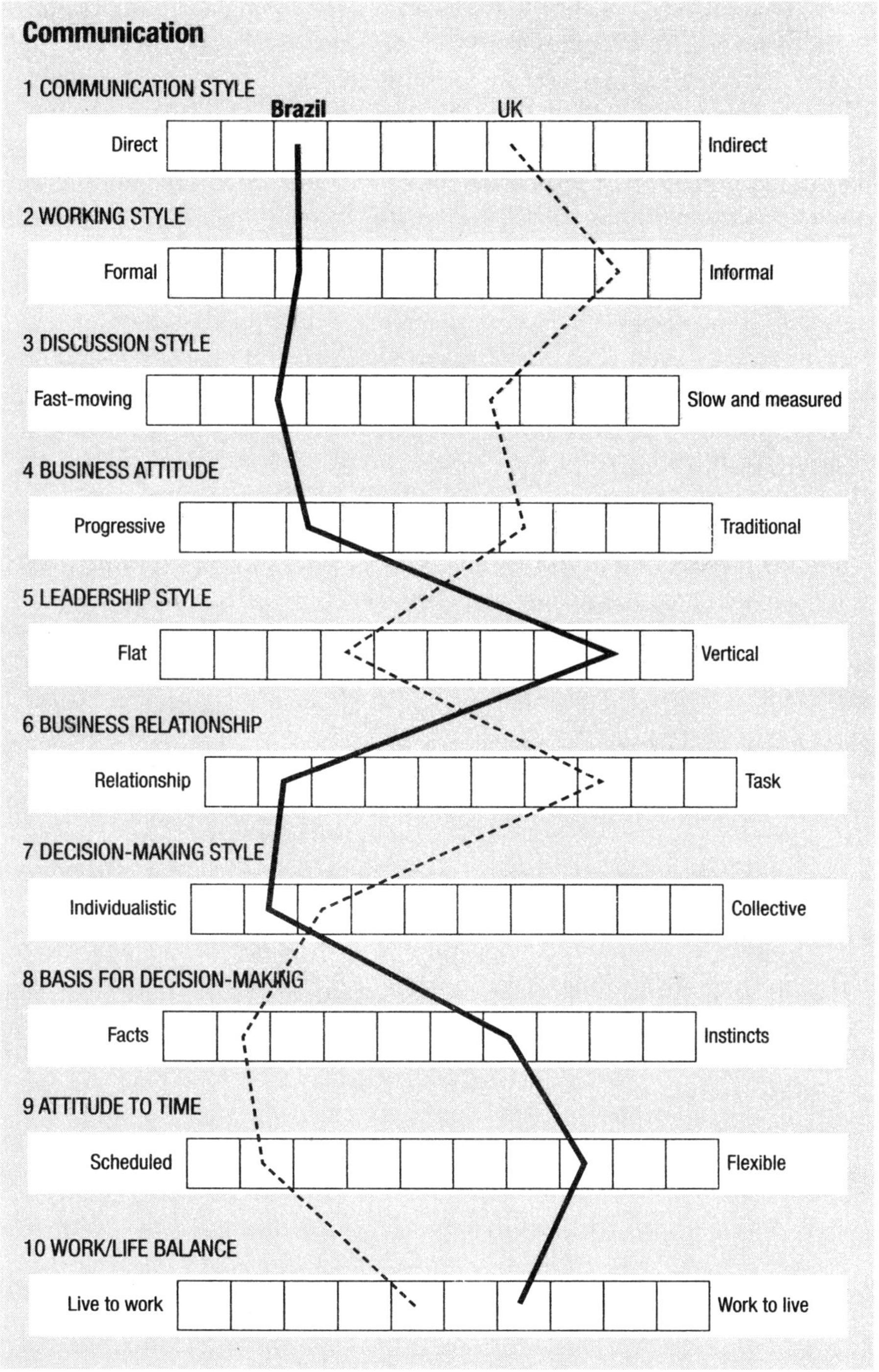

Communication

Warm, friendly and talkative is the Brazilian style. They form impressions less on what is said and more from your gestures and eye contact. They like to please and to be pleased by others, and this may lead on occasions to an unwillingness to deal with unpleasant subjects. They like bold imaginative visions, and sometimes shy away from detailed long-term planning in favour of short-term solutions.

So chat first, then get round to the business. Brazilians need to feel that you appreciate them as a person. What Americans and northern Europeans may consider unnecessary socializing is simply a Brazilian's way of feeling comfortable with you. Treat the office secretary as your new best friend: she will advise you on procedures, dress codes and a multitude of other details. Brazil is proud of its Brazilian-Portuguese identity, so all documentation, including business cards and letters, should be in Portuguese and English, never in Spanish.

Brazilians consider the European mode of presentation to be rather over-cautious, so be prepared to be bold. They are interested in ideas, so they will want to know your vision, supported by facts. But style, eloquence, expressiveness and body language are also important. Try to maintain strong eye contact, and show your human side. Keep your presentations short – around 30 minutes – and allow time for discussion.

Forms of address in Brazil can be quite formal, as Brazilians are used to distinctions of age and rank. Even if you are on first name terms with someone, you will probably use a term of respect, such as *Seu Pedro, Dona Ana* or *Doutor Francisco* (for bosses). Address strangers as *O Senhor* or *O Senhora*. One of the key issues in Brazil is rank inequality within the population. This means that people will always be polite to foreigners, but may be very informal with junior staff. They might also get quite upset if not addressed formally themselves. This mixture of informality and formality in Brazil can take a bit of getting used to.

Organization

Brazilians work very hard, but don't expect them to be on time. Employees usually are, but executives often arrive late and stay late, so slow down a little. The best times for appointments are around 10am, and between 3pm and 5pm. Expect people to say one thing and do another in Brazil: your word is not regarded as an absolute bond.

Meetings and negotiations

It's best to schedule only two or three meetings a day; remember that you must start them with coffee and socializing before you discuss work. A typical meeting might last around two hours. The seating plan in meetings is usually arranged on a hierarchical basis. The style of the gathering will be formal, but structured so that more casual conversation is possible: Brazilians like to discuss and analyze situations from all sides. Expect the debate to be lively and overlapping: they don't mind interruption. Neither do they expect to keep to an agenda: they prefer to complete the business at hand rather than cut it short because of time schedules. Don't expect clear-cut yes or no answers, and don't try to impose tight deadlines.

Brazilian people are talkative, with lots of body language, and will be quite emotional. Argument and debate are valued, but it's important to avoid direct confrontation in meetings: try and look for constructive solutions. If there is disagreement, it may be expressed in terms such as, 'It's your money', or 'That's a courageous decision.' Disagreements will normally be resolved face- to-face, without recourse to writing or to a third party.

Meetings usually end in a decision, but it could be modified before it is implemented. Demonstrating trust (while investigating the reality of a proposal) and giving people the benefit of the doubt is important. Personal loyalty is the key to successful negotiation in Brazil.

Team-working

Seniority and experience tend to be the criteria for team selection. The pace of work may be slow although Brazilians do put in the hours and deadlines are treated as flexible. Highly structured business practices also tend to work against a team, as does a degree of arrogance and bossiness often displayed by managers.

Leadership and decision-making

In Brazil a team is a group of individuals bound together by a strong leader whom they regard as a superior. Brazilian managers will consult with key stakeholders, but the function of team meetings is often simply to give orders and instructions. The process can appear autocratic to northern Europeans and Americans, but managers are also expected to demonstrate a duty of care towards subordinates, which means taking a personal interest in them.

Socializing and gift-giving

Lunch is normally a two-hour affair between 12 noon and 2pm. Dinner starts from 7pm, but dinner parties may not begin until 10pm. Formal business entertainment usually takes place somewhere smart and prestigious. If you're entertaining a business associate, ask his secretary to recommend a restaurant. Business is usually discussed during coffee at the end of the meal. A couple of general points: punctuality is not important in Brazil; smoking is common.

Great gifts: Scotch or champagne; something for the children for home visits.

Avoid giving: anything black or purple (associated with funerals), knives (the breaking of a relationship) or handkerchiefs (grief).

Conversation topics

Ice-breakers	Ice-makers
The richness and variety of the Brazilian music scene	The 1982 World Cup, when Brazil lost 3-2 to Italy in the quarter finals: it hurts the nation to this day
Brazil's beautiful beaches: ask for tips on the best ones	The failed airline Varig, once the international pride of Brazil
New young Brazilian football stars, a great opener for discussion	Crime and policing, not something Brazilians are proud of

Doing business in Russia

Doing business in Russia

Five Ways to Succeed	Five Ways to Fail
Be patient	Criticize Russia
Be firm, even tough, in your negotiations – the Russians value leadership and strength	Compromise too early in a negotiation
Respect the Russian calendar: their meeting times may not be the same as yours	Show disunity in the team
Pay attention to the hierarchy: it's important to give due respect to the boss.	Neglect to check what lies behind the prosperous front
Show personal warmth: Russians build business on personal relationships	Use 'hard sell' rather than 'academic sell' tactics in negotiating

Overview

If you're going to be dealing with Russia, you'd better first consider the great topic of the 'Russian Soul'. Note that we said consider, and not understand, because even the Russians and some of their greatest writers continually debate the subject. Russians are certainly different from Westerners: they themselves claim that they are more spiritual. The vastness of their land, the harsh winters, and the country's tragic-glorious history have all contributed to the forging of the Russian soul.

Remember that Russia lost tens of millions of people – some historians claim 40 million – during Stalin's purges in the 1930s, and up to 27 million in the Second World War. From all this, Russians maintain a sense of endurance and faith in life, and they do not seem to make the clear distinction between hard logic and emotion that is prevalent in many Western business cultures. They often value intuition more than rationality. Certainly, Russians will want to feel that they like you before they do business with you.

Destiny now appears to be rewarding Russia's fortitude. Oil and gas revenues have transformed its economic situation and its world standing after its loss of superpower status in the 1990s. There is an expanding middle class, and a consumer economy thrives, at least in major cities. However, for the business community, Russia can still seem a daunting prospect. The country derives the bulk of its export revenue from commodities, which can leave it exposed to fluctuating prices. It must modernize its manufacturing industry, reduce corruption and crime and make its banking and other business infrastructures more welcoming to foreign investors. Even so, Russia is now enjoying greater stability than at any time since the momentous dismantling of the USSR in the 1990s.

Values and attitudes

Billionaires who can buy British Premiership football teams with the cash in their back pocket may have given a false impression of what Russians are really like. Most of them share a highly communal and collective spirit. This dates not just from the decades of Communist rule in the twentieth century, but from long before the industrial era, when agrarian life was dominated by village communes and the traditional *artels*, cooperative associations of workers.

The analyst and former Russian Minister of Economics, Yevgeny Yasin, notes the following traditional values among his countrymen:

- An emphasis on spiritual principles and moral laws;
- A propensity for teamwork based on a history of collectivism;
- *Sobornost* – the community of the individual will and the endeavours of the people;
- The joy of working;
- A tendency to make far-reaching plans and sweeping actions.

Some of these can have unfortunate reverse implications – collectivism can lead to the suppression of individuality and the creep of authoritarianism – but overall he believes that the Russian people's qualities can enable to them to adapt to their challenges.

Cultural style

Russian business depends on good relationships. Proceedings usually start formally, but the business will only develop if good informal bonds are created. Russians would describe themselves as polychronic and relaxed about time: it's more important to complete the business in hand rather than stick to strict timetables. Initially, Russians may appear reserved, but they are happiest in an environment where they can freely express their emotions.

Russia/UK cultural styles – a comparison

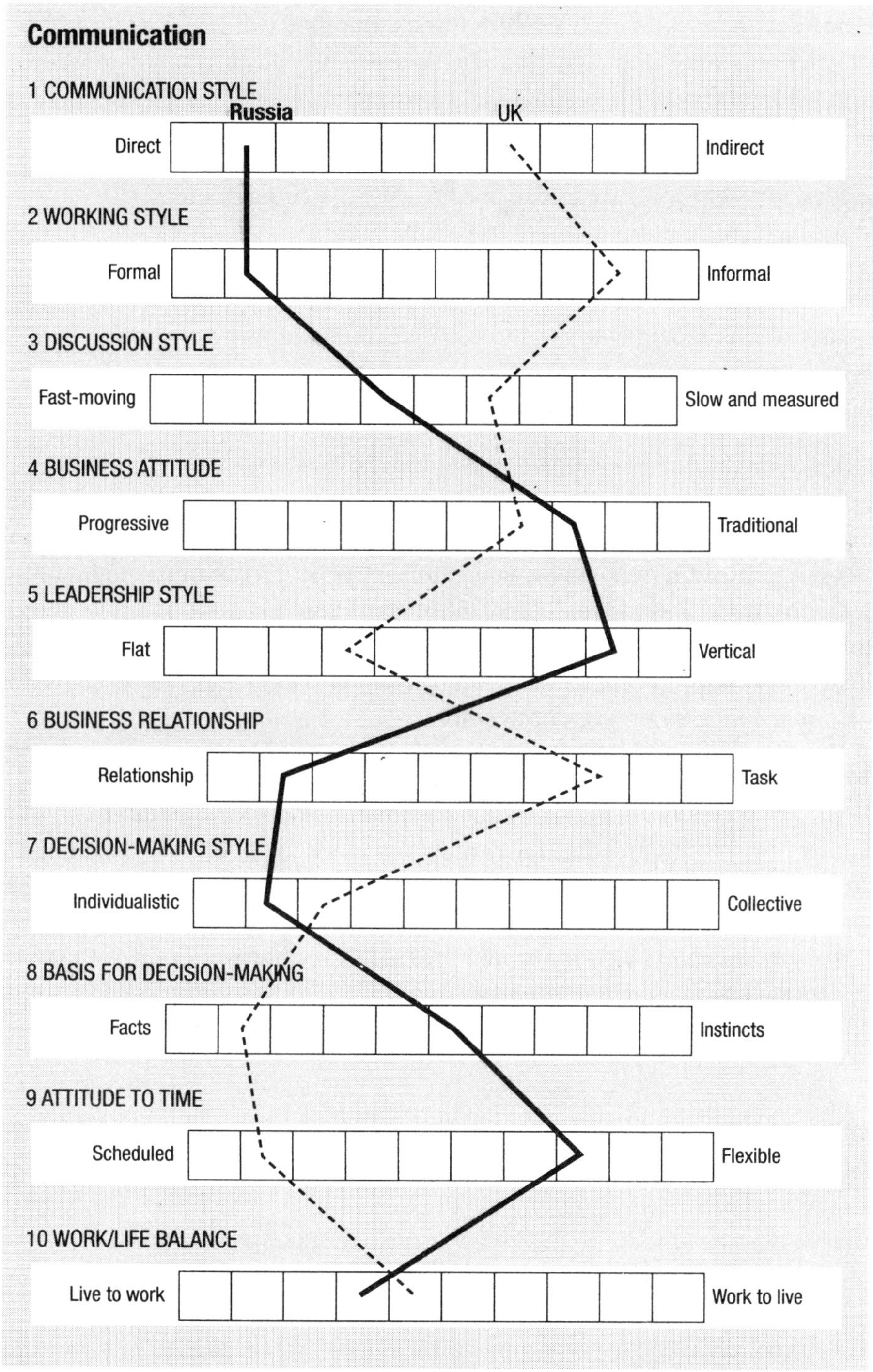

Communication

Good speaking skills are valued in Russia, but they will also note your tone of voice and body language. Russians appreciate a warm, relaxed approach, and will often ask you personal questions about your family and life in your home country. They can be quite tactile with people they regards as friends, but they are also direct and blunt, and mean what they say. This is unlike most relationship-focused countries, but learn to appreciate their candour rather than fear it.

Russians are interested in the credibility of the speaker in terms of experience, qualifications and knowledge and you must establish this. Strong eye contact is important, and you should shake hands firmly. It will help if you have your business card printed in two languages – yours and Russian.

Russians have a moderate attention span of 30-45 minutes. They will not appreciate you starting off with a joke, so keep your presentation serious, and include facts and technical details. But given what we've already said about the Russian personality, you can feel free to inject some emotion into your proposals. Russians enjoy looking at new ideas, but they distrust anything that sounds too official. Avoid words such as 'aggressive' and 'compromise': instead, talk about meeting each other halfway, or propose actions that depend on equal concessions from both sides.

Russians are sensitive to what they consider *nyeculturny* (uncultured) behaviour. This includes swearing, not depositing outer garments in the *garderobe,* lounging and standing with hands in pockets, shouting or laughing loudly in public and whistling indoors. People shake hands on meeting and leave-taking (older men may kiss a woman's hand). Smiling on greeting is not automatic (it helps to explain the tradition of surly service in Russian restaurants, shops and hotels), but shaking fists and the American A-OK gesture is considered rude.

Organization

Business hours are 9am-5pm Monday to Friday. It's important to allow plenty of time for appointments. Meetings can start late and run much longer than planned: punctuality is not generally a Russian virtue.

Meetings and negotiations

Meetings in Russia tend to be long, and often followed by meals. They're also quite formal, reflecting the hierarchical structure of Russian business, although it is important to preserve *uravnilovka* – egalitarianism, or the idea that nobody is better than anybody else. You should respect this formality in your style and dress, especially at first encounters. Russians may start and finish late, so be flexible in timing. Meetings may also be subject to interruptions.

When it comes to negotiating in Russia, good personal relationships are what get you through. Your counterpart should like you and trust you. Russian business depends to some extent on *blat*, a network of contacts and favour. Although it is less strong than it was once was, it will help if you can operate in the spirit of *blat*.

Most business is done face-to-face, so frequent visits or phone calls to Russia are important. Russians have a variable negotiation style ranging from extreme patience – sitting you out – to strong confrontation. Stay calm: patience is also the strongest card that you can play. Russian negotiations may proceed by concession, so it's important to build some into your proposal and offer them at appropriate moments.

If there is disagreement, try to show that you understand their difficulties. Be direct and straightforward. Share in their soul-searching of what is wrong or causing problems. Talk in terms of personal recommendation rather than of direct orders or regulations. Build up trust through clarity of action, keep your inner circle small and at all times aim to build trust.

However, it is important to monitor subsequent performance. Don't put facts before feelings and don't be sophisticated or devious because Russians are privately quite straightforward.

Russians often send a written confirmation after an agreement has been reached to protect themselves. They are, however, prepared to renegotiate the fine print of a contract after it has been signed if it seems appropriate.

Team-working

Teams need to be built on individual trust, so it's important to establish a personal link with each member of the group you're dealing with, and to know them well. Asking advice is important, and is not seen as a weakness. Once people cooperate with you, it is then important not to disappoint them. Make sure the working process is highly organized and structured, and that you and they know who is responsible for what. Unofficial channels and processes are as important as official ones, and can cut through red tape.

Team strengths in Russia tend to be their ability to forge relationships, and come up with imaginative solutions. They're less strong on implementing and completing tasks. Team members are selected primarily on their competence for the role, although educational qualifications and family connections can also be influential. The team leader makes all decisions, and is usually well connected to other decision-makers.

Leadership and decision-making

It's important to bear in mind that Russia only began to evolve from its combination of traditional patterns and Soviet coercion in the early 1990s, so it is hardly surprising that Russian business tends to be hierarchical. The top man in the company makes all the decisions, which has two corollaries: it slows down the process, and it means that you must make sure that you're negotiating with the right person.

In Russia, it's who you know, not what you know. As in many other countries, the exchange of favours ensures that things get done: in Russia, this system is known as *blat*. Although women have equal status to men in many areas of business, especially in academia and administration, at top levels posts are mainly held by men. Women visitors may be subject to 'old world' courtesy and gallantry, but may also feel patronized as senior Russian businessmen are less used to dealing with female executives on an equal basis. Russian senior managers, both men and women, tend to dress to impress, and observe some formality in their attire and public behaviour. You should do the same.

Socializing and gift-giving

Don't go empty-handed: gifts may be exchanged with a foreign visitor if a meeting has gone well. Russian executives appreciate the offer of good quality presents, especially those carrying a well-known logo. On the other hand, a small business gift may not be treated seriously.

An invitation to a Russian home is something to be prized – you should definitely accept. Dinners tend to take place early (around 6pm), and it's important to prepare something complimentary to say as toasting the host, the country and the relationship is common.

In a meeting, the table may be laid with *zakuski* (snacks) and even vodka. If so, eat and drink sparingly. If you are hosting the meeting it will be appreciated if you provide some snacks, but alcohol is not necessary.

Great gifts: good quality brand-name products. Flowers, alcohol or a luxury food item are appreciated at a home visit.

Avoid giving: Poor-quality items – the days when you could get away with secondhand jeans, tights or magazines are 30 years out of date.

Conversation topics

Ice-breakers	Ice-makers
Russian culture, literature and art	Chechnya
Russian achievements	Criticize Russia (even if Russians do it)
World War Two (the Great Patriotic War in Russia)	The Communist period

Doing business in the United Kingdom

Doing business in the United Kingdom

Five Ways to Succeed	Five Ways to Fail
Deliver on time, without drama	Boast about your achievements
Arrive at meetings punctually	Talk for an hour in a presentation
If you're having difficulties, ask advice immediately rather than risk missing a deadline	Phone people in the evening about work
Check at the end of a meeting exactly what the Brits expect of you	Let a colleague down once he or she believes they can depend on you
Join them for a beer after work, or in the gym (many Brits now avoid alcohol)	Be patronizing to women

Overview

A group of north-west European islands, and a member of the EU since 1973, the UK is a monarchy that never seems quite sure whether its key alliance lies with Europe, the USA or the Commonwealth. It has always resisted joining the Eurozone, maintains sterling as its currency and opts out of much of the European Union's Common Agricultural Policy. It claims a 'special relationship' with the USA that extends back to the two countries' common roots (the Pilgrim Fathers sailed from Plymouth, on Britain's south-west coast, to America in 1611), and remains a leading member of the Commonwealth, a loose association of countries that were formerly part of the British Empire. In some of them (Canada, for example) the British monarch is still considered Head of State.

Its 60 million population and common language (English) conceal quite deep social divisions. First there are the four main nationalities; English (the majority), Scots, Welsh and Northern Irish. Then there are the main migrant groups who have settled in the UK from Commonwealth countries, principally the West Indies, India and Pakistan and most recently the Central and Eastern European arrivals from the new EU entrants in 2004. Finally, within England itself there is a traditional rivalry between the old industrial north and the more affluent south.

Britain claims that it is a multicultural country with strict laws against discrimination by race, religion, gender, age, disability and sexual orientation,as well as respect for human rights. This policy has, however, been thrown into question by the 7/11 terrorist bombings of 2005 and debates about religious dress and separatism. Economically, the UK is placed seventh in Goldman Sach's forecast of the world's richest countries in 2050. Its strength lies in the City of London's financial services sector and in Britons' personal wealth in a buoyant property market.

You would imagine that a nation whose language has become the global business language would be easy to understand. But this is not always the case with the British. They remain an idiosyncratic island race: frustratingly insular, reluctant to display overt emotion, and ambiguous in what they say.

The British are often uneasy and nervous when dealing with other people, even amongst themselves. Perhaps this explains their reliance on their notoriously unpredictable weather as a subject of small talk. It's a shield to save having to talk about – heaven forbid! – one's personal life or feelings. Americans get exasperated by the British fear of not saying clearly what they feel and what they want, and this impassive, undemonstrative approach also confuses many other cultures. You should, of course, remember the differences between the UK's four different cultures: the Scots can be healthily frank, while the Irish and Welsh regard themselves as far more open and passionate than the English.

Despite these drawbacks, combined with the devastating economic blows of two world wars and the loss of empire in the twentieth century, Britain has emerged into the twenty-first century as one of the world's major trading nations. The Brits themselves exist in a curious mix of regret for a lost idyllic past, when life was supposedly less tense and less violent, and a relaxed contemporary hedonism.

Values and attitudes

Just like any other culture, Britain is full of paradoxes. On the one hand, the British continue to believe in the values of tradition, caution, restraint and fair play. They support the underdog, tolerate eccentricity (often by ignoring it) and think that taking part is more important than winning. Modesty and politeness are also important to them. This, combined with their zeal for personal privacy, can produce bizarre effects such as a reluctance to say what they actually do in their working life. If asked at a party what his job is, a Briton might say, 'I'm in advertising,' when in fact he's the high-performing CEO of a major advertising agency.

The British are also famous for their legendary ironic and self-deprecating humour. They find it useful as an ice-breaker at meetings, to defuse tension and cover potentially embarrassing moments. The difficulty for visitors is that they just don't get what's being said, or, even worse, take it literally. Britons working internationally, or dealing with foreign clients in their own country, should develop more awareness of this pitfall and modify what they're saying or writing accordingly.

What has changed in Britain in recent decades is that the country has become much more informal in its social and business customs, and has shed much of its former respect for institutions, title and age. In this it follows the American model. People use first names very quickly, even to bosses, and the words 'Sir' and 'Madam' are now mainly used only by sales assistants in shops. Britons do, however, maintain a generally high level of respect for the law and for procedures, which largely explains the absence of corruption in British business and politics.

This combination of tradition and rapid change can make life confusing for the foreigner in Britain. The secret is to watch and listen carefully, and to learn to read between the lines to try and establish what the British are really saying. In this respect Britain is closer to some Eastern cultures than Western ones. It can take years to fully decipher British codes, but this is also true of any culture where much of what is truly meant remains unspoken.

Cultural style

Britain is a systems society, very much governed by a strong legal system and a principle of fair play. The job comes first, the relationship second and professionalism comes before friendship or a relationship. Once renowned for its formality, Britain has become one of the world's most informal business communities with all levels of society on first name terms. This informality is crucial to successful communication, and many foreign business people, used to the stereotypical image of a 1950s' English male in bowler hat and pin-stripe suit, carrying a rolled umbrella, still fail to recognize it.

UK cultural style

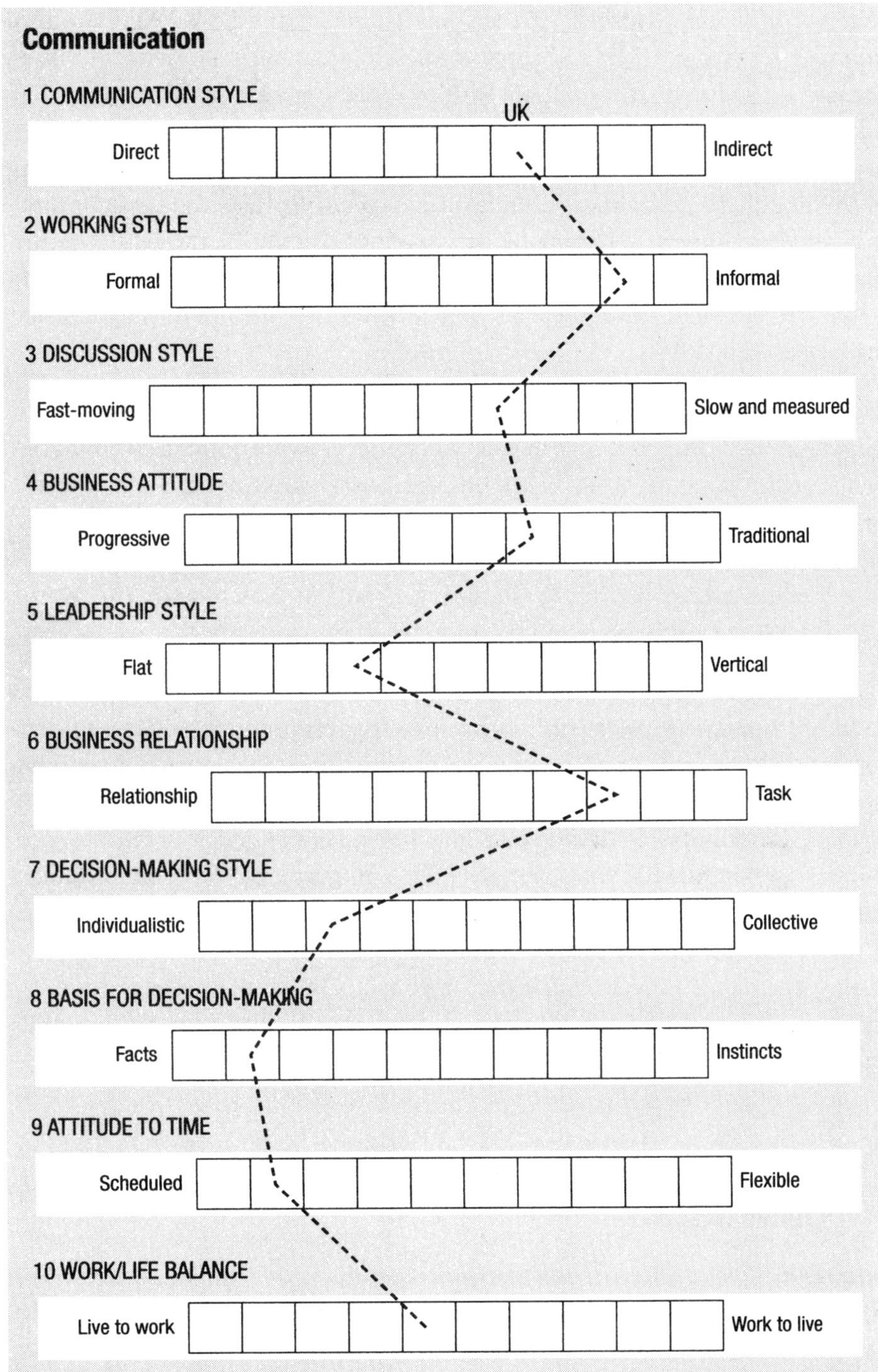

Communication

As we have already seen, Britain has copied many social and business mannerisms from the USA. People use first names almost immediately: many bosses actively encourage their staff to call them by their first name. This informality even extends to those you are dealing with purely by phone or email: the person you have just contacted responds using your first name even though they may know nothing about you. The practice is uncomfortable to many foreigners, and has one very obvious drawback. If the relationship goes wrong and disagreement sets in, you are left in an uncomfortable position: having to address someone in a friendly way when you are feeling anything but that.

British style is to be courteous and friendly but detached. It's polite to shake hands at the beginning and end of meetings. However, if you're a frequent visitor to a company, you will not be expected to shake hands with everyone in the office, only with those with whom you're dealing directly. You'll receive a limp, tenuous handshake from a surprising number of Britons: it's their nervousness at confronting someone new, combined with the British reluctance to reveal too much emotion too soon.

The British are practical, empirical people, and distrust too much theory, philosophizing and idealism. So pack your presentations full of attainable objectives, concrete detail and provable statistics. Time your presentation to last around 20 to 40 minutes, depending on the gravity of your proposal, and allow opportunity for debate and questions. People will concentrate more on the content of what you say than on how you say it or your body language. Remember that even if your audience is wildly excited about your project, their response may be muted: it's that British reserve at work, that fear of being seen to be too enthusiastic. If your audience is highly divided, the discussion is unlikely to be heated: a sense of calm and proportion usually prevails in British business.

Organization

The British are renowned worldwide for their punctuality, so ensure that you're there on time. Some British managers can get agitated if someone is as little as two or three minutes late. However, road congestion and rail disruption are common in the UK, and the Brits are becoming more tolerant towards people who are delayed by genuine travel problems. You can defuse any tension by getting the mobile phone number of the person you're going to meet: if you do get into a jam, call or text to let them know what's happened and when you expect to arrive.

Office hours tend to start at 8.30am or 9am, although many professions in London, such as the media, tend to arrive at 10am and leave correspondingly later in the evening. As in the USA, eating lunch at your workstation while surfing the web is becoming commonplace.

Meetings and negotiations

A formal business meeting in Britain will generally run to an agenda. If the discussion wanders too far from it, the chairperson may feel uncomfortable and try to drag everyone back on line. If important new matters arise in these digressions, the chair will often suggest that they are put on the agenda at the next meeting, or, if urgent, addressed rapidly by a sub-group of people outside the meeting. Meetings generally end on time.

Following the American example, British meetings can be highly egalitarian affairs. Managers are often happy to sit beside staff and not at the top of the table, and will try to draw everyone into the discussion. The ideal is to achieve consensus so that everyone feels that they 'own' the decision. The British like to arrive at decisions and action points in their meetings, which managers are then expected to follow up. The focus is on action rather than going through an exhaustive discussion of options.

In debates the British tend to avoid dogmatic and absolute statements, and use words such as 'perhaps' and 'maybe' to imply that alternative points of view might be valid. In negotiations they are often willing to compromise to achieve a win-win situation in which both parties can feel that the agreement offers a reasonable deal and prospects of further cooperation.

Team-working

Operating in management teams is a basic principle of British business. This includes sharing information, regular briefings and teams taking credit for success (or getting angry if the boss does so without crediting them.) Team members are chosen for their experience and qualifications, but also on the basis of 'usefulness'. The team leader is responsible for setting the objectives and tasks, but team members take responsibility for implementation: delegation is an important principle of British management.

Consultation is important, although team members will normally abide by majority decisions. However, the way of giving feedback can sometimes be quite adversarial. Criticism should not be seen as an attack on personal competence.

Leadership and decision-making

American management approaches and methods have also influenced this area of British business. Power is often devolved downwards, and people are expected to 'champion' and to take responsibility for their particular projects. Britain operates on a 'tight' time environment, so managers are also expected to deliver on schedule, or have a pretty good reason for why it's not possible. The more enlightened companies welcome input from any member of staff, no matter how modest their experience.

British managers often have fewer academic and technical qualifications compared to their equivalents in other countries, but tend to compensate for this by having more on-the-job experience. Some cultures regard British practices as unprofessional and slack: 'muddling through' is the British term for pulling everything together in the end, but this approach does not impress the Germans, for example.

The general management attitude in the UK is warm but detached, and relationships tend to be functional rather than personal. If confrontation emerges, it will be resolved face-to-face by focusing on the issues rather than on the personalities.

Socializing and gift-giving

'Going for a pint' after work is common in Britain. Join in: it's a good place to make friends and get to know the Brits, and you don't have to drink alcohol. Despite their reputation for reserve, the British are quite quick to invite visitors to their homes for dinner or for lunch at the weekend. If you are asked, don't arrive more than 15 minutes late, or you risk disrupting the hosts' timing. The evening will probably finish by 10pm or 11pm. Take wine: Britain is not a major wine-growing culture, so 'bringing a bottle' is an accepted convention. You may also want to take flowers or some chocolates for your hostess. Dress is almost always smart casual in out-of-office occasions.

Gift-giving is not necessary to the business process: it is more common to invite people to a good lunch to express appreciation. If you wish to offer a present, something from your country is always acceptable: remember that the British tradition is to open gifts immediately so that both giver and receiver can share the pleasure.

Great gifts: Wine, chocolate, a speciality from your own country.

Avoid giving: Most presents are acceptable. Maybe ask a florist about appropriate flowers. Red roses or white lilies may send the wrong message.

Conversation topics

Ice-breakers	Ice-makers
British weather – it never fails	Religion, politics and immigration
Property prices – but don't ask someone directly what theirs is worth	People's salaries and personal worth
Laments about traffic, parking and public transport	'Why do British people put their parents in homes?'

Doing business in Germany

Doing business in Germany

Five Ways to Succeed	Five Ways to Fail
Demonstrate efficiency and punctuality	Be disorganized and ignore due process
Be straightforward and direct	Promise and fail to deliver
Do what you say you will do	Do things without consultation
Find out the rules and follow them	Go over the heads of line managers or reports
Respect the management hierarchy	Be over-familiar with colleagues

Overview

Germany's economic potential in the 21st century remains a topic of hot debate among cynics and optimists. Some believe that the world's biggest exporter, and its third largest economy, can shrug off the sluggish performance that has been a feature of recent decades and compete effectively with energetic nations to the east, both in Europe and in Asia. Others claim that any changes that Germany is making to its internal systems are inadequate, and that any business surges and unemployment dips that the Germans experience may be only temporary.

The country is weighed down by problems typical of Western European nations. Its social costs and taxes are high, and its population is ageing and unwilling to surrender privileges. In addition, Germany continues to modernize and invest in the east of the country, pumping millions into the former Soviet satellite territory. All this, and the threat of jobs disappearing eastwards from its manufacturing sector, which is already suffering unemployment problems. The government is struggling to address all these challenges, and it is hard to imagine that a country so rich in resources will not manage to throw off at least some of its shackles.

Geographically, Germany has three main areas, the lowlands in the north, the uplands in the centre and the mountains in the south. There are sixteen states, or *Länder*, with the federal capital in Berlin. Like many parts of Europe, Germany preserves a cultural difference between its Lutheran north and its Roman Catholic south (Frankfurt and below). Southerners tend to be more expansive than their northern compatriots.

Values and attitudes

Efficiency is imperative to the Germans. In business they seek *Ordnung* (order) and *Klarheit* (clarity) to achieve an organized system, and they expect a strong work ethic, reliability and honesty from their employees and partners. Formality, punctuality, fairness and obedience to authority are other German characteristics. All of this means that the Germans excel at the detailed planning of projects, and completing them on time and to specification.

The tone of many work environments can be serious and formal, which probably contributes to the misconception that Germans lack a sense of humour. But talk to foreign business people who have worked in Germany, and they'll give you a different version: when the Germans are off-duty, they can be plenty of fun.

Incredibly, nearly 70 years after the end of hostilities, a minority of visitors to Germany finds it necessary to raise the subject of the Second World War in the context of business meetings. Sadly, some of these insensitives are British, probably swayed unconsciously by views in the country's notoriously xenophobic tabloid press. But today's Germany is a new one, run by different generations, and nothing angers them more than those outdated jibes. Focus on contemporary European, business and world issues if you want to succeed in Germany.

Many visitors remark on the difference between German business and domestic life. The friendliness and coziness (*Gemütlichkeit*) of German homes contrast starkly with the utilitarian nature of many of their offices. For Germans, light conversation about everyday things (*Unterhaltung*) is kept for the kitchen table. In bars a table is kept for regular clients to drink and talk. Although it is changing, Germans still maintain a stronger separation between home and office than Britons or Americans do. *'Dienst ist Dienst und Schnaps ist Schnaps'* – work is work and play (drink) is play' – is an important distinction in their culture.

Truth and duty are important values for Germans. They are brought up to believe that using their language correctly and precisely is a point of honour, and that to say what you mean and mean what you say is important. This leads to a degree of directness that can come across as rude or arrogant to foreigners, although this is rarely intentional. Germans, on the other hand, can find the British style of indirect and non-committal communication quite hard to take.

Germans also have a strong sense of social responsibility and citizenship. This affects everything from their attitude to organization to their recycling habits. By and large they show tolerance to foreigners, but they're prepared to remind them of their social responsibilities, such as how to put out the rubbish, when to wash or not wash cars, and when to make noise. What the British sometimes see as intolerable intrusion on personal liberty, the Germans simply regard as good citizenship.

Doing things thoroughly (*Gründlichkeit*) and in the right way is also a German value. Within limits, they would rather things happened later (as long as they are well-informed in advance) than with lower quality by taking short cuts.

Cultural style

German and British cultural behaviour is broadly comparable and is different in degree rather than by type of behaviour. We are equally time-conscious, task- and systems-minded, and reserved in our emotions. The one difference is that British business tends to be less formal in style and approach.

Germany/UK cultural styles – a comparison

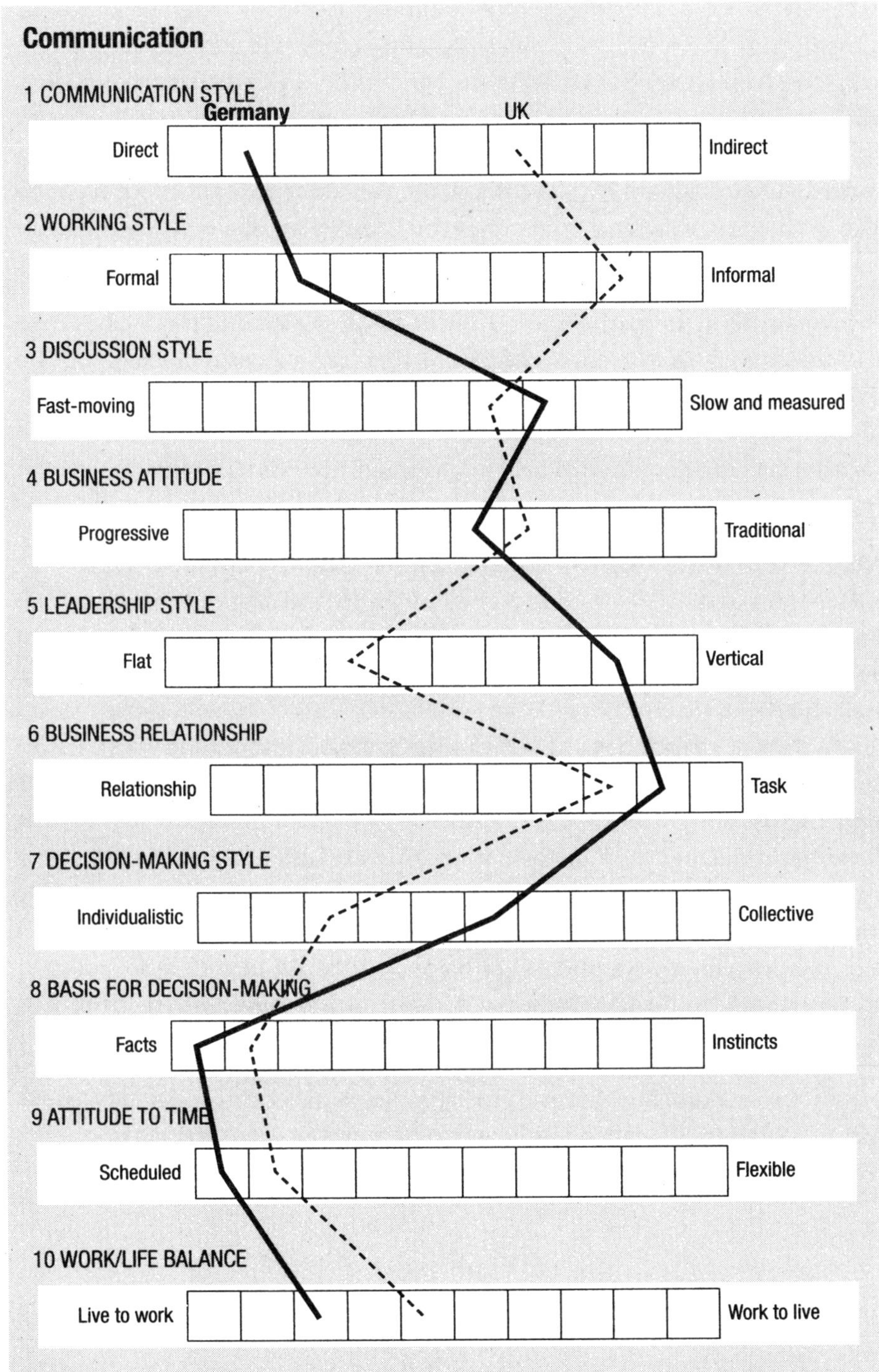

Communication

Germany is still a surname culture. Although Germans may use your first name outside the office, in business meetings they will address each other, including women, by surnames alone. Naturally, they're experts at decoding when to switch between surnames and first names. British and American visitors to Germany should forget the matey office culture that exists in their home countries, where employees are often encouraged to address even the MD or CEO by his or her first name. You'll look a bit of a cowboy if you do that in Germany.

Shaking hands at the beginning and end of business meetings and the business day is essential. Good working relationships can be easily formed, but be careful not to lapse into over-familiarity. Formality is important in office dealings, and endearments and diminutives – using the short form of someone's name – are not acceptable. When addressing women, use *Frau Schmidt* rather than *Fraulein Schmidt*, except for young people.

When you're presenting to a German audience, they will expect to hear the full technical details of your idea. They prefer logical arguments rather than emotional 'hunch' type proposals, and the content is more important for them than body language. They also look for well worked-out proposals, with evidence that it has been tried or piloted successfully elsewhere, and will appreciate an 'academic' sell, stressing the benefits and pointing out and dealing with possible issues rather than a 'hard sell'. They feel perfectly capable of making up their own minds on the evidence presented. The attention span in German meetings is usually long – up to an hour. They will ask detailed questions and expect in-depth answers. They also have a great respect for the truth as they see it, and this may lead them to appear unusually outspoken at times. As a rule, expect politeness but don't look for flattery. It's best to avoid jokes in presentations or formal discussions, and during office hours generally. Audiences are unlikely to interrupt you except to seek clarification.

It used to be traditional in Germany to follow up phone or email communications with a written confirmation by conventional mail, but even German managers are now saying that life is too short to observe this at all times.

Organization

The office tone in Germany tends to be quiet and measured, and the working environment clean and well-ordered. A clear desk is admired, and there's a tendency towards a closed-door culture rather than open-plan arrangements. Working hours in Germany tend to be from 8am to 5pm or 5.30pm. People often eat lunch in the office or the office café for 30 minutes or an hour.

Meetings and negotiations

Meetings in Germany are used to implement planning, brief participants and agree decisions. The pace may be slow if technical issues are presented in detail, and the agenda will be followed in order. The discussion will seek consensus and common ground, reliable partners and long-term profit. Be punctual, dress formally, observe the hierarchical seating plan, and be serious in your approach. Jokes to lighten the atmosphere are generally not appreciated in meetings.

Team-working

A typical team in a German company will be formed of individuals selected for particular technical competencies. Everyone will have a strong sense of their position in the organization's hierarchy, and will conform to company procedures; they will also regard deadlines as fixed. Progress might be slow and methodical, but the leader will be expected to give firm and confident direction.

Leadership and decision-making

Management tends to be by consensus and consultation, backed by a great deal of research. Juniors show seniors considerable respect. Equally, you should respect the hierarchy: never split or undermine superiors in German organizations, and do not bypass people by going higher to complain or search for decisions. Propose constructive alternatives rather than offering criticism. Differences of opinion are best dealt with in face-to-face discussions rather than via a third party or on paper.

German managers often spend more years at university than their counterparts in other countries, and may not enter the workforce until they are 27 or even older. German managers and business leaders may have doctorates, and the appellation *Herr Doktor* is not uncommon. Key factors in promotion in Germany are a person's education and qualifications, track record and seniority. Managers change jobs less often than their British and US colleagues; there is no difference in the status and treatment of men and women in business.

Socializing and gift-giving

Germans have a much more rigid definition of friendship than exists in Britain. In Germany a friend is a close friend for life, and the relationship with a foreigner will be initiated from the German side. If you speak a little German, never use *Du* (the informal way to say 'you') to a colleague until he or she invites you to do so. Keep to the formal *Sie* form.

Evening business dinners take place from 7pm. They're usually formal affairs, so wear a lounge suit or a jacket and tie; a trouser suit is appropriate for women. Titles may be used (*Herr Professor, Frau Doktor*), and there might be a formal seating plan. The host will propose any toasts, and you can then reciprocate: don't touch glasses until the first toast has been raised. You can talk business before or after the meal, but not during dinner. Remember that out of hours business contacts are discouraged in Germany.

Great gifts: unwrapped flowers, chocolates, and presents from your region. Wrap presents properly, except flowers.

Avoid giving: lilies and chrysanthemums (associated with funerals), and intimate gifts such as perfume or jewellery; be careful about wine – many Germans have good cellars.

Conversation topics

Ice-breakers	Ice-makers
Show an interest in German and European affairs	Premature talk about your hosts' private life and personal circumstances
Overseas travel and holidays – Germans are great travellers	Germany's role in World War Two
Sport, especially football and the UEFA and World Cup competitions	'Five-one', harking back to England's defeat of Germany in a 2001 World Cup qualifier

Doing business in France

Doing business in France

Five Ways to Succeed	Five Ways to Fail
Understand the free market v social contract debate in France	Do it all in English – if you have no French, apologize
Show appreciation of French culture	Ignore the French intellectual approach
Make sure that French guests eat and drink well	Swear and drink too much
Maintain a degree of formality until you're invited to use first names	Dig up the old clichés about Anglo-French conflict
Be logical and consistent in negotiations, and when you reach a decision, stick with it	Decline lunch invitations and buy a sandwich to eat at your desk

Overview

If you've ever felt a little overawed about the prospect of making a business trip to France, don't worry – your reaction is normal. The French can seem so unnervingly cool and worldly, and sometimes aloof, especially to Britons and Americans. It's hardly surprising: they're great thinkers, and they value intelligence and eloquence. Philosophy is a part of a French child's education, and logical thinking and a passion for abstract argument are inherent in the people.

This can cause problems for visitors from more pragmatic cultures, such as Britain and the USA, who often claim that the French are 'difficult'. But this simplistic dismissal ignores the contribution that they have made to philosophy, literature, science and the arts over centuries. The French are rigorous debaters, and they enjoy exercising this skill. Travel with a well-prepared proposition, think through the answers to all the awkward questions they could bring up, and learn from the experience.

The French are very conscious of the status of being French, and invest in big, imaginative projects aimed at increasing their international prestige. You see the architectural expressions of these ambitions every time you walk around Paris. The French also feel frustrated that their beloved language is rapidly losing ground to English in global business and diplomatic circles, so if you can talk at least some *français*, it will help to earn the respect of your new colleagues.

There are close links in France between industry and government, and the top echelons of both are educated at the *Grandes Écoles*, graduate schools entered by competitive examination. To be an *énarque*, a graduate of the *École Nationale d'Administration*, is to be marked as a future political or business leader. The structure of the state is mirrored by its major businesses, which are often centralized, ordered, legalistic and elitist.

New president Nicolas Sarkozy is now trying to deal with the crisis of self-confidence that has affected France in recent years. Its tax burden remains one of the highest in Europe, and unemployment hovers around 10%. Most French people accept that the country must adapt in the face of globalization, yet no one seems to want to surrender the privileges bequeathed by their social system. While comfortably-off Britons scour *La France Profonde* in search of second homes, many younger French people openly express their admiration for Anglo-Saxon business models, and some 200,000-300,000 are said to be working in London. It's important to see France in context, however: it retains rich agricultural, manufacturing and service sectors, and boasts one of the world's lowest poverty rates of only 6% (more than 20% of children live in poverty in the USA and 15% in the UK, according to Unicef).

Values and attitudes

Building relationships is important in French business, and it's a process that French people do not like to rush. Lunches and dinners are important opportunities to develop these bonds. Although shorter lunch breaks are becoming more common, much of France stops work between 12 noon and 2pm, and in August many firms close down for the annual summer break.

The French are quite formal in public and preserve the distinction between the familiar *tu* and the formal *vous*, two different ways of saying 'you'. Use *vous* with people you know until they invite you to use *tu*. Saying *Bonjour monsieur* or *Bonjour madame* is important in greetings: it preserves a degree of formality until you get to know people.

The French often criticize the British for inconsistency – not following through on decisions and changing their minds after something has apparently been decided. In turn, the British accuse the French of 'selfishness' – acting in their own national and commercial interest at the expense of others. To succeed in doing business in France it is vital to escape these stereotypes, and accept that there is a French way of doing things to which the British need to conform.

Cultural style

The French tend to be more relationship-oriented than the British, although this varies according to the business or profession you're operating in. It's therefore not surprising to find that entertainment plays a larger part in French business than in the UK. In the office the French are more formal than the British, and it's easy for UK visitors to underestimate this. In Paris time is considered to be more important than in the south, but the French consider themselves to be generally less time-sensitive than the British. They also tend to find the British much less prepared to show their emotions in the business environment than they are.

France/UK cultural styles – a comparison

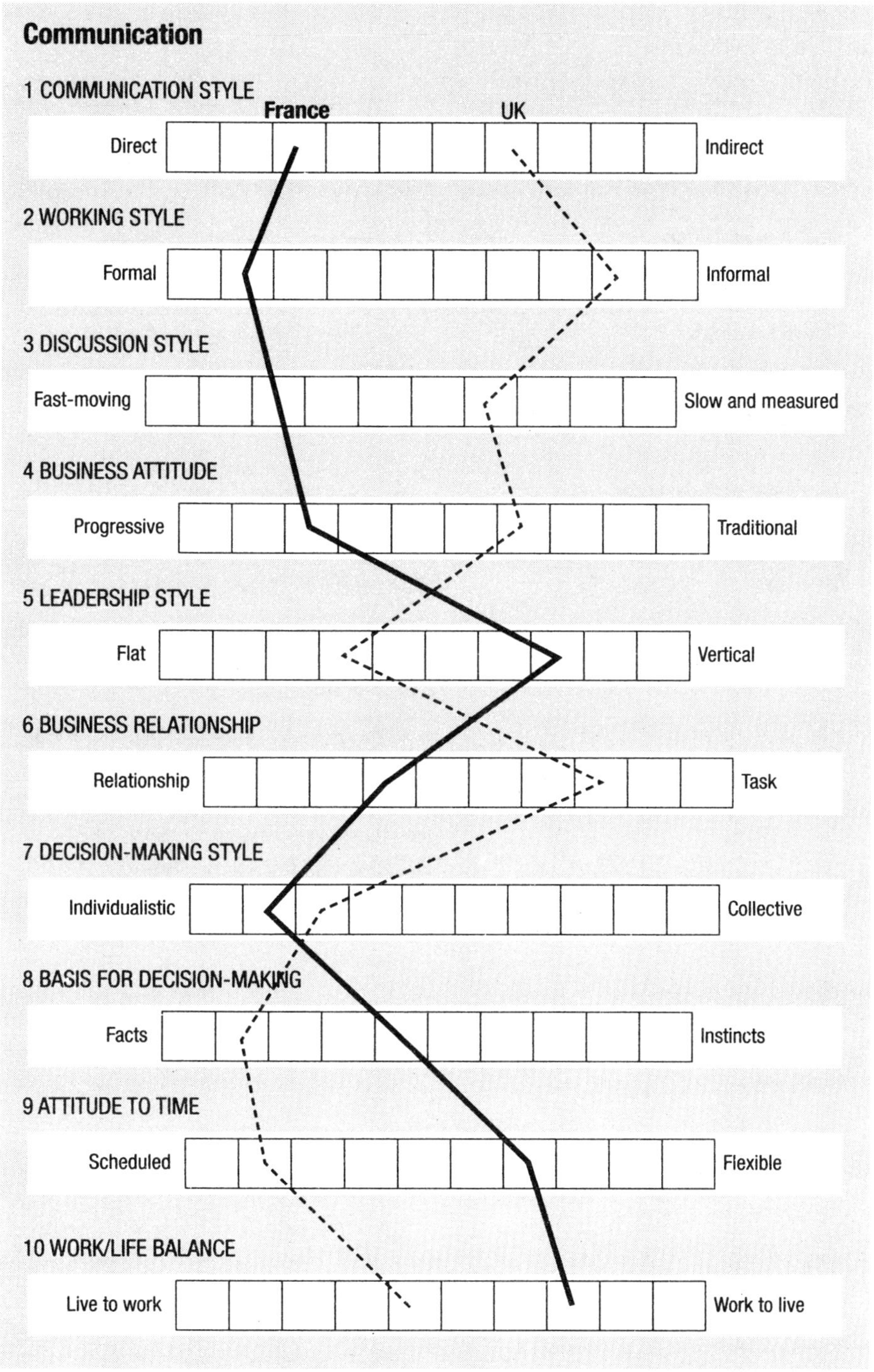

What people misunderstand about the French

Many foreigners misinterpret the French. This table may help to avoid some potential collisions.

Foreigners say...	**The French say...**
The French are obstinate	We believe we are right
They're too emotional	We are Latin, but we also believe in rationality
They're too direct	This reflects the precision of the French language
They talk too much	We build up logical arguments
They never get to the point	We like to consider all aspects of a question before making a decision
They can't keep to the agenda	We believe everything is related
They're fussy	We have a clear idea of what we want, and we argue for it
They have extravagant ideas	We have vision but we also understand detail
They're poor team workers	We are individualistic in our own lives but our government exercises strong central control – we manage the two
They prefer ideas to facts	Statistics can prove anything: ideas are what move people
They're opinionated	We know what's best for France

Communication

The French love of logic and elegance means that you should be explicit and clear in what you are saying. Listen also for the logic behind the communication when a French person is speaking. Focus on the content of what you want to express, but remember that body language is also important in France. Demonstrate eagerness and enthusiasm for what you believe in, and use gestures for emphasis if you feel comfortable doing so. However, this is not an art that comes easily to most people from Anglo-Saxon cultures, so it's probably better to keep to your natural style rather than look like an overactive TV presenter.

The French are often categorical when they speak, and feel happy to express their disagreements directly and openly. Don't be put off by the Gallic '*Bouf!*', a dismissive snort or sniff that indicates dissent. Rely on factual evidence to prove your case, but demonstrate that you understand other points of view, even if you disagree with them. The French enjoy using wit in business discussions, but avoid criticizing France.

Assume a relatively short attention span of about 20 minutes when you are addressing a French audience, so keep your presentation moving briskly. Stress the style, imaginative features and elegance of your idea or product, and expect active audience involvement and questions.

Organization

The 35-hour working week introduced in the Socialist era in an attempt to create more jobs has effectively been relaxed in France for private companies. They can now offer employees up to 13 hours overtime, allowing them to put in up to 48 hours a week - the maximum allowed by the European Union. Business leaders had complained that the 35-hour week, introduced in 1998, had failed to create jobs and was uncompetitive. However, the limit has not been scrapped - it continues in force in France's large public sector and will remain the standard working week in the private sector.

Meetings and negotiations

The purpose of business meetings in France is coordination, briefing and allocation of tasks rather than to arrive at decisions. Given the French desire to debate intellectual propositions as well as practical points, you should outline the general principles of your idea before you get into the details. Rationality and logic are important to them: simply having a 'warm feeling' for something will not do, so go in armed with plenty of knowledge about your product, your market and its trends, and what the opposition is up to.

An agenda might be circulated, but no one will expect to keep to it. French meetings can be long and wordy, and the debate can become an intellectual exercise. The French believe that clarity of thought is achieved through intensive discussion, so it is important not to rush the proceedings. Expect to be questioned if there is imprecision in your proposition.

Meetings are usually formal occasions. Dress well, and expect a hierarchical seating arrangement. Surnames and formal introductions are used, and jackets are usually kept on. The style of the meeting will probably be polite and formal: use respect at all times. The French like to find out your position without revealing theirs until late in the discussion. Their approach is likely to be perceptive and opportunistic, but cautious.

Team-working

The criterion for selecting team members is specialization in a field required by the work or project. A strong leader will be the point of reference for all decisions, and relationships between team members are often based on competition rather than collaboration. This is something that comes from France's rigourous education system. Individual team members may act within their competence (or sometimes extend it) without waiting for group consensus. The authority of the team leader is essential in ensuring group harmony and completion of goals.

Leadership and decision-making

It's important to be *correct* in style and manner and to be seen as *sérieux* (professional) in France. The PDG – *président directeur général* – decides the strategy, and managers draw up and execute the plan. The French say, *une entreprise n'est pas une démocratie* – a business is not a democracy.

French companies take time to reach decisions, and prefer to examine a problem or proposition from every angle. It is considered rude to end a meeting if the business to be conducted has not been concluded, which can affect overall punctuality. There is a stress on comprehensive, well-structured and well-written reports and studies.

Socializing and gift-giving

Business entertaining in France is usually formal in style and takes place in restaurants. Check the dress code with your hosts: smart casual is increasingly acceptable. Smoking is a declining habit even among the French, although you'll often see people lighting up at the table, and certainly in the bar, without any embarrassment. Britons often see a visit to France as a reason to indulge in a little too much *vin*, but resist this. Drunkenness or over-familiar talk after too many glasses is not seen as cool by the French. Likewise, leave at home those tired references to the supposedly ancient rivalry between England and France: they've all been dragged out so many times before.

French people keep their private and public lives very separate, and tend not to invite visitors to their homes until real bonds have been established. Smoking is common in people's homes, but it's courteous to ask before you light up. Chewing gum at meetings and social events is considered rude.

Great gifts: flowers, in odd numbers and not yellow; also avoid chrysanthemums (associated with funerals) and carnations (may be seen as a sign of bad will). Chocolates or liqueur.

Avoid giving: wine – it may suggest they don't know their vintages.

Conversation topics

Ice-breakers	Ice-makers
France's fascinating regions	Compare French v UK unemployment rates
Food and wine	Ancient Franco-British rivalries: a well-outworn topic
Six Nations rugby, World Cup football	Why you've abandoned French wine for New World varieties

Doing business in Italy

Doing business in Italy

Five Ways to Succeed	Five Ways to Fail
Build good personal relationships and keep in contact	Criticize or belittle Italy and its economy
Show appreciation of Italy and especially of your partner's region	Remain solely on a business footing
Remember that the top man or woman makes the decisions	Decline invitations to eat or drink with your hosts
Dress carefully and in coordinated fashion for meetings: in Italy clothes do make the man (or woman)	Wear jeans and trainers to the office on a Friday
Name Italian products that you own or have enjoyed	Make jokes involving the Pope

Overview

With some 90% of its native inhabitants speaking Italian, Italy remains a remarkably homogenous population. However, that is threatened by two issues, one long existing and one more recent. The enduring one is the division between the north and south. This is often expressed as the tension between the richer, more industrialized region and the *mezzogiorno*, the more rural and poorer south. A feature of postwar life in Italy was the migration of southern Italians to industrial cities such as Milan, although more recently the south has benefited from considerable national funds and – after Italy became a founder member of the European Economic Community in 1957 – of European investment for infrastructure and development. Even today there are differences in lifestyle and perceived wealth between the two regions. A more recent fear is that of immigration, particularly from Albania and Libya, once an Italian protectorate.

It's important to remember that as well as the familiar boot of the Italian mainland, the islands of Sicily and Sardinia both form part of the country. Italy also contains two mini-states, San Marino and the Vatican State. The Principality of Monaco, ruled by the Grimaldi family, considers itself to be Italian, despite being surrounded by France.

Italy is a Mediterranean country but extends upwards into the Alps in the north-west and to Austria in the north-east. The people of Trieste, Turin and Milan have more in common with each other than any of them do with Rome or Naples.

Italy used to be a collection of city states loosely held together under the rule of the Austro Hungarian empire until 1861, when the country was unified. But the regions jealously guard their cultural independence: indeed, Italians embrace the concept of *campanalismo*, loyalty to the sound of your local church bell or campanile. Some say the only time the country gets together is to celebrate the success of Azurri, the national soccer team!

While many northern Europeans dream of owning a house in the Tuscan sun, Italians get on with daily life – and that's not always easy for them. Italy shares some problems with other 'old European' countries – an ageing population, high welfare costs and labour-market rigidities. It also has to contend with its own unique difficulties. In recent years its growth has generally been the slowest in the European Union. Embarrassingly for national pride, the World Economic Forum in 2006-07 rated Italy only 42nd of 125 nations in its annual competitiveness league (although in fairness, India and China were placed 43rd and 54th). Added to this, Italy has to cope with high levels of organized crime and the controversy over immigration, even though the industrial north clearly needs labour. Tax avoidance is a national pastime, and experts claim that the underground economy accounts for between 15% and 27% of GDP. On top of all this, Italy has to import around 75% of its energy needs and most of its raw materials.

A distinctive feature of the Italian economy – and what gives Italian products so much charisma – is its huge number of energetic small firms, many of them family-owned. Around 90% of Italian businesses have less than ten employees. However, this vibrant SME (small and medium-sized enterprises) sector is vulnerable to competition from lower-cost Asian products.

None of this detracts from the sheer fascination of being in Italy and in interacting with Italians. Their cultural heritage is vast and varied, from the

Roman Empire to the Renaissance, to contemporary motorized emblems such as Ferrari and Ducati. Now they must find a direction for their future development. And all this being said, Goldman Sachs still predicts that Italy will be the world's 10th largest economy in 2050.

Values and attitudes

An Italian's most immediate loyalty is to the family. Family ties are more important here than in any other country, with the possible exception of Spain, and mean far more to an Italian than political rules and regulations or company policy.

Italians are proud, and sensitive about their world reputation. A critical article in the *Financial Times* or *The Economist* can turn into a national event, responded to and discussed in the national press and on TV. They appreciate that their country is justly famed for its cuisine, wine, art, architecture and quality of life, but they are also intensely aware that its bureaucracy and business administration do not match the standards of other European countries. Italy also remains sensitive about its Fascist period in the thirties, especially when the movement experiences recurrences, and by the extremes of wealth and poverty in the north and south of the country.

Keep in mind all these things when doing business in Italy, and remember also that Italians respect age, seniority and power. This means that the business structure is very hierarchical.

Cultural style

The Italian cultural style is to build relationships, from which business can grow. This involves eating and drinking with business partners and getting to know each other's families. The business relationship remains quite formal and quite top-down with decisions being taken at top level. Doing the business and taking the time needed is more important than bending the business to the time for Italians and they are not afraid to show their human side in business when they trust their business partner. Italian and British cultural styles can be compared like this.

Italy/UK cultural styles – a comparison

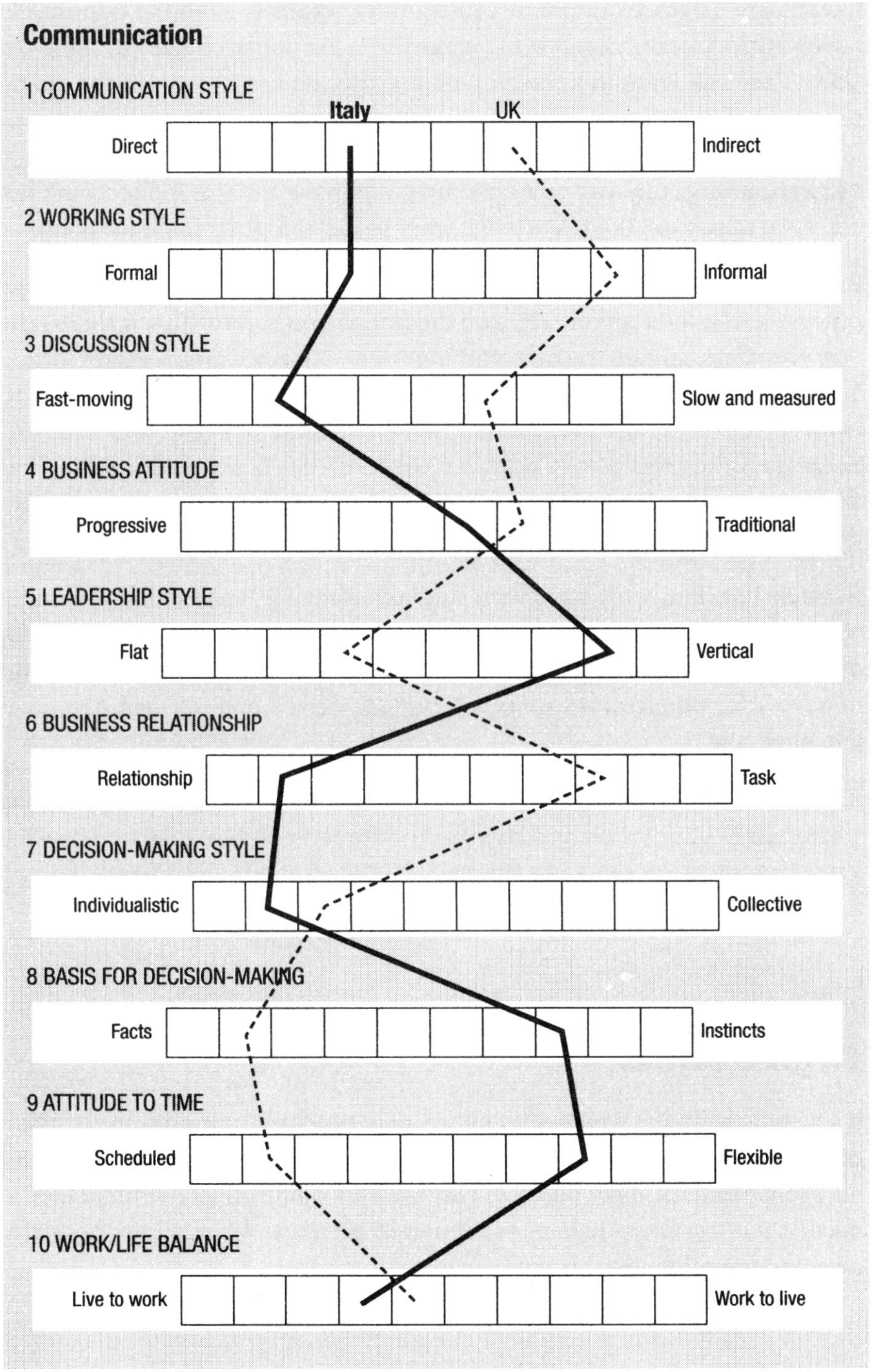

Communication

Italians are driven by intuition and emotion, which is often the opposite to how business is conducted in many northern European countries and in the USA. They will want to know you before they do business with you, so be prepared to chat about your family and personal life, your experiences in life and your impressions of Italy, without being obviously gushing. Your demeanour and the way you open up could have a major influence on the outcome of any dealings. They will want to feel that they can trust you.

Be aware also of the importance of *bella figura* in Italy. It means the way you present and conduct yourself, and the image you create. This includes the way you dress, so pick the best clothing from your wardrobe for both formal and casual wear. If necessary, buy something in which you feel really good before you go. You're never going to match the inherent style of the Italians, but at least you should leave behind those scuffed shoes and the bad ties that don't match your shirts. Italians, apparently, are Europe's biggest spenders on clothes and shoes.

Because Italy is synonymous with style and elegance, ensure that any visual material you hand out or show, including audio-visual presentations, is well-designed. It's also useful to have your card printed in Italian on one side, and to have your title clearly expressed. Include details of a relevant degree, if you have one.

Italian presentations tend to be short – 30 minutes is ample. Listeners are interested in your vision and style and in the presentation quality. They like a moderate to hard sell and a discussion of market opportunities. Allowing time for discussion is important.

Organization

It's normal to shake hands with everyone when you enter someone's office or when a meeting begins and ends, and to establish good eye contact. You may sense that it's appropriate to wait until a woman offers her hand before making the first move. Italians are generally punctual, especially in the north, so get to appointments on time.

Protocols, rules and procedures are often ignored in Italy, where managers focus on getting the essentials done without principles or rules getting in their way. This may be unnerving to visitors from cultures with more fixed patterns, but you have to learn to adjust to it in Italy.

Meetings and negotiations

Don't expect to reach decisions in an initial meeting with Italians. At this stage it will be about finding out who you are and seeing if a relationship can evolve. If you push too hard at this stage, you will appear brusque – and it will weaken your eventual negotiating position. You may find that even at subsequent meetings no actual decisions will be reached: these gatherings are more to encourage debate and constructive criticism, while the boss rules on the outcome later. If your proposal involves dealing with the Italian bureaucratic or legal systems, expect to suffer lengthy delays, so build that into your schedule.

Italians cut across one another during meetings, and their discussions may become very heated. Don't be alarmed by this, as it's quite normal and not seen as at all rude by the participants.

Team-working

Tasks are delegated to trusted individuals. Appraisals and job descriptions are rarely used, and the key indicators monitored in Italian businesses are cash flow, turnover and gross profit.

Leadership and decision-making

In an Italian company the *presidente* is assisted by a board of directors (*consiglio d'amministrazione*) and an MD (*amministratore delegate*). A *direttore* is a departmental manager. Other titles tend to be meaningless: power lies with the boss and things are done well only with his or her personal supervision or involvement. Organigrams are usually for foreign colleagues, and may have no relevance within the company. Your best move as a foreign business person is to find out who is the prime decision-maker in an organization.

True hierarchies in Italian firms are based on networks of people who have built up personal alliances across the organization. The primary attributes of a manager are flexibility and pragmatism; different departments will have different management styles depending on the boss.

Women are highly respected in the home but less so in the workplace. Courtesy is important but so may be flirting. Make clear your position in the company and make sure your junior colleagues defer to you. You may find it difficult to pay the bill in a restaurant as the Italian host will normally expect to pay and men would normally expect to pay for women in the group.

Socializing and gift-giving

Timekeeping is a little more relaxed for social events than it is for business, so you can arrive between 15 and 30 minutes late for most of these functions. Italians tend not to exchange business cards at social events, but instead carry a calling card, which bears their contact details. If you're in Italy for a short time you may have no option but to rely only on business cards, but anyone settling there for a while, or even making frequent visits, should consider using a calling card.

It's appropriate to take wine or chocolates if you are invited to someone's home for dinner. Make sure that it's a decent bottle, because Italians know their wine. If you're taking flowers, avoid red and yellow – the former implies secrecy, and the latter jealousy.

Great gifts: Small items of real quality, alcohol, delicacies or crafts from your country; maybe flowers or chocolates for junior personnel.

Avoid giving: chrysanthemums (linked with funerals) and even numbers of flowers. Brooches, handkerchiefs and knives are said to be associated with sadness.

Conversation topics

Ice-breakers	Ice-makers
Conversation about your family and background	'I used to have a Fiat but it rusted to bits'
Italian art, music and films	Asking 'What do you do?' when you've just met
Sport, especially football	'Is Italy still dominated by the Mafia?'

Fact files

Fact files

Facts about Brazil

Name	Federative Republic of Brazil
Size	8.5 million sq km; occupies nearly half the area of Latin America
Population	188 million
Capital and main cities	Brasilia (2m), Sao Paulo (20m), Rio de Janeiro (6m)
Ethnic make-up	White 53.7%, mulatto (mixed white and black) 38.5%, black 6.2%
Economy	Agriculture, oil, textiles, shoes, chemicals, cement, lumber, iron ore, tin, steel, aircraft, motor vehicles, other machinery and equipment
GDP per head	US$8,600 (2006 estimate)
Language	Portuguese
English usage	Few Brazilians are fluent in English; most understand Spanish
Religion	Catholic 73.6%, Protestant 15.4%, spiritualist 1.3%
Currency	Real
Climate	Mostly tropical, temperate in south
Visas	Not required for citizens of the UK and most other EC countries, compulsory for US citizens

Facts about China

Name	People's Republic of China
Size	9.6 million sq km; half the size of Russia
Population	1.3 bn
Capital and main cities	Beijing (12m), Shanghai (14.1m), Tianjin (10.2m), Chennai (6.6m)
Ethnic make-up	Han Chinese 92%, other nationalities including Zhuang, Uygur, Tibetan, Mongol and Korean 8%
Economy	Agriculture, mining and ore processing, iron, steel, aluminium, coal, petroleum, machinery, defence, textiles, chemicals, cars, locomotives, ships, aircraft, telecommunications, consumer products including footwear, toys, and electronics
GDP per head	US $7,600 (2006 est)
Language	Mandarin Chinese, with many local dialects
English usage	Huge numbers are studying, but best to use a translator for negotiations
Religion	Officially atheistic, but there are five State-registered religions: Daoism, Buddhism, Islam, Catholic and Protestant Christianity
Currency	Yuan or Renminbi
Climate	Tropical in south to sub-arctic in north
Visas	Compulsory for EU and US citizens

Facts about France

Name	French Republic
Size	547,030sq km; more than twice as big as the UK
Population	61 million
Capital and main cities	Paris (2.14m), Marseilles (807,000), Lyons (515,000)
Ethnic make-up	France does not record data on ethnic groups
Economy	Aerospace, automotive, pharmaceuticals, industrial machinery, food and drink, tourism
GDP per head	US$30,100 (2006 est)
Language	French
English usage	Many French professionals are fluent; many French speak basic working English
Religion	Roman Catholic 83%-88%, Muslim 5%-10%, Protestant 2%, Jewish 1%, unaffiliated 4%
Currency	Euro
Climate	Mild summers, cool winters; hot summers, mild winters on Mediterranean
Visas	Not required for citizens of the EC or USA

Facts about Germany

Name	Federal Republic of Germany
Size	357,021 sq km; nearly half as big again as the UK
Population	82.4 million
Capital and main cities	Berlin (3.4m), Hamburg (1.7m), Munich (1.2m), Cologne (1m)
Ethnic make-up	German 91.5%, Turkish 2.4%, other 6.1% (mainly Greek, Italian, Polish, Russian, Serbo-Croatian, Spanish)
Economy	Automotive, chemicals, telecommunications, machine tools, banking, insurance
GDP per head	US$31,400 (2006 est)
Language	German
English usage	Many German professionals are fluent; many others speak good working English
Religion	Protestant 34%, Roman Catholic 34%, Muslim 3.7%, unaffiliated or other 28.3%
Currency	Euro
Climate	Cold, cloudy and wet winters; warm, sometimes wet summers
Visas	Not required for citizens of the EC and USA

Facts about India

Name	Republic of India
Size	3.3 million sq km: world's seventh largest country
Population	1.1 billion
Capital and main cities	New Delhi (13.7), Kolkata (13.2m), Mumbai (10m), Bangalore (7.2m), Chennai (4.25m)
Ethnic make-up	Indo-Aryan 72%, Dravidian 25%, Mongoloid and other 3%
Economy	Agriculture, textiles, chemicals, food processing, steel, transport equipment, software services
GDP per head	US$3,700 (2006 est)
Language	Hindi is the official language, but there are more than 20 other official languages
English usage	English has associate status as a language; most professionals speak it
Religion	Hindu 80.5%, Muslim 13.4%, plus Christians, Sikhs, Buddhists, Jain and others
Currency	Rupee
Climate	Tropical monsoon in south to temperate in north
Visas	Compulsory for EU and US citizens

Facts about Italy

Name	Italian Republic
Size	301,000 sq km; about 20% larger than the UK
Population	58.1 million
Capital and main cities	Rome (2.6m), Milan (1.3m), Naples (1.0m), Turin (0.9m)
Ethnic make-up	Italian, with clusters of German-, French-, Greek- and Slovene-Italians
Economy	Engineering, automotive, chemicals, electronics, textiles and clothing, tourism
GDP per head	US$29,700 (2006 est)
Language	Italian, with German in South Tyrol, French on Swiss/French border, Slovene on Slovene border
English usage	Reasonable in business community, except in the south
Religion	Catholic 83%, Jewish, Protestant and Muslim minorities
Currency	Euro
Climate	Mediterranean in south, Alpine in north
Visas	Not required for citizens of the EU and USA

Facts about Japan

Name	Japan
Size	378,000 sq km; 1.5 times the size of the UK
Population	127.5 million
Capital and main cities	Tokyo (8.5m), Yokohama (3.4m), Osaka (2.5m)
Ethnic make-up	Japanese 99%
Economy	Motor vehicles, electronic equipment, machine tools, steel and nonferrous metals, ships, chemicals, textiles, fishing, processed foods
GDP per head	US$33,100 (2006 est)
Language	Japanese
English usage	Varies widely; many Japanese can speak and read English but have difficulty conversing in it
Religion	80% adhere to more than one religion: Shinto 106.2m, Buddhist 95.8m, Christian 1.8m
Currency	Yen
Climate	Tropical in south to cool temperate in north
Visas	Not required for citizens of the EC or USA

Facts about Russia

Name	The Russian Federation
Size	17.1 million sq km; the world's biggest country in area spans 11 time zones and is nearly twice the size of the USA
Population	142.9 million (2006 est)
Capital and main cities	Moscow (10m), St Petersburg (4.6m), Novosibirsk (1.4m)
Ethnic make-up	81.5% Russian, 3.8% Tatar, 3% Ukrainian (more than 100 nationalities in all)
Economy	Minerals and gas extraction, iron, steel, chemicals, aircraft and space vehicles, defense equipment, shipbuilding, agricultural machinery, food, wood products, clothing
GDP per head	$12,100 (2006 est)
Language	Russian, plus many minority languages
English usage	Younger Russians have a good grasp; use a translator for negotiations
Religion	Russian Orthodox 15-20%, Muslim 10-15%, other Christian 2% (figures for practising worshippers)
Currency	Rouble
Climate	Warm summers in steppes to cool on Arctic coast, cool winters on Black Sea to frigid in Siberia
Visas	Compulsory for citizens of the EU and US

Facts about the UK

Name	United Kingdom
Size	244,820 sq km; just over half the size of California
Population	60.5 million
Capital and main cities	London (7.5m), Birmingham (1m), Leeds (723,000), Glasgow (578,000), Edinburgh (458,000), Manchester (437,000)
Ethnic make-up	White 92.1% (English 83.6%, Scottish 8.6%, Welsh 4.9%, Northern Irish 2.9%), black 2%, Pakistani/Bangladeshi 1.9%, Indian 1.7%
Economy	Financial services, coal, gas, oil, pharmaceuticals, machine tools, electric power equipment, automation equipment, railroad equipment, aircraft, motor vehicles, electronics and communications equipment, food processing, textiles, clothing
GDP per head	US$31,400 (2006 est)
Language	English, Welsh (26% of Welsh population)
English usage	Universal
Religion	Christian 41m, Muslim 1.58m, Hindu 558,000, Sikh 336,000
Currency	Pound Sterling
Climate	Temperate; more than half the days are overcast
Visas	Not required for citizens of the EU or US

Facts about the USA

Name	USA
Size	9.6 million sq km; half the size of Russia
Population	298.4 million
Capital and main cities	Washington DC (550,000), New York (8.1m), Los Angeles (3.8m), Chicago (2.8m)
Ethnic make-up	White 81.7%, black 12.9%, Asian 4.2 %, Amerindian 1% (US does not list Hispanics as a category, but there are about 40m in the country)
Economy	Oil, steel, automotive, aerospace, telecommunications, chemicals,electronics, food processing, agriculture, lumber, mining
GDP per head	$43,500 (2006 est)
Language	English 82.1%, Spanish 10.7%
English usage	Universal
Religion	Protestant 52%, Catholic 24%, Mormon 2%, Jewish 1%, Muslim 1%
Currency	Dollar
Climate	Mostly temperate, tropical in Florida, arid in the south-west
Visas	Not required for citizens of the UK and most other EC countries